Supersuming Subsumption

Historical Materialism Book Series

The Historical Materialism Book Series is a major publishing initiative of the radical left. The capitalist crisis of the twenty-first century has been met by a resurgence of interest in critical Marxist theory. At the same time, the publishing institutions committed to Marxism have contracted markedly since the high point of the 1970s. The Historical Materialism Book Series is dedicated to addressing this situation by making available important works of Marxist theory. The aim of the series is to publish important theoretical contributions as the basis for vigorous intellectual debate and exchange on the left.

The peer-reviewed series publishes original monographs, translated texts, and reprints of classics across the bounds of academic disciplinary agendas and across the divisions of the left. The series is particularly concerned to encourage the internationalization of Marxist debate and aims to translate significant studies from beyond the English-speaking world.

For a full list of titles in the Historical Materialism Book Series available in paperback from Haymarket Books, visit: www.haymarketbooks.org/series_collections/1-historical-materialism.

Supersuming Subsumption

Theory and Politics

Marco Briziarelli

Haymarket Books
Chicago, IL

First published in 2024 by Brill Academic Publishers, The Netherlands
© 2024 Koninklijke Brill NV, Leiden, The Netherlands

Published in paperback in 2025 by
Haymarket Books
P.O. Box 180165
Chicago, IL 60618
773-583-7884
www.haymarketbooks.org

ISBN: 979-8-88890-360-5

Distributed to the trade in the US through Consortium Book Sales and Distribution (www.cbsd.com) and internationally through Ingram Publisher Services International (www.ingramcontent.com).

This book was published with the generous support of Lannan Foundation, Wallace Action Fund, and the Marguerite Casey Foundation.

Special discounts are available for bulk purchases by organizations and institutions. Please call 773-583-7884 or email info@haymarketbooks.org for more information.

Cover art and design by David Mabb. Cover art is developed from *Painting 45, Long Live the New! Kazimir Malevich drawing painted on 'Arbutus' wallpaper by Kathleen Kersey for Morris & Co*, paint and wallpaper on canvas (2016).

Printed in the United States.

Library of Congress Cataloging-in-Publication data is available.

To Sara. La totalità.

∴

Contents

1 **All That Is Solid about Subsumption Melts into the Air** 1
   1. A Tentative Definition 8
   2. The Question of Subsumption: An Incomplete but Totalising Abstraction 11
   3. Subsumptive Relations as a Theory of Power Relations: Unstable Hegemony 21
   4. The Structure of the Book: Subsumptive Relations and Subsumptive Scenarios 27

2 **Defining a Legacy** 34
   1. Defining Subsumption: A First Approximation to Logic and Material Tension 35
   2. Critical Genealogy: The Kantian–Hegelian Trajectory 41
   3. The Legacy of Kant and Hegel in Marx 44
   4. Systemic Dispossession and Systemic Subsumption 53
   5. The Marginal Centrality of Subsumption in Marx 57
   6. Marx's Multiple Subsumptions: Formal, Real, Hybrid and Ideal 60
      6.1 *Surplus Values* 64
      6.2 *Formal Subsumption* 69
      6.3 *Real Subsumption* 74
      6.4 *Hybrid Subsumption and Ideal Subsumption* 86
   7. Selective Traditions of Subsumptions: Two Main Narratives of Totalisations 90
      7.1 *Subsumption: Systematic Dialectic and Historical Dialectic* 91

3 **From Subsumption to Subsumptive Relations** 101
   1. The Terrain of Class Struggle Relations 106
   2. Subsumptive Relations and Hegemony 111
   3. Integral and Welfare State 121
   4. The Legal Hegemonic Apparatus 127
      4.1 *Legally Formal and Informal Subsumptive Relations* 132
   5. UnFreedom of Labour 135

4 **Determinate Supersumption: Molar and Molecular** 140
   1. Molar Determinate Supersumption 145
   2. Molecular Determinate Supersumption 150
      2.1 *Tactics and Strategies* 151

2.2 *Subjection and Subsumption*   153
2.3 *Consuming Subjectivities*   158

5 **Subsuming Communication: The Rising of the Translation Machine and Data-Subjects/Objects**   173
   1 Communication: Relational Labour and Labour of Relations   176
   2 Translatability and Translational Labour   178
       2.1 *Communicative Fixed Capital*   183
   3 Digital Platforms as Translation Machines   187
   4 Who Is Exactly a Translational Worker …?   193
   5 Data Subjects and Data Objects   196
   6 Active Supersumptive Politics: Freire and the 150-Hours Laboratory on Communication   202

6 **Domesticated Living Bodies and the Social Space of Subsumption**   210
   1 Space and Subsumption   212
   2 The Covid-19 and Determinate Supersumption   217
       2.1 *Social Spatial Fixes*   218
   3 Digital Abstract Space   221
   4 The Contradictory Facets of Domestication, or Subsumption as Always   227
       4.1 La perruque, *Gamification and a Rhetoric of Choice*   232

7 **Conclusions: Two 'Futures' of Work**   244
   1 The 'First Future of Work': Remote Working and Class Relations   248
   2 Another Future of Work, or Cryptocurrency as Technological Fetish   250

Bibliography   255
Index   270

CHAPTER 1

All That Is Solid about Subsumption Melts into the Air

There is a mode of vital experience – experience of space and time, of the self and others, of life's possibilities and perils – that is shared by men and women all over the world today. I will call this body of experience 'modernity'. To be modern is to find ourselves in an environment that promises us adventure, power, joy, growth, transformation of ourselves and the world – and, at the same time, that threatens to destroy everything we have, everything we know, everything we are. Modern environments and experiences cut across all boundaries of geography and ethnicity, of class and nationality, of religion and ideology: in this sense, modernity can be said to unite all mankind. But it is a paradoxical unity, a unity of disunity: it pours us all into a maelstrom of perpetual disintegration and renewal, of struggle and contradiction, of ambiguity and anguish. To be modern is to be part of a universe in which, as Marx said, 'all that is solid melts into air'.[1]

∴

It's possible that I shall make an ass of myself. But in that case one can always get out of it with a little dialectic. I have, of course, so worded my proposition as to be right either way.[2]

∴

The main purpose of this book is to extrapolate from the Marxian understanding of subsumption – and my own socially historically situated reading of it – a dynamic and holistic theory of capitalist social power relations, to bring such a notion to the core of an anti-capitalist analysis of everyday practices.

---

1 Berman 1982, p. 15.
2 Marx and Engels 2010, pp. 40, 152.

The objective may seem counter-intuitive because, despite a recent and renewed interest in the subject, subsumption remains a fairly under-explored category, being either used as a 'floating signifier' by critical literature prevalent in the humanities to describe a vague wide-ranging tendency of capital to colonise social life, or, alternatively, lingering at the fringes of specialised Marxist scholarships, used as an introductory/transitory topic before one moves on either to surplus-value theory or historical analyses of capitalist development.

What intrigues me about this notion is my nebulous intuition of its great explanatory power, and the frustration deriving from the difficulty in pinpointing its precise significance in relation to the grand horizon of capitalist phenomena. This category may concurrently refer to a broad variety of meanings: 'subordination', 'subjection', 'integration', 'mediation', 'superimposition', 'substitution', 'power relation', 'sublation', 'incorporation', 'alienation', 'abstraction', 'exploitation', 'colonisation', and even 'territorialisation'. Yet, while Marx does not directly and explicitly define subsumption in his *opus operatum*,[3] it is exactly in this rich but undefined semantic region[4] that several key capitalist processes seem to intersect each other, and it is to here that I consistently find myself returning.

My interest in subsumption has its own journey. This work represents the elaboration of personal reflections that span several years of relatively vague, accidental, but also more and more frequent encounters with this notion. It possibly started on the occasion of the 2007–8 crisis, just before my return to academic studies. I was living in Spain, working for a textile company, when the global financial crisis shocked a considerable part of the world, in Southern Europe with particular intensity. The whole of Spanish society was hit quite abruptly: massive unemployment reaching the double-digits, widespread bankruptcies, the violent bursting of the local real estate bubble, and serious issues of public debt re-financialisation.

---

[3] Marx elaborates on subsumption in *Capital*, Volume I, in the 'Results of the Immediate Process of Production', the *Manuscripts 1863–66*, and in the *Grundrisse*: Marx 1973; Marx 1990; Moseley 2015b.

[4] It is no accident that in this book I link Marx to Gramsci via the need for symptomatic readings. While due to rather different circumstances, we see in both cases the need to return again and again to an interpretation that constantly re-defines and qualifies the significance of a particular term *vis-à-vis* the whole theoretical environment created by a given thinker; this obliges the critical reader to walk a hard and perilous but also enriching path. The award for our effort is that we hit three birds with the same stone, we get a concrete sense of the author's: 1) method of presentation; 2) method of dissent; 3) a relational definition of the term about which we were inquiring.

In the context of such a multi-layered crisis, together with millions of fellow workers, I found myself unemployed, with no prospect of finding a decent job, or any kind of job, for quite some time. My company, like many other well-established productive activities in the Comunidad Valenciana region, went bankrupt. That was for me my first experience of crisis as someone with financial responsibilities, a mortgage, and a family. It was not as quasi-instantaneous as the Covid-19 crisis but, all of sudden, the word capitalism and its powerful rhetoric seemed to have lost its meaning.

A small digression. As an Italian born and raised in an upper working-class family in a semi-rural upper-working-class city like Perugia, I always felt that places like Italy, Spain, and Greece were far from that 'virtuoso' and architectonic balanced economic system described by Marx in *Capital*, Volume I, capitalism in its pure forms. For that matter, they were also far from what I experienced in my years of living in the United States, a place which seems to be operating free of the burdens of history, that is, mostly no feudalism, no corporative thinking, no Vatican ... Conversely, capitalism in Southern Europe seemed to me just a layer of a huge palimpsest, and thus as something quite dissimilar to an actual capitalist base or structure. You could walk inside the most capitalist spaces, in semiotic terms, like a branch of a chain restaurant such as McDonald's, defined by the procedural promise of providing the same product/experience globally, and you could still see signs of a deeply rooted way of living not compatible but coexisting with capital: chaotic lines at the cash register, 'unprofessional' personnel, people ordering items that were not on the menu. In sum, this is to say that if subsumption was to signify capitalist colonisation of social life, then my life experience led me towards two working hypotheses: I was either living in an enclave that has resisted its subsuming power, or subsumption appeared to be a relatively superficial phenomenon rather than an anthropological one.

Linked to that and returning to the 2007–8 crisis, what was striking to me was that those social relations previously shaped by capitalist firms, that is, relations such as value, wage-labour and commodity exchange, partially but significantly withdrew into a quasi-pre-capitalist stage. I could see how rapidly capitalist social relations were being replaced by older 'informal', pre-capitalist logic. Take the example of the job market. I have just mentioned I was laid off and was looking for an occupation. By sending out resumés, attending job fairs, opening accounts in off and online job search agencies, and finally doing numerous job interviews, I could see how the job market very rapidly transitioned from being the arena of the coercive law of competition and demand/offer logics pure to clientelism, nepotism and the informal economy; furthermore, the practical ways in which capital and labour interacted, such as during job negotiations, had been 'purified' of the rhetoric of a free and just market economy – where employer and job seeker are ideologically depicted as equal buyer-sellers of commodities – and had returned to draconian crude power relations. Marx says in *Capital* that 'Between equal rights, force decides',[5] but when the fiction of equal rights vanishes, force becomes cruder and more violent – or at least, this was my experience both in Italy and Spain. As a result, people (such as myself!) found themselves accepting lumpenproletariat salaries of 700 euros per month for a precarious job, working beyond schedule, which pushed workers, especially young workers, down below the poverty line. Thus, everything that was allegedly subsumed, colonised and reshaped by capital reverted into something very different.

This impression crystallised even more clearly during the bizarre experience of lockdown amid Covid-19. During these long months of generalised shutdown of 'normal' social and economic life, whenever I could get out of my house I would observe with a mesmerised gaze the social space of the city so abruptly transformed: the once so lively commercial spaces of malls and busy main streets emptied, shops with their shutters closed. All lively economic activity was almost entirely replaced by the explosive proliferation of micro-logistics: couriers, people using their pandemic puppies as an excuse to walk outside, an abundance of police. Certain things struck me and added up to the idea I was maturing about subsumption: the fragility of a particular spatial configuration of capital accumulation and its circulatory system; new emerging social activities that seemed to be de-subsuming previously capital-incorporated social dynamics simultaneously working as 'fix'; temporary solutions.

Many aspects of this scenario *à la* post or *à la* pre-capitalism brought me to radically revise my initial teleological understanding of capitalism and its subsumptive dynamic, as a narrative of a generalised unstoppable progression of capital. When I visualised how capitalism wages its war against and within society, to use the metaphors of another critical thinker for this project, Antonio Gramsci, instead of a frontal attack, I saw instead a fairly heterogeneous 'push and pull': altercations, guerrilla warfare. Instead of a pure space of capitalism colonising everything, I started seeing frequently uncoordinated conquering expeditions, often failing, or winning by force and by fortune.

Furthermore, since the Covid outbreak, and now living the slow and dull process of returning to 'normality', I have been trying to make sense of yet

---

5 Marx 1990, p. 434.

another configuration of capital, this time concerning my work as a professor involved in teaching classes, which have all migrated to online formats due to the Covid-19 lockdown. How should I consider that change in the labour process from a subsumptive point of view? Social physical isolation, increased connectivity, intensification of ICTs, my questionable professional attire at home ..., sharing working space with Susana, Emma and the annoying dog Moxi. Was remote working a liberation from the coercive aspect of wage-labour? I am not sure. It was hard to tell whether sourdough pizza and the incorporation of Thursdays into Aperitivo time was a symptom of a better working life or some kind of compensatory sublimation.

Again, the subsumption bell was ringing, but I didn't know which way to turn. The real question is of course not a matter of language – even though, as a communication and media scholar, I think that giving voice to/articulating phenomena, for example by writing books, is extremely important – but rather about how people live, coexist, survive and fight the social arrangement of life called capitalism. This brings me to the subtitle of this book, 'theory and politics'. The narration I have offered so far seems at first sight quite far from both the theoretical and the political, but again, the bell is always ringing – it depends on if, where, when and how you want to respond. For instance, how should I interpret all the life experiences I have just recounted? Are those the issues of a self-contained psyche or broader social conditions? Are they theoretical or political? Or, more specifically, should I approach the question of subsumption as a theoretical or a political issue?

In my mind, there are two main related but distinct ways to understand this. 'Theory and politics' is both a journey of systematic discovery as well as a crucial synthesis. First, as I will elaborate in more detail later on, my approach to subsumption follows the Marxian path from 'simple abstract' to 'complex concrete', from the artificial and forceful 'purity' of a concept to the messy richness of an historically determined practice such as politics. It is not a linear path but a dialectical one according to which, for example, the complex concrete cannot be interpreted without the abstracting effort of theorising. So, it is not a *telos* from theory to politics but an active dialogue in the sense that a given theory implicitly reflects a political project and a given politics rests on primordial theoretical assumptions about what it means to do politics, i.e., to define the subject and its political objectives.

Secondly, and linked to that dialogue, 'theory and politics' entails Gramscian praxis: a synthesis between theory and politics. The validity of admittedly rather abstruse terms such as subsumption cannot only apply in the context of inaccessible technical language, in the same way that abstractions when used to understand reality must always be real and rational abstractions. This synthesis is for Gramsci both a normative goal for transformative action and also an epistemological assumption. In this sense, Gramsci poses and answers a fundamental question, which I think can help a theory and politics of subsumption:

> Can the modern theory be in opposition to the 'spontaneous' feelings of the masses? ('Spontaneists' in the sense that they are not the result of any systematic educational activity on the part of an already conscious leading group, but have been formed through everyday experience illuminated by 'common sense' that is, by the traditional popular conception of the world).[6]

He responds that there is no opposition but a 'quantitative' difference of degree, not one of quality: 'A reciprocal "reduction" so to speak, a passage from one to the other and vice versa, must be possible'.[7] The question in my mind comes down to the tension most of us in academia feel between theoretical awareness and empirical experience and the fact that 'fancy' technical terms such as subsumption acquire meaning only in the embodied everyday lives of people. As I mentioned, abstractions are useful when operating as rational abstractions, in which rationality is understood as practical rather than ideal logic.

The politics that I refer to in this book are almost pre-political and possibly prefigurative. I am referring to those necessary unstructured and tactical forms of antagonistic subsumptive relations in everyday working and living. These elements, which I will define as 'molecular', materialise through the unevenness of unstable subsumption; this is then potentially brought to the surface by an active and more organised political engagement. In this book, I will give a real concrete social existence to those practices, such as translational labour and *la perruque*, that counteract the tendency to treat subsumption as an abstract substance of thought. This is my small contribution to politicising subsumption.

Given this normative emphasis on a 'practical' and experience-oriented subsumption, why bother with abstractions and theory? Why not simply find effective and immediate representations of the 'reality' of subsumption? Still, theory and politics cannot be understood in isolation. This can be understood in two main senses. First, in a social reality dominated by the capitalist mode

---

6 Gramsci 1971, pp. 198–9.
7 Gramsci 1971, p. 199.

of production, there is no such thing as immediacy, which also means, there is no such thing as clear-cut and stable theory or definitions. Thus, pushing back against immediacy brings mediation, mediation in plural brings a complex interconnected totality, whose comprehension necessarily implies abstractions.

Secondly, no theory is innocent; theory can be subject to both political projects and political disputation. *Capital*, arguably Marx's most important effort to produce a scientific critique of capitalism, one that was intended to be acknowledged by scientifically-minded readers, is a beautiful network of slippery slopes inhabited by werewolves, ghosts, animals undergoing metamorphosis, ever-changing social forms of representation, people acting as social characters in a world-as-stage ...

In this context, subsumption is at the same time the cause, the disease and the cure for abstractions. Later on, I will argue that subsumption agglutinates several moments and layers of capitalist phenomena, due to the fact that it constitutes a fundamental perspective on the (imperfect) totalising dynamic of capitalist development. As per the title of this introductory chapter, which echoes both the well-known passage from Marx and Engels's *Manifesto*[8] but also Berman's later essay,[9] subsumption is in the end mostly about the larger dialectical experience of modernity, which reflects how capitalism has pushed society into a restless open-ended process of change:

> In its mystified form, dialectic became the fashion in Germany, because it seemed to transfigure and glorify the existing state of things. In its rational form it is a scandal and abomination to bourgeoisdom and its doctrinaire professors, because it includes in its comprehension and affirmative recognition of the existing state of things, at the same time also, the recognition of the negation of that state, of its inevitable breaking up; because it regards every historically developed social form as in fluid movement, and therefore takes into account its transient nature not less than its momentary existence; because it lets nothing impose upon it, and is in its essence critical and revolutionary.[10]

---

8   Marx and Engels. 1848/2004.
9   Berman 1982.
10 Marx 1990.

1   A Tentative Definition

Related to the so-called 'question of subsumption'[11] that Andres Sáenz de Sicilia so correctly posed, an important objective of this book is to conceptualise subsumption as a heuristic category that can indeed cut across different levels of abstractions by mediating the tension that arises when linking them together. My goal is to treat it as an articulatory notion that is capable of grasping both the totalising tendencies of capitalism but also the unstable and incomplete nature of such a totalising process.

To accomplish that, the first task of this book is to define the term, which always entails a theoretical and political effort to advance the study of a given subject matter:

> There is, however, one difficulty we could not spare the reader: the use of certain terms in a sense different from what they have, not only in common life but in ordinary political economy. But this was unavoidable. Every new aspect of a science involves a revolution in the technical terms of that science. This is best shown by chemistry, where the whole of the terminology is radically changed about once in twenty years, and where you will hardly find a single organic compound that has not gone through a whole series of different names. Political Economy has generally been content to take, just as they were, the terms of commercial and industrial life, and to operate with them, entirely failing to see that by so doing, it confined itself within the narrow circle of ideas expressed by those terms.[12]

As I have already mentioned, while Marx does not define it, and despite the lively and open discussion about what Marx ultimately wanted to do with the concept, I think that he also offers important theoretical coordinates to make sense of subsumption. In my case, I have been particularly inspired by the powerful introduction to the *Grundrisse*.[13] Specifically, I think of three passages that end up providing the pillars of my argument. Let me briefly review them.

---

11   Sáenz de Sicilia 2016. His study represents a *conditio sine qua non* of this work, in my view the first thorough and systematic engagement with subsumption. It has provided great insights for this book, as well as an opportunity to push his attempt to answer the 'question of subsumption' even further.
12   Marx 1990.
13   Marx 1973.

In the introduction, starting to elucidate his particular account of political economy, Marx makes the following claim:

> Thus production, distribution, exchange and consumption form a regular syllogism; production is the generality, distribution and exchange the particularity, and consumption the singularity in which the whole is joined together.[14]

This statement above synthesises for me the main motivation to write this book: I think about subsumption as a perspective that potentially links singularity, particularity and generality, which in my view also implies combining the insights emerging in the current Marxist debate about historical and systematic dialectics.[15] This is what I meant earlier when I said I wanted to treat subsumption as a category cutting across several levels/scales of abstraction, which are exemplified in this book by the dialectical relations between general and particular, by objective and subjective, logical and historical and molecular and molar.

Secondly, Marx argues that while for classical political economy 'production, distribution, exchange, and consumption form a regular syllogism', for him those moments of capital's general development are dialectically united, which for me signals a way to approach the totalising process that I think subsumption entails. The quote given in the last paragraph continues:

> This is admittedly a coherence, but a shallow one. Production is determined by general natural laws, distribution by social accident, and the latter may therefore promote production to a greater or lesser extent; exchange stands between the two as formal social movement; and the concluding act, consumption, which is conceived not only as a terminal point but also as an end-in-itself, actually belongs outside economics except in so far as it reacts in turn upon the point of departure and initiates the whole process anew.[16]

---

14   Marx 1973, p. 89.
15   As Chris Arthur (2009) insists, while there is a consistent body of Marxist literature that acknowledge the central importance of dialectics, scholars tend to either understand it as a 'sequence of historical stages' (p. 112), that is, historical dialectics, or as 'the structural relations and contradictory moments of a given system' (p. 112), that is, systematic dialectics.
16   Marx 1973, p. 89.

Subsumption describes an effort to reproduce over time and space an adequate social environment aimed at maintaining a stable surplus-value production. Surplus-value production is not only *not* guaranteed, but its production consists of forcing and limiting a complex social process to produce one specific outcome out of innumerable and unpredictable possibilities. Thus, in this effort to turn an intractable social field into a controlled environment for surplus-value production, capital unveils the tendency for subsumptive dynamics in relation to all social moments and all social spheres.

Accordingly, I will claim that subsumption is necessarily always social subsumption made by subsumptive relations. This also means that the links between those moments and spheres in the general cycle of reproduction of capital cannot be thought in deterministic ways, and they certainly cannot be understood as identities (that is, 'regular syllogism') either. This assumption in my view also points to another important feature: subsumption is a process without guarantees and must be understood together with its determinate negation, which I will call *determinate supersumption*. Dialectically enough, determinate supersumption points at the same time to crises of subsumption, which is to say moments where subsumption can slow down, regress, be diverted, or inverted, as well as new opportunities to ramp up subsumption, producing new waves of subsumption, or new social territories in which subsumption operates as a fix, that is, a temporal solution, a space/time displacement for those crises.

Finally, in the last passage, Marx provides me with enough material to attempt a first provisional (re-)definition of subsumption:

> Production predominates not only over itself, in the antithetical definition of production, but over the other moments as well. ... A definite production thus determines a definite consumption, distribution and exchange as well as *definite relations between these different moments*. Admittedly, however, *in its one-sided form*, production is itself determined by the other moments.[17]

In this particular usage, 'production' does not refer to the manufacturing of products but to surplus-value, the ultimate goal of a capitalist system. From this quote I infer that the power relation implied by subsumption consists of a social process infused by power. Its dialectical, social and totalising nature leads to me to frame subsumption as a hegemonic power relation that functions as a hegemonic apparatus.

---

17 Marx 1973, p. 99.

Thus, based on the discussion so far, I provide here a tentative definition of subsumption as the totalising hegemonic apparatus attempting to eliminate any obstacle preventing a consistent production of surplus-value. It is a negative definition because, according to the argument of this book, trying to secure surplus-value production across the whole circuit of production, distribution, exchange and consumption means constantly overcoming opposing and hijacking forces. It is dialectically negative, because, as we shall see by examining the link with 'fixed capital' and 'fixes', the subsumption process frequently advances by a 'negation of the negation' dynamic. It is also a hegemonic kind of power relation because to try to secure a consistent flow of surplus-value it must engage society as a whole, at different levels (for example, politico-economic, ideological, social and cultural) and constitute adequate subjectivities moving across the coercion and consent axis.

2 The Question of Subsumption: An Incomplete but Totalising Abstraction

Certainly, I am not the only one nor the first to have noticed the following paradox about subsumption: that a category potentially so revealing of the so-called general *modus operandi* of capital – for example, its dynamicity, its perpetual need to expand, its abstracting power – has also been played down by Marx and most of his interpreters. Skillman,[18] who in my view has gotten closest to providing an answer to that question, argues that subsumption was almost completely erased because of its complex overdetermination. As a concept interacting with the overall narrative of *Capital*, it would have forced Marx to deal with two potentially incompatible perspectives: a value theoretic narrative about surplus-value production; and an historic one, mostly about the alleged linear progression from 'primitive' forms of accumulation to formal and real subsumption and finally total subsumption. The two perspectives are not simply divergent but also operate at different levels of abstraction. To put it in Kozo Uno's terms,[19] in his triadic model of levels of abstraction applied to Marx's analysis of capital, the value-theoretic line would supposedly work at the level of 'generality', as part of the 'Principles of Political Economy', while the historical one would work at the level of 'particularity', operating at the level of 'the Stage Theory of Capitalist Development'.

---

18   Skillman 2013.
19   Uno 1980, p. 62.

Such a distinction is also consistent with the particular way – at least according to David Harvey –[20] in which Marx has conceptualised the three volumes of capital: while being an holistic approach aimed at treating capitalism as a totality, it also analytically and artificially isolates synchronic views on capitalism. Thus, in each volume, Marx posits certain assumptions, such as granting no-problematic status to aspects that otherwise may impair the general understanding of capital accumulation, so that he can study a particular aspect using a simplified scheme of dependent and independent variables.[21] For example, while Volume I understands capital by technological dynamism and assumes the absence of any problem of realisation of value, Volume II assumes technology to be constant and starts analysing circulatory issues of realisation beyond the sphere of production.

In my view, following this method of combining but also distinguishing 'in Vitro' (value theoretic) and 'in vivo' (historical) moments, Marx probably decided to play down subsumption because it would have obliged him to combine those two dimensions and mix the general and the particular levels of abstraction I have just mentioned. It was probably a problem cutting across what he defines as strategic differentiation between a 'method of inquiry' in relation to a particular topic and its communicability, that is, the method of presentation.[22]

As I have mentioned earlier, the issue with subsumption is that involves abstractions in various imbricated ways: it produces both capitalist abstractions and abstract theorisations to grasp those abstractions. This is not a para-

---

20   Harvey 2017.
21   This represents an important way in which Marx demonstrates its dialectical approach to abstraction. In this sense, Volume I and II represent to abstract renditions of what it means to take capitalism in its pure forms. Its value is twofold: it is a strategic move to understand a dynamic and complex mechanism, and it is a rhetorical move, to construct an immanent critique of classical political economy.
22   In the 1872 preface to the second German edition of *Capital*, Marx differentiates between method inquiry and method of inquiry:
> Of course the method of presentation must differ in form from that of inquiry. The latter has to appropriate the material in detail, to analyse its different forms of development, to trace out their inner connexion. Only after this work is done, can the actual movement be adequately described. If this is done successfully, if the life of the subject-matter is ideally reflected as in a mirror, then it may appear as if we had before us a mere a priori construction. My dialectic method is not only different from the Hegelian, but is its direct opposite. To Hegel, the life process of the human brain, that is, the process of thinking, which, under the name of 'the Idea', he even transforms into an independent subject, is the demiurgos of the real world, and the real world is only the external, phenomenal form of 'the Idea.' With me, on the contrary, the ideal is nothing else than the material world reflected by the human mind and translated into forms of thought.

dox, since, as Marx mentions in the introduction to the *Grundrisse*, the aim is to reconstruct in the head by the force of abstraction the totality of capitalism:

> ... the method of rising from the abstract to the concrete is only the way in which thought appropriates the concrete, reproduces it as the concrete in the mind. ... a product, rather, of the working-up of observation and conception into concepts. The totality as it appears in the head, as a totality of thoughts, is a product of a thinking head, which appropriates the world in the only way it can, a way different from the artistic, religious, practical and mental appropriation of this world. The real subject retains its autonomous existence outside the head just as before; namely as long as the head's conduct is merely speculative, merely theoretical. Hence, in the theoretical method, too, the subject, society, must always be kept in mind as the presupposition.[23]

The method set out above is designed to capture a complexity that develops both in social space and social time. Marx and Engels famously claimed that 'the bourgeoisie cannot exist without constantly revolutionising the instruments of production, and thereby the relations of production'.[24] This revolutionary character of capitalism consists in engaging hypostatic elements, putting them in motion, and trying to increase both the magnitude and the speed of such motion. In this context, despite its most accepted translation,[25] subsumption cannot be simply understood as a subordination process to capitalism, but also as a mobilisation, that is, a process of reformulating every element by movement instead of stasis, it is a force that always tries to win any inertia and overcome the barrier. For this reason, in Chapter 5 I will talk about subsumption both as a process of translating meanings from the outside into the inside of capitalist grammar, as well as something that produces a general condition of translatability, which allows those meanings to circulate inside capitalist circuits. I will also be arguing that even 'fixed capital', in its machinic combination of living and dead labour, appears to be a continuous dynamic between fixity and movement.

The mobilisation described above is realised through a kind of fetishism implemented, for a change, by abstraction. By that, I refer to the process of rallying complexity by eliminating from it any element that goes against a

---

23   Marx 1973, pp. 101–2.
24   Marx and Engels 2010, 40, p. 487.
25   Camatte 1988.

logistic ratio, by making complexity not so complex, simple, qualitatively indifferent, translatable and quantifiable.[26] Thus, in the first instance, the abstraction triggered by subsumption trades concrete heaviness, concrete complexity and static inertia, with equivalence, speed and movement. I say the first instance, because quantitative changes, even when motivated by the goal of producing equivalence or commensurability, always eventually turn into qualitative changes. This aspect already reveals the overall complexity implied by trying to understand subsumption, which, for example, comparing different kinds, such as formal, real, hybrid and ideal, transform the labour process and the worker subjectivity in qualitative terms as well. As I will discuss with the help of Henry Lefebvre in Chapter 6, the project of producing a space *ad hoc* for capitalism, trying to grind down any element foreign to capital, ends up creating its dialectical other, differential space. This is the recurrent moral of the story of a dialectical approach to subsumption.

While subsumption, when understood as 'the tip of the spear' of capitalist conquest, appears to operate through the vitalism of a Futurist painting and Marinetti's glorification of the future, such constant revolution is not a linear path but rather appears as an uneven course characterised by interruptions, regression, accelerations, deceleration and re-routings. This is one of the main counter-narratives that emerges through the re-examination of subsumption by its dialectical other, determinate supersumption. Indeed, subsumption represents a formidable force but is constantly threatened by dynamics that negate it, slow it down, and divert it. For this reason, to put it in Gramscian spatial terms, subsumption as a conquering force operates only infrequently by frontal attacks and more often by a war of position, often needing multiple assaults to win its colonising war.

As in the case of the hegemonic side of subsumption, determinate supersumption is an imperfect description, it is a metaphor that acquires more significance only by gaining increasingly more determinations throughout the narration of this book. Determinate supersumption simultaneously pushes against, and produces, at the subjective level, the conditions for subsumption. Thus, the perspective provided by the dialectical unity between subsumption and determinate supersumption enriches our understanding of capitalism in the following way: the revolutionary element of capitalism, its technological and organisational dynamism, is not understood simply in terms of acceler-

---

26 Following Marx's example, there are two main ways in which I used abstractions here: as a useful moment of simplification of concrete reality; and as an instrumental simplification of reality realised by capital in its 'terraforming' operations *vis-à-vis* the social.

ating capital accumulation but also as a continuous struggle against its own limits, its dysfunctionalities and, ultimately, its contradictory nature.

In order to deconstruct subsumption, we need to unleash the mess of real social intercourse; that is, we need to suspend the operational assumptions that Marx poses in the first volume of *Capital* of a perfectly functioning market, of fair value exchange, and assume instead that the cycle of valorisation, realisation and distribution is under constant threat of interruption, crisis, devaluation, and unsound capital speculation. Each of these moments disrupts capital's reproduction of the conditions for the production of surplus-value, as well as the condition that guarantees capital's command over the labour process, and obliges us to think of subsumption not as a definitely accomplished stage but as a battleground of class warfare. In this sense, subsumption acts as a solvent and as the cement of class composition as well as the cement and solvent of hegemonic relations between classes.

It is interesting in this sense to notice how class struggle, that is, how the subsumption of workers under capitalist forms such as wage-labour, does not really get a lot of attention in the first volume of *Capital* when subsumption is introduced. Mindful of Marx's plan as enunciated in the *Grundrisse*, the reason seems clear: class struggle is always historic and geographically context-specific, it therefore belongs to the study of 'particularities' rather than 'generalities'. It represents a way to avoid inserting historical contingency into its account of capitalist production, in its pure state, as a perfectly functioning and self-contained sphere.

But can we keep separated particularities and generality when it comes to a category such as subsumption that is designed to deal with such a relation? The link between abstraction and subsumption is, to say the least, twofold and in both cases tied to the capability of a more 'powerful', more general element or actor to incorporate and subordinate the 'lower' more specific element and actor. First, as we shall see, especially by the perspective advanced in this book, subsumption describes mainly subsumptive social relations inhabited by asymmetric power relations. Second, subsumption is an abstraction from people in a fetishistic sense: it describes how social processes initiated by people take on a life of their own independent from people and exert active mastery over people. Along this line of thinking, Dunayevskaya[27] claims that Marx's labour theory of value would be better described as 'value theory of labour', to the degree that the social process of production controls workers instead of the opposite.

---

27   Dunayevskaya 1988, p. 138.

The general tendency of capitalism is the colonising of all human productive activities. Since, by my assumption, all human activities are inherently productive, subsumption is a totalising process of capitalist (re-)production, which describes active processes of adaptation, mediation and unification of heterogeneous realities. Thus, studying subsumption sheds light on capitalism as a social form.

The link between subsumption and abstraction in the capitalist context is so vital that I would go as far as to paraphrase the famous opening of *Capital*: 'In societies where current capitalist conditions of production prevail, life is presented as an immense accumulation of abstractions', which tends to rule us and to saturate our consciousness with layers of complexity, fetishisms, and also – as Debord[28] would say – 'separation perfected'. We live immersed in a reality comprising two reciprocally completing principles of unfulfillment and alienation: people make history but not under the condition of their own making, on the one hand; and capital makes history but not under the condition of its own making, on the other. In other words, we are dominated by abstractions created by ourselves when involved in capitalist relations.

How do abstractions rule the (capitalist) world? Material production of life, that is, productive practices come to be mediated and constituted by capitalist relations such as value, commodity and wage forms. Those forms tend to shape both practices and relations by replacing qualitative difference – inherent to complexity – with quantitative variations, inherent to an 'abstracted', ergo, impoverished reality, thus impoverishing individuals, along with contingent practices such as concrete labour, in order to make them equivalent and therefore exchangeable. Talking about the abstract domination of the value form, Moishe Postone claims that it is the reification of abstract labour that transforms qualitative specificity into quantitative exchangeability, a social mediation that dominates individuals:

> I conceptualise capitalism in terms of an historically specific form of social interdependence with an impersonal and seemingly objective character. This form of interdependence is affected by historically unique forms of social relations that are constituted by determinate forms of social practice and, yet, become quasi-independent of the people engaged in these practices. The result is a new increasingly abstract form of domination – one that subjects people to impersonal structural imperatives and constraints that cannot be adequately grasped in terms of con-

---

28   Debord 1995.

crete domination (for example, personal or group domination), and that generates an ongoing historical dynamic. In reconceptualising the social relations and forms of domination that characterise capitalism, I shall attempt to provide the basis for a theory of practice capable of analysing the systemic characteristics of modern society, such as its historically dynamic character, its processes of rationalisation, its particular form of economic 'growth', and its determinate mode of producing.[29]

Postone explains that the form of domination brought up by capitalism does not consist of people ruling over other people, but a power exerted by an abstract social structure that we created, which, through capitalist forms such as capital and commodities, goes beyond class domination. This is the sense in which Marx claims that in capitalism both labour and capital are alienated: because they are both compelled to reproduce capital. As Alfred Sohn-Rethel[30] claims, subsumption stands on an existing terrain of abstraction of the exchange principle, understood both in the general sense of exchangeability and commensurability of otherwise heterogeneous elements (such as the use-value of commodities or my concrete labour), but also in relation to the specific freedom of the labour market, where free sellers of labour-power confront free buyers of labour-power as fundamentally equal.

Considering both capital's social totality and its core abstracting principle of exchange, I claim in this book that subsumption, therefore, is better understood in terms of subsumptive relations. The reframing is in my view crucial: from a theoretical notion to a practical, lived and fluid social ensemble of relations; from the apparent stability and linear *telos* of capitalist progression to the instability, contradictions and relationality of the social field; from subsumption as an abstraction to a humanist perspective that aims at recognising human practices,[31] which is to say, *à la* Sartre, that while history may escape us, we are still making it.[32]

---

29   Postone 1993, p. 3.
30   Sohn-Rethel 1978.
31   Among other reasons, subsumption can be understood as totalising when considered as an 'abstraction machine': I will discuss this in Chapter 6. In this sense, I would claim that recuperating this rather obscure, technical notion helps us understand how capitalism produces powerful abstractions that contribute to creating what David Harvey has defined as universal alienation: Harvey 2020. Universal alienation is not just the worker's alienation; it signals, together with its more violent and cruel manifestations, that capitalism has failed to deliver the utopian component of its social/political/economic project: a happy and safe life for all.
32   Sartre 1991.

The paradox of the subsumption–abstraction nexus must be found in the implied tension between completeness and incompleteness. On the one hand, subsumption as a totalising process of socialisation of capital aspires to its own completeness. When Marx in the *Grundrisse* claims that methodologically, in trying to reconstruct a mental representation of the totality of a given socio-economic formation, we cannot simply start by following the chronological order of economic stages/moments, he refers to the fact that any given totality reconfigures the meaning and positionality of each element like money, landed property or debt. This form-giving agency of the social whole represents a fundamental function of subsumption which, by reincorporating and subordinating, reshapes labour and commodities into their adequate social forms. Thus, subsumption means simultaneously absorption into the totality and reshaping to adjust the newly absorbed element in relation to the totality, thus implying that the closed totality is better understood as an open process of totalisation.

However, on the other hand, subsumption tends to achieve its goals through abstraction, that is, simplification/impoverishment of complexity, which ultimately leads to the non-fulfilment of totalising aspirations. In fact, as its Latin etymology discloses, *ab-trahere*, the word involves pulling away reality, therefore leading to a reality that is incomplete, and this is what makes it difficult to grasp: it involves removal from concrete reality, not real complexity. For Hegel and Marx, the abstract describes the element with the fewest determinations; when we speak of the concrete, we speak of a complex combination of determinations. Abstraction is a neoliberal imperative of the 'travel light' variety; it exists in order to make total capital circulation more fluid and to increase the speed of its turnover.

Nevertheless, regardless of simplicity or complexity, the less we understand those abstractions, the more dominant and naturalised they become, and thus less available to be acted upon. Thus, quasi-universal abstraction, from the humanist standpoint of this work, relates directly to quasi-universal alienation, understood as the lack of capacity for conscious and consequential action upon the world.

While aspiring to describe subsumption as a real and concrete social and political process, as a militant theoretical intervention this book can be understood as an attempt to mobilise abstract thought so as to reconstruct and explain capitalist abstractions. I will accordingly enrich, therefore make progressively more concrete, a relatively abstract understanding of subsumption, along with its dialectical flipside, determinate supersumption.

My expansion of subsumption follows the Marxian method of enriching through the mental reconstruction and interpretation of the social phenomenon. Ernest Mandel[33] argues that Marx's method starts from material concrete phenomena such as industry, production and cities, which are then mediated by the theoretical abstract which allows for the reconstruction of concrete totality. We pass from the 'real concrete', as the superficial phenomenological appearance mediated by analytical activity that breaks the indeterminate whole into parts – that is, abstractions – to the 'thought concrete', as the mental reconstruction and interpretation of the social phenomenon; this represents my attempt to show how, as a concrete abstraction, subsumption constantly links systematic and historic social dynamics.

Such reconstruction is needed because the collective ensemble of social practices is mostly not transparent to us practitioners.[34] Thus, the reality of collective practical activity can only be indirectly attested to by exposing its symptomatic (because fetishistic) misrepresentation both in individual consciousness and the theoretical consciousness that takes its cue from the latter. Therefore, the critique of political economy is necessary. I thus propose a symptomatic reading both of social realities and of Marx: trying in both cases to find subsumption where it is not explicitly manifest and to reclaim its centrality where it appears to be only marginal. In my case, this means not only looking at subsumptive relations but also at the possibility of their coming undone, their determinate negation.

As Althusser and Balibar[35] suggest, similarly to Ricoeur's[36] take on the hermeneutic circle, symptomatic readings consist in making implicit meanings or problematic nodes explicit, depicting them against the backdrop of the entire conceptual and historical framework. This requires mediation and dialectical thinking. In this sense, enriching subsumption by means of determinate negation is a way to rehearse the general dialectical movements that propel Marx's analysis, which rejects immediacy as something that – as György Lukács observed – provides a static image that denies social-historical change:

> For anyone who sees things in such immediacy, every true change must seem incomprehensible. The undeniable fact of change must then appear to be a catastrophe, a sudden, unexpected turn of events that comes from outside and eliminates all mediations. If change is to be understood at all it is necessary to elevate their interrelatedness and the interaction between these 'relations' and the 'objects' to the same plane of reality.

---

33 Mandel 1976.
34 Brassier 2020.
35 Althusser, Balibar, Establet, Macherey and Rancière 2015.
36 Ricoeur 1981.

The greater the distance from the pure immediacy the larger the net encompassing the 'relations', and the more complete the integration of the 'objects' within the system of relations, the sooner change will cease to be impenetrable and catastrophic, the sooner it will become comprehensible.[37]

This method may appear then to oppose abstraction (created by subsumption) by way of abstraction, as a strategic moment of inquiry. However, there is an important difference between a momentary reduction of complexity of a given phenomenon, occurring in a larger process of reconstruction of a given phenomenon, and the real abstractions created by capitalism, which amount to an ontological condition, referring to those social dynamics, frequently opaque and invisible, that operate beyond individual will, with impersonal and systemic logic. The former can be considered an adequate tool critically to dissect the latter.

As Tony Smith claims: 'The task of thought is first to pierce through the appearances to that depth level … and then to proceed to the mediations that connect the depth level with the given appearances'.[38] In this sense, the task of abstracting thought is opposite to abstract ontology, because it aims at reconstructing the richness of reality, that is, the concrete. Marx has a specific definition of the concrete in mind, one much closer to its Latin etymological root, that is, an organic whole made of distinct but united parts in a totalised whole. I have already quoted part of this passage, but it is important to return to it, as Marx claims:

> The concrete is concrete because it is the concentration of many determinations, hence the unity of the diverse. It appears in the process of thinking, therefore, as a process of concentration, as a result, not as a point of departure, even though it is the point of departure in reality and hence also the point of departure for observation and conception. Along the first path the full conception was evaporated to yield an abstract determination; along the second, the abstract determinations lead towards a reproduction of the concrete by way of thought. … the method of rising from the abstract to the concrete is only the way in which thought appropriates the concrete, reproduces it as the concrete in the mind.[39]

---

37 Lukács 1971, pp. 153–41.
38 Smith 1990, p. 371.
39 Marx 1973, p. 101.

Based on the reasoning above, for instance, abstract labour as understood by Marx represents a reduction of the richness of concrete human labour so that it becomes exchangeable and quantifiable. Abstract labour, like subsumption in its inevitable incompleteness, is a metonymy gone bad, where a limited part, that is, abstract labour, aims at superimposing itself on the whole, concrete labour. This forceful reduction is the product of subsumptive processes, where a whole is exchanged for a part and where a complex historical practice is exchanged for ahistorical generality.

While in its received understanding subsumption is the process of metabolising particularities under the general dominance of capital, in this book I approach subsumption not only to rediscover particularities but also to look at those singularities that negate the systemic balance or that transform the whole. In this sense, while it is not the only issue at stake, the most important singularity that needs to be considered is the living and embodied worker. I will draw on the one hand on the Workerist and Autonomia approaches, and on the work of Enrique Dussel, to talk about an intersubjective and supra-individual kind of subjectivity, capable of class composition and re-composition as well as, sporadically, social and political eruptions; and on the other hand I will draw from Gramsci's insights about the molecular level, where individual and transindividual experience may erupt into a radical social movement.

The will to reintegrate the rich concreteness of particularities and singularities represents my recipe against abstractions and abstract thinking. At the time of writing, it is easy to see how dangerous it is to neglect those objective but intangible, impersonal and systemic realities that escape everyday notice. The typical law of motion of those abstractions describes dynamics that seem to operate at another level from our daily lives – until they touch the ground, like bolts of lightning with their destructive power. These abstractions may be called 'housing bubbles', 'supply chain crises', and of course 'the fall of the rate of profit'. In other words, when abstraction finally becomes manifest by concreteness, it usually does so in explosive destructive ways. I will show how subsumption/supersumption passes from being the point of entry to abstractions (for example, abstract labour, alienation, exchange-value, etcetera) to become a dialectic portrait of particularities, and even of potential singularities.

3 Subsumptive Relations as a Theory of Power Relations: Unstable Hegemony

I intend significantly to expand the frame of interpretation of subsumption, developing it on a broader and richer social scale than the sphere of production in which Marx seems to place it. I would claim that subsumption constitutes a socialising force capable of reshaping social relations in a fashion adequate to capital and of operationalising those social relations as powerful means of socialisation. Possibly, the most eloquent example of this is the establishment of the commodity form and the principle of exchange behind it as the basic social relation. Let us consider the process of commodification of labour, that is, the subsumption of work under exchange-value. This dynamic implies a twofold subsumption: the subsumption of use-value under exchange-value, which corresponds to the subsumption of concrete labour under abstract labour. Labour as a commodity implies the need for the products of labour to be exchanged, which entails a sphere of universal and abstract economic equivalence. At the same time, subsumption becomes a socialising force because the exchange principle sustaining commodification articulates goods as well as economic subjects who are both producing and consuming, selling and buying. This dynamic takes place while operating in social relations that are both coercive and consensual: while most of us need to submit to wage-labour to earn money to buy commodities, our socialisation is fundamental here because we enter the C–M–C circuit as a particular subjectivity with needs, wants and desires. Thus, subsumption must secure both the stability and the adequate transition from one moment of capital to another: while subsumption in the sphere of production generates surplus-value, subsumption in the broader social realm secures valorisation through its realisation, which means the management of consumption and the maintenance of effective demand in the form of concrete subjects who are able and willing to buy commodities.

To make sense of this multilayered aspect of subsumption, in this book I interpret subsumption using two sets of assumptions, 1) subsumptive relations are permeated by power, and 2) I synthesise my perspective with the Gramscian notion of hegemony.[40] Now, trying to interpret a fairly obscure and intricate term such as subsumption with another that, to say the least, has produced lively and extensive debates over its meaning[41] sounds like an aggravating task, more prone to produce confusion than clarity. While my study is mostly about subsumption, I think the connection with hegemony is so important that examining the two concepts in terms of their reciprocal relations and translatability may indeed provide significant insights into the conceptualisation of each respectively.

---

40   Gramsci 1975.
41   See Anderson 1976 – Thomas 2007.

Both notions describe totalising dynamics, asymmetric power relations and mediated class antagonism. However, while hegemony mostly tends to be used to describe a reality removed from the 'hidden abode of production', subsumption seems to experience the reverse issue, being relegated to such a realm. What do we gain by combining them? Essentially, a more adequate exploration of their broader sphere of agency.

On the one hand, Gramscian hegemony significantly contributes to the defetishising of subsumption. Both as a periodising tool[42] and as a *telos* of capitalist colonisation of social life,[43] subsumption tends to be theorised as a linear progression, following the narrative of primitive accumulation-formal subsumption-real subsumption. I thus reframe it as 'subsumptive relations'. The integration of subsumptive relations into a framework of hegemony leads to a much-needed opening up and dialecticisation of the former, pointing to their instability, exposure to crisis, susceptibility to diversion, need for constant reproduction, negotiability – comprising both coercion and consent – and even the possibility of their negation. As a result, the frame of interpretation of subsumption expands to a broader social scale – similar to the Workerist vision of the social factory,[44] but without the dismissal of the value theory of labour and the overstated subjectivist tendencies of some strands of Autonomia.[45]

On the other hand, subsumptive relations contribute to developing Gramsci's wish, expressed in the *Americanismo e Fordismo* fragments of *Quaderni*,[46] to bring back the materialist basis of hegemony, that is, to grasp it in direct relation to the labour process and (surplus) value production. Furthermore, without downplaying hegemony's political side, subsumptive relations add to hegemony a perspective on capitalist abstractions, the systemic ways in which a given system reproduces itself. For instance, the subsuming power of the exchange principle becomes a hegemonic socialising force: it articulates the circulation of commodities as well as the existence of subjects who operate within social relations of production and consumption that are both coercive and consensual, in the sense that, while most of us need to submit to wage-labour to earn money to buy commodities, our socialisation through the C–M–C circuit also requires our needs, wants and desires. Thus, subsumption in the broader social realm secures the valorisation process through its realisation and its social reproduction by producing subjects. This implies that the general

---

42 See Camatte 1988 – and Vercellone 2007.
43 See Debord 1995 – Hardt and Negri 2000.
44 Tronti 1966.
45 Wright 2002.
46 Gramsci 1975.

principle of exchange and the liberal ideologies conveyed by 'freedom, equality, property and Bentham'[47] become hegemonic. However, such hegemony is still unstable and susceptible to crisis: the abrupt transition to remote working during the Covid-19 pandemic, for example, sheds light on the tensions between a digital technology that acts like expanding fixed capital, subsuming the domestic sphere, and people renegotiating their neoliberal understanding of work and productivity.

I understand hegemony as a way to grasp a social totality[48] integrated, coordinated and reproduced by power relations that alternatively and to a variable degree, over time, combine coercive and consensual means. As Gramsci claims,[49] hegemony emerges in the first instance in the sphere of production, but then extends beyond the manufacturing sphere as well as the merely economic, reconfiguring worldviews, communication, social practices, values, and social, cultural and political institutions. In my view, understanding subsumptive relations as hegemonic provides an adequate framework to look at the dynamicity, volatility and the openness of subsumption. It is a way to grasp subsumption by the complex ensemble of social and historical conditions that both allow for its production, reproduction, transformation and, last but not the least, the possibility of its negation.

Subsumptive relations describe how specific form of class warfare, born inside the sphere of production, becomes a general principle of power and class domination, based on a combination of violent and coercive alongside consensual and ideological means. It is a complicated power relation that mediates important tensions inside and outside the labour process. In the synthesis of such tensions, subsumption indeed suggests a window onto the contradictory generality of capital, which here Marx describes so well:

> Capital itself is the moving contradiction, in that it presses to reduce labour-time to a minimum, while it posits labour-time, on the other side, as the sole measure and source of wealth. ... On the one side, ... it calls to life all the powers of science and of nature ... to make the creation of wealth independent (relatively) of the labour-time employed on it. On the other side, it wants to use labour-time as the measuring rod for the giant social forces thereby created ...[50]

---

47   Marx 1990, p. 280.
48   Jay 1984.
49   Gramsci 1975.
50   Marx 1973, p. 706.

While this passage is most of the time mentioned in reference to the tensions inside the valorisation process, what it provides in my view is an alternative approach to subsumption and the power relations inside and outside the labour process. If, as Marx puts it, the increase of the most adequate kind of fixed capital, that is, machinery, technology, applied science, collective knowledge and communication practices, displaces the pivotal role of living labour, then why on earth should capital insist on reasserting the labour theory of value and using it as a measure?

The reason, as David Noble[51] has already observed, is that managing socially necessary labour-time through the disciplinary apparatus of technology means managing productivity as well as the class relations between capitalists and workers. This is, in my view, the central contradiction that should lead to a rethink of the notion of subsumption: the integration of workers via a series of capitalist forms such as commodities, wage-labour, and capital, in a context of vast employment of fixed capital, such as the technological infrastructure of platform capitalism, creates a tension between expelling workers from the forms just mentioned while also trying to control them.

Such control cannot be described as pure domination because it is based on 'freedom', equality, property and Bentham on the one hand and the constitution of capital-subsumed kinds of subjectivity on the other. First, as Marx mentions several times in *Capital*, the worker is subordinated but independent. Such independence derives from the fact that workers and capitalists enter into contact by the juridical form of a contract, which is a relation between two wills that mirrors the economic relation.[52] Marx notices how the worker is twofold free, free of alternatives to sustain his/her life and free as an agent who decides to whom to sell his or her labour force. Those terms of the labour contract ground the capitalist's control over the use of the labour power, as a rightful owner of this commodity that he or she has fairly bought. The legalisation of such a power relation corresponds to the naturalisation of an ideological fiction of free choice (of buying and selling labour-power) because, as mentioned, the worker is compelled to sell his/her labour-power.

Secondly, subsumption stands at the intersection of de-subjectivising processes such as the abstraction of labour, as well as its opposite, the production of subjection: production of subjects and their disposition towards and internalisation of power. Accordingly, we need to look at the molecular level because, after all, what the power relations implied by subsumption aspire to is exactly

---

51   Noble 1983.
52   Marx 1990, p. 178.

the containment of worker subjectivity as a practical and embodied consciousness – one that is not always adequate to capital and that can even be antagonistic to it. Subsumption operates at the intersection of molecular and molar levels. As per Gramsci's take on this concept, molecular describes 'the organic process that constantly is produced by the manufacturing of personal and collective subjectivity, by will and consent, and by action'.[53]

As I will exemplify later, subsumed subjectivities describe for example how neoliberal subjects internalise control and surveillance, which become self-control and self-surveillance. The concept also accounts for self-exploitation, for example when labouring remotely outside the office or factory, a phenomenon that increased during the period of Covid-19 restrictions. On the topic of subjectivities, subsumption needs to be further examined. For example, when the worker is subsumed by a commodity economy, the worker assumes several roles, e.g., as the seller of labour-power but also as the buyer of commodities. Especially in the second case, subsumption under the commodity form does not actually imply a simple and literal subordination in terms of power relations: while indeed the worker becomes increasingly dependent on commodities in order to live (commercialised food, clothes, etc), he faces the capitalist as any other buyer.

To recap what said so far, subsumption, as an articulate conception of power, aspiring to command all productive sites within a given social formation, must be expanded in its theorisation so as to grasp its totalising dynamic. When understood in its expanded sense, as a form of social relations, and dialectically, subsumption goes beyond the received understanding of subordination, submission and domination; it also involves integration, internalisation and all other conditions that are understood as contingent, unstable, reversible and negotiated. Camatte claims that:

> Subsumption means rather more than just submission. Subsumieren really means 'to include in something', 'to subordinate', 'to implicate', so it seems that Marx wanted to indicate that capital makes its own substance out of labour, that capital incorporates labour inside itself and makes it into capital.[54]

In this sense, a more concrete (in the Marxian sense) theorisation of subsumption should open to the total social process, in its polyformic nature, multiple

---

53 Marchi 2021, p. 73.
54 Camatte 1988, p. 106.

sites, multiple determinations and outcomes, and in this sense Gramsci's holistic understanding of hegemony seems the most adequate.

4 The Structure of the Book: Subsumptive Relations and Subsumptive Scenarios

As I have already mentioned, this study starts from the abstract and moves to the concrete in order to enrich the theory and the politics of subsumption; it is a journey of discovery through different scales of abstractions. Accordingly, the book is structured as follows: after a first portion of the book dedicated to a mostly theoretical discussion, in the second part of the book I concretise the discussion by engaging with social and historical conditions characterised by digital and spatial 'fixes' used to overcome crises that are currently taking place in digital, informational and platform economies. The current critical context provides a frame to look at the contradictory and dynamic relations illuminated by subsumptive processes. My general assumption is that during times of crisis, a sustained reproduction of the conditions of possibility for subsumptive processes may experience an *impasse*, thus the ever-present tension between subsumption and supersumption may become more visible.

To see how this 'subsumptive' narrative unravels, let us examine each chapter in detail. Following the introduction, in Chapter 2 I provide a critical review of the recent intellectual history of subsumption. I first consider the trajectory linking Kant, Hegel and Marx, as well as the ways in which Marx's use of the term goes beyond its use by his predecessors, while preserving important elements of their approaches. I will also dedicate a considerable portion of the chapter to how Marx understood subsumption at different stages of his work and across different publications. I will also discuss the link between surplus-value and subsumption and the different social configurations that capitalism produces to secure surplus-value: formal, real, hybrid and ideal subsumption.

Reviewing the post-Marxian literature, I claim that subsumption has emerged in the last decades as an important analytical category for contemporary critical theory, one that is prevalently used in rather broad terms to describe the *telos* of increasing subordination of people's lives under capitalist forms. However, I argue that its prevalent received usages limit the potential of the notion, as they obscure its relational and dialectical nature. In this sense, I identify two main approaches in most contemporary understandings, which both build on a similar assumption: subsumption sheds light on both capitalism as a totality and as a process of totalisation. Those two tendencies depart from this broad but significant common base and develop, in an almost homological manner, the already mentioned distinction between systematic/value and historic dialectic: hence, subsumption as a totalising mechanism of closed/locked totality propelled by its inner self-reproducing core; and subsumption as a totalising mechanism that describes how capitalism changes over time in order to reproduce itself.

Overall, I see a common problem in both bodies of literature: subsumption remains abstract as a power relational almost solely based on submission, domination and subordination,[55] which is correct but also incomplete, because subsumption almost systematically establishes contradictory and mutable relations, which may temporally turn the table or make capital–labour-power relations more symmetric. In this case, dialectics characterises those power relations that are inhabited by multiple internal and constitutive tensions: between coercion (for example, labour compelling needs to sell labour-power) and consent (the emancipatory aspect of being the owner of our own labour-power); between subordination and independence; between formal/legal equality and material asymmetries (for example, between equal rights force decides); between reciprocal necessities of subsuming agent/agency and the subsumed element.

While the two main lines of interpretation examined in Chapter 2 provide formidable insights into capitalist phenomena, they both also run the risk of fetishising subsumption. Fetishised, that is, to the degree in which they treat subsumption as an automatic, clear-cut and one-sided outcome rather than a contradictory social process. In the strand of the literature that tends to understand subsumption as periodisation, the fetishism relates mostly to the teleology of capitalism, as if this mode of production had a pre-scripted historical development. In the other strand of literature, subsumption tends to be understood as another kind of *telos*, not simply in history, but in terms of totality, in other words, as if capitalism constituted a linear progression towards its completion, thus a closed totality, saturating the social. According to this vision, the totality seems to operate as if it were moved by what Althusser defines as an expressive causality.[56] These tendencies display a potential fetish character because they tend to hide the contradictory social relations implied by subsumption processes and to treat subsumption as an autonomous agent with a life of its own (this being the fetish as such …).[57]

---

55 See Adorno 2005; Marcuse 1968.
56 Althusser, Balibar, Establet, Macherey and Rancière 2015.
57 As Marx would say, we are dominated by real abstractions such as subsumption, but its material base is still people, historically engaged in a contradictory social intercourse. This is because abstraction is not metaphysical or mystical, but the outcome of human organ-

In Chapter 3, I proceed to reinterpret subsumption, building on what I consider the published literature to have missed and my sense of how its intuitions can be advanced. Based on the just-mentioned shortcoming in the existing literature, I expand and open up the notion of subsumption into contradictory, indeterminate *subsumptive relations*. Subsumption is not simply accomplished – as a matter of fact, according to this book's main thesis, it is never completely accomplished – but needs to be constantly sustained in order to counteract its determinate 'other', which in Chapter 4 I will define as determinate supersumption. I will argue for the pressing need carefully to examine each case of subsumption so as to keep track of these indissoluble but analytically distinguishable elements: the subsuming agent acting upon a subsumed object under historic-specific capitalist forms.[58]

A crucial element of this perspective is provided by the state, understood as a Gramscian integral state, that is, integration between civil and political society, marketplace and legal framework, coercion and freedom, private and public life, and the construction of hegemony. In relation to the integral state, I will examine two aspects: the role played by 'the legal' framework as a form given to subsumptive relations, in relation to which I will also consider the welfare state, as an example of determinate supersumption, ambiguously composing and decomposing subsumptive relations. I will also consider the subsumption of consumption.

---

ised practice. Such a process is open because founded on a productive kind of tension between two co-constitutive historic principles: 'people make history, but not and under the condition of their own making'; and 'capital abstractions' (such as subsumption) make history but not under the condition of their own making.

58　The analytical distinction above is needed not simply to capture and dissect the subsumptive relations but, most importantly, to try to keep track of their dynamism and their fluidity. That is because the subsuming syntax relation between its composing elements can radically change over time or even synchronically comprise multiple contradictory subsuming relations. This is exemplified by granting to the subsumed element a variable degree of independence or mutual compelling relations (for example, both capital and labour confront each other as alienated): sometimes latent, sometimes explicit, and sometimes only potential. As I will discuss throughout the book, such a dialectical nature is exemplified by living labour which is simultaneously subsumed under capitalist forms, but which also remains independent. Thus, based on this reinterpretation, subsumption may also imply inclusion, integration, transformation and a degree of perceived freedom. In this sense, I draw on Marx's perspective as best enunciated in *Grundrisse* that both capital and labour confront each other as alienated because compelled by forces and pressures that are both internal and external to their relation. It is the variable level of alienation, negotiation with such existing forces and pressures, that make their relation dynamic and changeable.

Together with the socialisation of subsumption as 'subsumptive relations', another way by which I convey my invitation to reinterpret subsumption is to shed light on its dialectical other, which I define as determinate supersumption. In this sense, Chapter 4 will first define determinate supersumption. Subsumption is a process without guarantees. Synthetically worded, subsumptive relations comprise two co-constitutive sides, subsumptive and determinate supersumptive dynamics.

Determinate supersumption is a constitutive relative negation of subsumption that reminds us that subsumptive relations must constantly be sustained in order to overcome both inertia and the forces that push against the productive process: for example, in the labour process, measures reinforcing capital's command over labour – such as labour control and disciplinisation, monitoring technology – sustain subsumptive relations against phenomena such as sabotage, slowdowns and 'pilfering' or 'fiddling'. Thus, I claim that without these opposing forces subsumption could not be reproduced. I will show how such a notion has political implications because it points to the reversibility of subordinating power relations established by subsumptive processes.

I will examine determinate supersumption at two different levels: molar and molecular, which are inextricably mediated by the class dimension. While in many ways, the molar level was explored in Chapter 3 and was exemplified by the integral state, I here explore the structural tension that tends to disturb subsumptive relations even in its own operations, which is to say inherent contradictions embedded for instance in value theory. Objectively, at the level of broader relations of production, such a notion indicates a tension between a constant violent divorcing of workers from their means of production and an equally constant relative reappropriation of the means of production – this reappropriation is increasingly mediated by technology such ICT. In other words, this perspective articulates the synchronic nature of primitive accumulation and/or accumulation by dispossession to subsumptive dynamics as a continuous interplay between separating and rejoining living labour from its means of production, alienation and dis-alienation for it.

Determinate supersumption perspective invites us to look more closely at hybrid forms, which for instance go beyond formal subsumption. For example, black market labour, unregistered companies, informal economy and illicit business all constitute important aspects of the economy of most countries as well as pointing to the diversity and unevenness of capitalist development. Based on such a perspective, I consider the coexistence in the valorisation process of absolute, relative surplus-value and anti-value; the relationship between the informal economy and informal subsumption; precarisation as determinate supersumption; simultaneously 'advanced' real subsumption as well as reversion to formal subsumption.

However, despite the crucial importance of those objective contradictions that constitute determinate supersumption, in Chapter 4 the molecular level will be privileged as a perspective that rejects both the component of determinism that received understandings of subsumption convey, as well as the tendency to understand subsumption overwhelming as an abstract and fetishised force.

Molecularly, living labour is considered as exteriority or interior transcendentality that can never be completely exhausted by subsumptive relations. Homologically to the importance of distinguishing between production/realisation and value/price to show how the valorisation process gets fulfilled only conditionally, upon the sale of commodities produced, we can describe the same dynamics in the relations of subjection. In other words, if subsumptive relations mainly describe power relations of capital over labour so that the former can extract surplus-value from the latter, then subsumption is not completely realised if it does not control the consumer's effective demand and people's wants, needs and desires. That is where subsumptive relations become productive or (in-)adequate subjectivities. As per the case of determinate supersumption in productive relations, such a perspective not only shows the way in which subsumptive relations concern the capitalist social totality, but also the numerous points in which subsumption may encounter its supersumptive other and overcome it.

In the second part of the book, I move towards the more concrete. In order to exemplify key aspects of subsumptive relations and their productive tensions through determinate supersumption, I examine the context of emerging labour practices implemented by information and communication technologies (ICTs). In fact, as I will argue in Chapters 5 and 6, the need to revise, dynamise and qualify subsumption becomes evident when we consider subsumption in relation to both media/communication practices and living labour's subjectivities: for instance, the thesis of people's subjectivity being shaped by capitalist forms such as neoliberal ideology obliges us to conceive subsumption beyond pure subordination, in that trickier hegemonic realm of coercion and consent, freedom and necessity. Such an ambiguous context explains why criticising the so-called gig/digital economy means dealing with a system that generates contradictory phenomena such as intensification of labour and dramatic precarity while also promoting a sense of self-realisation and passion for working.

In relation to those arguments, both the condition of translational labour/practices in Chapter 5 and spatial relations of domestication in Chapter 6 represent particularly exemplary cases of how subsumptive processes permeate communication but also approach the barrier of untranslatability. In Chapter 5, drawing from both Gramsci and Marx, I examine communication practices as a kind of fixed capital that produces 'translatability'. The assumption here draws from a varied body of literature that tends to read ICTs as 'linguistic machine', which do not only harness communication within the labour process but the power to create spoken and software language (such as coding for algorithms) capable of abstracting concrete linguistic and signifying practices (such as social semiosis) into abstract linguistic labour. The reproduction and circulation of meanings (and the value attached to it, like in a TV commercial) across subjects, cultures and social spheres always leave certain areas untranslated. That is why linguistic machines like algorithms, trying to establish universal translatability for human practices, will always need machine learning to keep training them.

In the second part of Chapter 5, I will provide three examples of how communication creates contradictory conditions of translation and subsumption by producing data, digitalised information that allows a faster and smoother circulation of valorised information. I will look at the case of work mediated by digital platforms: the micro-logistics task of delivery food apps and data-driven journalism. Finally I analyse the clearest example of supersumptive politics from the point of view of translational practices: the 150 hours project.

In Chapter 6, I describe how a Covid-19-Capitalism is currently looking for fixes. In this connection, the book presents a critical inquiry on current space and time fixes implemented through information communication technologies, which operate as entry points to new subsumptive configurations. I exemplify this last analytical chapter with the discussion of the so-called domestication of remote working subjects, platform algorithmic economy and its implementation through communicative translational practices.

Reflecting on the role of technology, not just as a fix for capital, but as a fix for capital developing in social-spatial terms, I employ Lefebvre's spatialised theory of capitalist development, especially concentrating on his notion of abstract space. I argue that social space, both concrete and abstract, represent a formidable way to examine subsumption in the realm where physical space, social relations, ideologically loaded perception and practices meet each other.

I will look at the home working as a result of Covid-19 restrictions as a context in which capital finds its temporary fix/solution by producing digital abstract space. It is a space of production constitutively mediated by digital technology that profoundly alters households. As a result, the worker experiences what Sergio Bologna and Andrea Fumagalli[59] call domestication. I will

---

59   Bologna and Fumagalli 1997.

argue that domestication is not simply a social factory moving into the household, it is a complex assessment of spatial relations in which subsumptive and supersumptive tendencies clash with each other at the molecular level of '*la perruque*' and gamified labour practices.

Finally, in Chapter 7, I conclude by briefly discussing two cautionary cases that provide me with the opportunity to reflect on the short and midterm future of work mediated by digital technology and by subsumptive relations. First, almost as a natural continuum of Chapter 6, I discuss the debate on remote working and why, despite the unchanged profitability and undeniable cost reduction for production, many companies insist on having their remote-working personnel return to work in the office. I claim that despite work intensification and longer hours – which show how in the hybrid realm of domesticized work we work more, and are more surveilled by digital connective technology – bosses want workers back because, assuming that it is easier to manage bodies that are physically present, they would rather maintain their power in terms of class relations than make short-term gains in surplus-value. This, in my view, shows that subsumption is both about surplus-value and hegemonic class relations.

The second case is about the rise (and current fall) of cryptocurrency and the aspiration of many techno-optimist to turn it into a universal currency – a digital money free from material production and from control by central authority. I argue that financial products such as Bitcoin can never become a universal currency because their libertarian and neoliberal conception dislodge them from the material economy. The issue is not simply that these financial products are anti-state; rather, their supporters imagine that technology can replace the ensemble of power relations that ramify across all of society – therefore well beyond the state – and guarantee a consistent production of surplus-value. In other words, fiat currencies are not simply backed by the centralised authority that libertarianism rejects so strongly, but by an entire hegemonic organisation of the production of value, that is, by that which the state ultimately reflects. Without such backing, I argue, cryptocurrencies are destined to remain volatile and unreliable.

CHAPTER 2

Defining a Legacy

> Alongside representations of nature and humanity itself, representations of the aims, means, stages and anticipated results of human activities on nature and society – representations which simultaneously organise a sequence of events and legitimise the location and status of agents in society.[1]

∴

This chapter offers a selective intellectual history of subsumption, which starts with a brief review of the critical tradition of German idealism as represented by Kant and Hegel, and especially concentrates on the crucial transition from Hegel to Marx. Then, I review Marx's usage of the term as it appears throughout his whole *opus operatum*, and particularly in the *Grundrisse*, *Theories of Surplus Value*, 'Results of the Direct Production Process' and *Capital*. Finally, in the second part of the chapter, I examine some of the most significant interpretations of the term, mostly developed in the twentieth-century Marxist literature.

The discussion of Kant, Hegel and Marx will be organised by a rationale that pushes further Andres Sáenz de Sicilia's[2] already well-established inquiry: gradually adding logical, social and historical determinations to my understanding of subsumption. While in this chapter I mostly accept and follow Sáenz de Sicilia's approach, I add an extra layer, that is, the political one, which I will then develop in the following chapters.

My review of Marx's approach to subsumption draws on what Skillman[3] defines as the tension between two coexisting – but not necessarily always compatible – lines of argument: the value-theoretic line of argument, which in relation to subsumption manifests with its links to surplus-value; and the

---

1 Godelier 1986, p. 11.
2 Sáenz de Sicilia's doctoral thesis represents a major source of inspiration for this manuscript. While I think his study ultimately stops short of really politicising subsumption and remains trapped at a fairly abstract conceptual level, his philosophical reflection of the link between subsumption and social form theory makes this work a seminal study in the literature on subsumption. As the reader will notice, I will consistently make reference to his ideas.
3 Skillman 2013.

historical one, which in relation to subsumption manifests through the historical reference to capitalist development, in terms of primitive accumulation, and allegedly a subsequent order of subsumption stages, such as formal–real–social–total.

While Skillman uses the distinction between the value-theoretic and the historical arguments to try to explain why 'The Results of the Immediate Process of Production' and its theoretical baggage – including the most robust Marxian treatment of subsumption – was not used as a chapter of the first volume of *Capital*, I utilise it to explain both the unresolved tensions in the Marxian conceptualisation of subsumption and how those tensions affected later readings of subsumption.

While the two narratives ultimately describe a general totalising tendency of subsumption, one tends to emphasise the expansion through social space and social time, while the other one tends to frame subsumption as symptomatic of an unstoppable absolute power of capitalism. On the one hand, subsumption is understood as a way to *periodise* capitalist development. That is a narrative characterised by a necessary incremental tendency that can be understood through relatively fixed historical stages. In particular, Jacque Camatte and Antonio Negri will be discussed as examples of the tendency to treat subsumption as a *telos* of *historical* progression, while authors like Chris Arthur, Patrick Murray and Eric-John Russell will be discussed as examples of treating subsumption as a *telos* of capitalism's *logical* development.

On the other hand, subsumption has alternatively been interpreted as a way to understand the techno-logic of capitalist development characterised by a mostly one-sided power relation. While the periodisation approach tends to reduce the dialectic of capital and labour to an all-encompassing story of the domination of the former over the latter, the techno-logical version tends to depict subsumption as bringing about a totalising ideologically saturated world completely remade in the image of capital and affected by technological determinism, a view developed most clearly in the work of Adorno and Debord. According to such a perspective, subsumption, even when comprehended in terms of subsumptive relations, tends to be approached in the reductive form of command and plain subordination.

1 Defining Subsumption: A First Approximation to Logic and Material Tension

Defining, signifying and re-signifying subsumption represents a major task of this book. Defining and determining then do not epitomise a point of departure but rather the point of arrival, through a process of dialectical movement that qualifies and delimits subsumption through determinate negation-qualification, contradiction and fluidification, but also significantly expands it by attaching it to notions such as subsumptive relations, determinate supersumption, hegemony and crisis.

So where do we start with subsumption? In the introduction, I have offered an already formed definition, but that does not really contain in itself an account of its own *raison d'être*. In this sense, this is what I am trying to provide here, a sort of reverse engineering to indicate where that definition comes from. It is a rather arbitrary endeavour that in my case leads to an 'etymological' approach. While words gain and lose meanings over time, the process of trying to uncover the original meaning of a given word frequently provides insights into how the words come to be used and how their meaning can transform or be reproduced over time.

The term subsumption comes from Latin *subsumere*. It is a word composed of two particles, *sub* + *sumere*. *Sub* is roughly translated as 'under' and *sumere* as to 'take'. The problem is that both elements are generic enough to assume a variety of meanings. For instance, literally 'to take under' in current English is essentially only used to describe protection and mentorship, as in the expression to 'take someone under one's wing'. On the other, to 'undertake' is more self-centred, is to take initiative in doing something, to commit and take a pledge. Moreover, *sumere* can be further translated as 'take up', 'take hold of', 'receive', 'spend', 'adopt', 'embrace' and 'assume'. Similarly, *sub* can be 'under', 'beneath', 'behind', 'from under', 'at the foot of'; also 'close to', 'up to', 'towards'; related to time, 'within', 'during'; or figurative, 'subject to', 'in the power of' and 'absorption'.

Common to all these connotations is a sense of acting upon, thus establishing a difference between an active and passive agent. Such an action shares some considerable semantic terrain with 'con+sumption'. Both *subsumption* and *consumption* may imply engagement and absorption, but while the former seems to lean more towards a logical/categorical absorption, the latter entails a physical wasting of a body that is materially used up. Thus, comparatively, subsumption synthetically means 'take under' as establishing a superiority/inferiority relation, while consumption means 'take in', implying a sort of internalisation by destruction and/or squandering.

So, you can consume a burger but not an institution, you can subsume an institution but not a burger. Is this really true? Part of the problem can be understood in terms of what Marx defined as metabolic relations. In *Capital*[4]

---

4 Marx 1990, pp. 138–9.

Marx theorises the material exchange linking people and nature as an inextricable combination of natural and physical conditions with human practices. Both the production and consumption of burgers and institutions represent for Marx a socially mediated and organised exchange of matter and energy, thus operating morphologically on quantitively (but maybe not qualitatively) different combinations of matter and energy. This is how Braverman explains it:

> Plants absorb moisture, minerals and sunlight, animals feed on plant life or prey on other animals. But to seize upon the materials of nature ready-made is not work; work is an activity that alters these materials from their natural state to improve their usefulness. The bird, the beaver, the spider, the bee and the termite, in building nests, dams, webs and hives, all may be said to work. Thus, the human species shares with others the activity of acting upon nature in a manner which changes its forms to make them more suitable for its needs.[5]

Such a social mediation, both in the case of a burger and institution, is primarily understood as human labour. Thus, from this point of view, subsumption and consumption are two aspects of the same labour-driven metabolic relation.

The semantic continuity and discontinuity between subsumption and consumption framed by the metabolic perspective are rather important in prefiguring an important argument advanced by this study. First, while I will gradually advance and refine an understanding of subsumption as subsumptive power relations, I will also stress, *vis-à-vis* much of the existing literature, that those power relations cannot be understood as absolute dominance or absolute integration of the weaker element/social group by the stronger one, but rather as more fluid and therefore more contradictory hegemonic relation in which the 'ruled' element is not consumed but integrated. Furthermore, without reducing an historical materialist perspective to a doctrine of physical matter, subsumption also entails sensuality, especially when it comes to workers' bodies and the biopolitics of managing them in the domains of both production and consumption.

Therefore, referring to the interaction between physical and social levels suggested by Marx's metabolic relations,[6] subsumption can only consume and

---

5 Braverman 1974, p. 36.
6 An important question that, due to space limitation, I will not really elaborate on here is

incorporate productively a given element, and can only do that without complete annihilation or absorption. Subsumption is not just contextualised in production but also in consumption, it is both consumptive production and productive consumption, which points, as I will discuss in Chapter 3, to the broader perspective of social subsumption.

There is also another important qualification about the distance between subsumption and consumption: between final consumption and productive consumption. While, thermodynamic-wise, consumption is never final – eating an apple turns into energy and residues of the digestive process – it is interesting to think of subsumption as productive consumption because the element subsumed is productive and also produces changes in the dynamic of subsumption. As Marx claims, 'the person objectifies himself in production, the thing subjectifies itself' in consumption;[7] in the same way, subsumption does not really consume the subsumed object, it actually reshapes it. This is one important characteristic of subsumption: it is a matrix of form, that is, a process of form-determination of forms, which ultimately brings us back to an understanding of subsumption as an interactive and immanent metabolising kind of relation.

Thus, the form-determining kind of consumption entertained here is unstable because it is based on the continuous interaction between the form of the subsuming agency and the form of the subsumed element.

In relation to the existing usages of term, apparently, my understanding seems to be at odds with how currently the notion is used outside the specialised and fairly marginal niche of Marxist studies. In fact, subsumption is currently utilised in its predominantly logical meaning, which is confirmed by its applications in the legal, rhetorical and computational fields. For example, in legal terms, subsumption defines an abstraction operation: a concrete event/action that can be assimilated under an abstract framework by a process of deduction, and the way evidentiary facts can be subsumed under concrete legal facts, which then can be interpreted by abstract legal norms. For instance, Cyras defines it as follows:

---

whether subsumption may encounter the same 'absolute limits of capital' that Mészáros associates with the ecological environment, which will illuminate the link between subsumption and consumption. According to Mészáros, all metabolic orders face absolute limits that they cannot transcend without forcing a radical transformation into a new mode of production: Mészáros 1995. The other option is Marx's metabolic rift, according to which capitalism cuts off its link with nature.

7 Marx 1973, p. 89.

> Subsumption refers to the application of the law, or more precisely, the application of a norm to a fact, thus concluding the legal qualification. ... Subsumption is central in making a legal decision. Legal qualification, which results in the subsumption procedure within the legal domain, is central for ontologies in law.[8]

As he explains it, providing legal qualification means for instance determining whether the death of a person can be defined as murder, manslaughter or as an act legally permitted during a conflict. Thus, subsumption implies two aspects that Cyras and Lachmayer defines as 'terminological subsumption' and 'normative subsumption'.[9] According to the former, subsumption means 'translating' the manifold factual manifestations of the social into an element contemplated by the law. Thus, the facts of a case are transformed into legal terms. According to the latter, once incorporated inside the semantic field of law, a legal norm can be applied, hence normative subsumption.

Terminological and normative subsumption describes a process that is not simply about formal logic, as in the case of implementing law and its concrete repercussions (for example, going to prison, paying a fine, winning a civic trial). The famous trope 'law and order', from a subsumption point of view, should be reformulated as a process 'order 1–law–order 2': ordering social facts according to a precise logic (order 1), a logic that can be translated into legal terms (law), which then are translated into a verdict, a diktat that re-establishes a social order (order 2). Thus, subsumption functions like a fairy tale understood in structural terms,[10] in which given acts (perpetrated by the disruptive agent) are terminologically defined and normatively condemned so that order can be restored. It is not a neutral passage of information between equally ranked orders of things, it is indeed a sort of metabolisation.

As I will elaborate in Chapter 5, subsumption in the legal sphere indicates the existence and the operations of a social translation machine. The question that we will have to answer is whether such a translation goes only one way or can be reversible. I can anticipate my short answer, it is indeed *partly* reversible.

Subsumption in the legal form hides a potential mystification that haunts interpretations of subsumption: the legal usage of subsumption betrays a logical ontology and the going back and forth – translation-wise – between logical and social ontology. As Marx argues in his critique of Hegel's legal philosophy,

---

8   Cyras and Lachmayer 2014, p. 330.
9   Cyras and Lachmayer 2014, p. 331.
10 Propp 1968.

the logical sphere is a form of representation of the social sphere, it is a mystification that tries to gain authority by claiming the existence of pure and neutral rational thought. Thus, rendering social facts imputable during a trial in legal logical terms, in order to process them into new social facts, implies a mystification of power.

As already mentioned, such a legal application derives from its original utilisation in logic/rhetoric. Interestingly enough, in rhetorical studies, subsumption represents the minor premise of a syllogism, the particular concrete example that can be subsumed under the general premise. What is indeed noteworthy about this is that, as we shall see in the next portion looking at its interpretation by Kant, Hegel and Marx, here subsumption refers to the particular element that can be subsumed under the general one. Thus, it refers more to the object of subsumption than to the dynamic of subsumption and its effects. Like in the well-known syllogism: 1) All men are mortal; 2) Socrates is a man; 3) therefore, Socrates is mortal.

Subsumption is the denomination of the premise of the syllogism, the conclusion containing the minor term, hence 'Socrates is a man'. In this sense, the object of subsumption can function as such because of its mediating potential between the general and the particular.

Similarly, in computer programming, robotics and linguistics, subsumption describes a kind of subclassifying between scales of abstraction such as types: type A is a subclass of type B, therefore type B is a superclass of type A. Accordingly, any element that meets type A's criteria also meets type B's criteria, because B's abstraction level is higher than A's, or, in terms of specifications, is less determined. This kind of subsumption is exemplified by the Liskov substitution principle.[11]

All these interpretations of subsumption have in common a description of a dynamic of assimilating the more specific element under a more general/abstract element, and such a dynamic is also consistently combined with a hierarchical structure according to which the subsuming category is not simply more general but capable of subordinating, controlling, assimilating the subsumed one in ways that are not reciprocal or revertible. As we shall see, when it comes to subsumption as a notion used to explain social dynamics, this represents a salient but not complete account of subsumption. As I have just mentioned, it seems to me that the coexistence or even the tension between the logical and the social involves a certain degree of mystification. In order to appreciate its richness, we must review its philosophical application.

---

11   Liskov and Wing 1994.

2 Critical Genealogy: The Kantian–Hegelian Trajectory

The reason to trace back the history of subsumption through Kant and Hegel is that it allows us to deconstruct a notion that comprises the logical, historical and social, especially when it comes to the Marxian and post-Marxist interpretations. In this sense, the logical/procedural definition so far discussed represents a component that will inform and mediate how Marx understands subsumption via the fundamental reading provided by Hegel, which, in turn, drew critically from previous thinkers like Kant.

In Kant, subsumption plays a fundamental role in integrating particular elements under the general/universal judgement, it constitutes an implementing mechanism of his overall project to link logical forms of judgement to rational practices, and the constitution of knowledge through critical assessments.[12] Subsumption is essentially a problem of ordering things according to their hierarchic status for the sake of creating knowledge. According to Sáenz de Sicilia, Kant's approach was as follows:

> He asked not how subsumption is possible in its formally logical sense, as an ordering connection of thought determinations, but rather, in analysing the conditions of possibility for any experience of an object, he asked how sensibility and the understanding – cognitive faculties that are 'entirely unhomogeneous' with one another, and thus generate representations that are different in kind – could be connected subsumptively.[13]

Subsumption by Kant's usage reflects more than a logical procedure, it is about sensible experience and 'how can sensations be adapted to concepts'.[14] According to such an interpretation, elements of a lower category get absorbed under a more general category, like incorporating a representation under a given concept; and those particulars can indeed be incorporated by concepts after having been processed by them. In this sense, Kant applies the syllogistic logic just mentioned according to which a given universal rule – such as 'all men are mortal' – is applied to a particular case – 'Caius is a man' – and from which an inferential judgement can flow, establishing all the implications of the rule within the particular – 'Caius is mortal'. Indeed, this kind of syllogistic judgement is the model for Kant's theory of rational cognition, within which sub-

---

12 Sáenz de Sicilia 2016.
13 Sáenz de Sicilia 2022, p. 39.
14 Sáenz de Sicilia 2022, p. 40.

sumption functions as the mediating act connecting particular representations with the predicates, or 'marks', of universal concepts.

For Kant, subsumption is a judgement, not a social condition or a praxis, a way logically to include or categorise experience, to introduce ordinal relations between elements that are not formally homogenous; thus it is a process of mediation and subordination dealing differences that need to be overcome for synthesis's sake. Kant links subsumption to the propositional capability binding together different representational elements under the same cognitive category. Thus, the subsuming action of linking together lower-order representations under the same concept is what for Kant guarantees the unity of consciousness and understanding of the world:

> Pure general logic deals with concepts, judgements and inferences, corresponding exactly to the functions and order of those powers of the mind, which are comprehended under the broad designation of understanding in general ... If the understanding in general is explained as the faculty of rules, then the power of judgement is the faculty of subsuming under rules, that is, of determining whether something stands under a given rule (*casus datae legis*) or not.[15]

This is a point that Sáenz de Sicilia stresses well, that is, the tendency since Kant, passing through Hegel and Marx, to go from a logical category to an historical one, and from an historical to a social one. That represents the passage from the cognition of an individual to the relationship between such an individual and a transindividual collectivity and its social forms. As I will show later on, my take pushes one step further into the political realm, in other words, it deals with the question of how a collective can act upon the social.

While in Kant the lower rank category – the less general, more particular one – is passively absorbed into the more general one, in Hegel conceptual subsumption is understood as a dynamic as relational and more interactive, according to which the particularity and the generality constitute each other. Thus, returning to my previous discussion of 'consumption' and 'subsumption', for Kant subsuming is indeed closer to consuming the lower order element, there is a sort of ethical sacrifice of difference for the greater good of a synthetic understanding of the world. My language here is of course deliberately suggestive, because the translation to the social and political seems to be rather direct.

---

15   Kant 1998, A130–132/B170–172.

Conversely, Hegel emphasises in dialectical terms the mediating function of subsumption already pointed out by Kant. However, while in Kant subsumption seems to be confined at the logical/formal level, for Hegel it acquires a social dimension associated for instance with individuals as particularities facing the general social structure. In this sense, as I have mentioned, the political implication is not absent either in Kant or in Hegel, but it is certainly not made explicit, or ready to be directly applied to the political. For instance, as in the case of my previous allusion to the 'sacrifice' of the lower element, particularities and generality are indeed dialectically linked, but the historical *telos* of human progress also leans towards the privilege of the general as a collective synthesis.

In Kant's theoretical structure, subsumption represents an organising principle that aims at ordering elements based on hierarchic logic and categorical belonging, distinguishing between degrees of particularity and generality. Ideally, through subsumption such an ordering system aims at achieving the most synthetic form of itself, because subsuming lower, less general element B under higher, more general element A means being to be able to say that every B can be considered to belong to A. Now, the question is whether B is being preserved, incorporated or ground under by subsumption. Returning to my previous discussion – of whether subsumption describes integration or consumption – this is the fundamental question that Hegel poses. His response differs significantly from Kant's. While in Kant the lower element B is ultimately absorbed/metabolised into the higher A, in Hegel the relational link and both elements are preserved.

Subsumption then becomes a social relational category. The main difference compared to Kant is that in Hegel subsumption entails social practices, social relations and social forms of existence rather than pure categories of thought or isolated objects and individuals. We are now dealing with the mediation of a third element that cannot be reduced to an internal trait already subsumed or an external one not yet subsumed. The mediating element also constitutes the common denominator that allows synthesis of the manifold into one.

As I previously did with consumption, it is useful to compare subsumption with another semantically related term, the Hegelian notion *par excellence*, sublation. Sublation in Hegel refers to a process that overcomes and preserves a given element at the same time. Therefore, the outcome of sublation is the conciliation of opposite aspects/tendencies of a given element. Compared to that, subsumption implies a hierarchical relation between ideas, principles and statements, a more general or a stronger category that incorporates a weaker or more particular. While both terms imply inclusion/incorporation of particular content by a universal form, subsumption qualifies that by a power relation:

that which is subsumed is 'brought under'. David Halliburton,[16] reflecting on this power relation aspect, claims that sublation implies a component of consent and a reflective acceptance of the 'negative side' that is not necessarily present in subsumption. As I will discuss later on, this represents an aspect that, when read symptomatically, while not manifest, is implicitly present in Marx and that I strive to recuperate: the idea that while subsumption implies asymmetrical power relations, they work with the same fluidity and dynamicity of hegemonic power relations, according to which the holistic and relational nature of such power relations implies a general instability, negotiation and even instances of table-turning.

3 The Legacy of Kant and Hegel in Marx

In Marx, both Kantian transcendental logic and Hegelian social logic fuse together into an historical materialist perspective on subsumption, according to which subsumptive relations are the outcome and precondition of a socially and historically determined metabolic relation between people and physical matter, that is, labour. It is labour that gives a specific form to both structured relations and use-value objects.[17]

Subsumption, as a logically and physically real condition as well, may well be understood as a homeostatic effort to push the necessary change (of state, of social form, and therefore status) inherent in any metabolic processes towards specific goals, that is, a necessary change adequate to preserve surplus-value production. Subsumption, as both logical and historic process, comprises the homeostatic imperative of preserving the conditions for surplus-value production, in spite of its metabolic tendency to gain more ground in order both to expand and overcome conjunctural crises.[18]

---

16 Halliburton 1997.

17 While its importance, especially in terms of embodiment and biopolitics, will be explored later on, I think it is important to here to insist on the crucial role played by physical matter. The move is not just rhetorical, that is, pushing back against idealism using a crude materialism of physical reality; rather, in the end the core of my argument is that subsumption is a specific kind of social relation that aspires to abstract generality. However, important limits to such an abstraction are indeed provided by rich concrete reality, including but not limited to bodies and matter at work.

18 Here begins to emerge a conceptual parallelism that I think is useful in following my argument: in many ways, the tension between metabolic and homeostatic is homologic to the logical and social-historical aspects of subsumption, and the negotiation of fixity and movement characterising fixed capital.

Chris Arthur, in his seminal text *The New Dialectic and Marx's Capital*, provides an interesting means to assess the importance of German Idealism, and in particular of Hegel, for the way in which Marx and his later interpreters have approached subsumption:

> Hegel is the great expert on how an ideality would have to build itself up, moment by moment, into a self-actualising whole. If then, as I believe, capital has in part an ideal reality, then if it can be shown to incarnate Hegel's blueprint it can claim to be self-sustaining. ... Hegel's logic can be drawn on in such a study of capitalism because capital is a very peculiar object, grounded in a process of real abstraction in exchange in much the same way as Hegel's dissolution and reconstruction of reality is predicated on the abstractive power of thought.[19]

Similarly, as Russell[20] describes it, Marx follows Hegel's method of conceptual retroactive grounding, according to which categories are incomplete if not understood through the more complex ones that come after them as well as through the whole, which is always presupposed. He provides the example of the logical journey from commodity to money and from money to capital.

Still, according to Russell there is a clear link between Hegel and Marx's take on subsumption, which he sees reflected in the homological relationship between Hegel's *Science of Logic* and Marx's *Capital*. Russell claims that those two works are moved by the same systematic dialectics according to which each of the respective categorial articulations is arranged to conceptualise an existent concrete whole. As opposed to an 'historical dialectic', for which the sequence of categories corresponds to their appearance in history – a causal succession of linear historical stages – the systematic or 'New Dialectics' emphasises the logical derivation of one category to the next. Russell argues that such dialectics work retroactively so that:

> Every partial category is only understood and justified through a subsequent more complex one, rather than by a progressive deduction or simple propositional definition. At each step in the exposition, the whole is presupposed.[21]

---

19   Arthur 2002, p. 8.
20   Russell 2015.
21   Russell 2015, p. 30.

He establishes a parallelism between how subsumption works conceptually in Hegel and in Marx, since the notion presupposes an immanent relational logic according to which the validity of a given set of categories is to be considered dependent on their reciprocal relations. While Hegel's primary example consists in the relation of subject and predicate, in Marx such immanence is exemplified by the relationship between the particular and multiple concrete labour processes and the universality of the valorisation process of capital. For Russell, the Hegelian interpretative key to subsumption helps understand Marx's conceptualisation of the reciprocally constitutive class relation: the self-valorisation of capital requires labour and labour requires an established organisation of production capable of producing surplus-value.

Differently from Eric-John Russell's reading of Hegel's interpretation of subsumption, for Levine,[22] subsumption was an act of conquest, a 'process through which one frame of reference absorbed and consequently annihilated another frame of reference',[23] thus suggesting a sort of metabolic process where the superior element consumes its prey. Levine claims that Hegel used subsumption to explain how, for instance, individuals would be absorbed and reshaped by different political systems, such as a liberal democracy, a revolution, or a dictatorship. For Levine, subsumption was a major force in Hegel's philosophy: his philosophy of history runs through subsumption, historical stages were the agencies of subsumption, and individuality was an object that was constantly subsumed by the passage of historical forms.

However, as Tony Smith points out,[24] lower categories are not absorbed, cancelled or completely overcome, but retained with their tensions and contradictions with each other. In relation to that, together with Arthur, authors such as Murray, Bellofiore and Fineschi and Smith[25] believe, to different degrees, in the coexistence of two kinds of dialectics propelling Marx's *Capital*, according to which events and elements follow historical and logical successions. Thus, according to Russell the so-called systematic dialectics – as opposed to historical dialectics – privileges:

> ... the logical derivation of one category to the next. Here, the expositional ordering of the categories addresses itself to the comprehension of a totality, one wherein systematically interconnected category express

---

22   Levine 2012.
23   Levine 2012, p. 90.
24   Smith 1990.
25   See Murray 2009; Bellofiore and Fineschi 2009, Smith 1990.

their moments as existing synchronically and mutually presupposing one another as elements within an architectonic whole.[26]

In this sense, I see subsumption as a key manifestation of the tension that pervades Marx's *opus operatum* between the historic and logical methods we just mentioned. Subsumption, as Sáenz de Sicilia eloquently puts it in his *The Problem of Subsumption*,[27] sheds light on the paradox of seeing capital as a self-referential totality that can sustain itself by its inner dynamics, and the fact that capitalism is inevitably tied to a social historic process that led to 'external' confrontations with competing economic models, by antagonising, negotiating and incorporating elements. Capital appears then to be a social organisation capable of reproducing its own condition of reproduction, but it cannot do that without interacting with what lies outside its totality by increasing incorporation and expansion. As we shall see later on, part of the problem is that the existing literature on subsumption reflects such a tension 'unreflectively': simplifying what evidently is a much more complex framework needed to assimilate rich theoretical discussions, scholars tended to either privilege the historic or the systematic dialectic.

The historic approach to dialectics, mainly represented by Adorno, Debord and Negri, privileges epochal and significant changes, while the systematic approach privileges internal coherence, and therefore is more resistant to change. My argument regarding these two main interpretations is that they both tend to regard subsumption as a symptom of the ineluctability and historical necessity of capital, in other words, whether it changes in order to remain or needs no change at all, capital, according to both subsumption narratives, seems to point towards the exhaustion of historical change.

I take on here the point that Sáenz de Sicilia[28] makes in his conclusions, that the problem of subsumption can be turned into an opportunity for subsumption as an explanatory category, due to its potentiality as a category that can cut across systematic and historic reasoning and thus actually mediate them, mediating history and systematism, elements internal and external to capitalism, change and inertia, human agency and structural constraints.

Marx's key break with Kant and Hegel consists precisely in his conceptualisation of subsumption as a fundamentally historical and sociological matter. More than a neutral matter, subsumption is for Marx an object of (limited but still) critical inquiry, which cannot be taken for granted. In fact, in Marx's

---

26   Russell 2015, pp. 29–30.
27   Sáenz de Sicilia 2016.
28   Sáenz de Sicilia 2016.

writings, subsumption always means identifying the concrete elements inhabiting such a process: subsumption of what, by what, under what. It is not, however, an absolute break, because when Marx uses the concept he retains the logical inclusion that characterised Kant's approach and that is partially retained in Hegel, as well as the meaning of subordination. For example, we see subsumption of particular concrete practices such as concrete labour under the abstract universality of value, abstracted, that is, removed from reality. In this reconceptualisation of labour, there is a reduction and a synthesis because the manifold gets reduced into one 'common denominator'; but also subsumption in the sense of putting a given element, such a labour process or a subject (such as an artisan) under capitalist command in the sphere of production.

While one of the goals of this chapter is to show how the category of subsumption is enriched by Marx compared to his predecessors, Levine[29] is right in strongly qualifying the rupture with Hegel, which could be alternatively defined as a complicated continuity. Levine, like Russell,[30] claims that, as for other aspects of the Hegelian legacy in Marx's thought, when it comes to the logic of subsumption, Marx retained important traits of Hegel's dialectical method but rejected the system and the social and political implications that Hegel derives from it. Levine pushes this argument to the point of claiming that until Marx published *Hegel's Philosophy of Right* in 1843, he was actually sympathetic to the notion of the Hegelian state and accepted that as the normative universal, subsuming individual and particular element into a higher more coherent whole.

After this phase, Marx radically departed from the celebration of the Prussian state as well from the moral-philosophic implications of the desired totality, in which the limitations of the particularities are supposedly overcome. In order to appreciate the continuities and discontinuities between Marx and Hegel, Marx's own effort to come to terms with Hegel may be very useful. In his critique of Hegel's conceptualization of the State,[31] Marx explicitly considers subsumption as a way to describe how Hegel regarded the process of integrating individuals under the Prussian state as the realisation of a positive process that overcomes individual particularity in the universality of the state. Such political subsumption would sublate the particularism of individual and social groups' interests, which enter into conflict with each other at the level of civil society; these would be elevated into the higher normative, moral and social

---

29   Levine 2012.
30   Russell 2015.
31   Marx, 1992.

organisation – the collective wealth – of the state. For Marx, this view was a fiction, because as a social and historical process involving the absorption of particular elements into a generality, the state always represented the interests of a given ruling class:

> Hegel does not inquire whether this mode of subsumption is adequate or rational. He simply holds fast to the *one* category and contents himself with searching for something corresponding to it in actual existence. Hegel thus provides his logic with a political body; he does not provide us with the logic of the body politic.[32]

In this well-known passage, Marx clarifies how his understanding of subsumption is coherent with a historical materialist method that intends to problematise and turn upside-down the link between rationality and social being. While Hegel is preoccupied to give a body, that is, a materiality, to the rational idea, Marx wants to provide a rational explanation for the actually existing social body, that is, actual people living and interacting with each other. Besides the impetus of the rhetoric, it is important to notice, as Levine insists, that Marx's approach is different from but not exactly opposed to Hegel. Marx's materialism is not the simple negation of Hegel's idealism: in fact the two positions share significant ground, because in the end neither can Hegel be considered to represent crude and absolute idealism, nor Marx crude and absolute materialism. So, for instance, the actuality of the body politic is not pure matter, because as Gramsci would maintain, that would reveal idealism underneath crude materialism; rather it represents human praxis as a synthesis of ideas and the action of concrete human circumstances.[33] Still, as Sáenz de Sicilia notices, subsumption for Marx does indeed begin with a metabolic action: 'Labour thus enacts the subsumption of physical material under a practical end, form-determination of the material which endows it with a novel or enhanced usability'.[34]

Hegel and Marx's meeting point, I would argue, can be found in the idea of concrete abstractions that are tied to associated life: both understand the importance of systemic dynamics that seem to function regardless of the intentions of the individuals involved. Hegel explains them with thought-abstraction and Marx with the crystallisation of human praxis taking place over time. Con-

---

32 Marx 1992a, p. 109.
33 Gramsci 1975, N 11 § 27.
34 Sáenz de Sicilia 2022, p. 42.

crete abstractions such as the state are indeed constitutive, but while for Hegel they are originally generative, for Marx they are historically derivative.

It is possibly on this occasion that, conceptually, subsumption and sublation are finally rejected as synonyms, and clearly disambiguated. Decisively, for Marx the educative function of the state in heightening the individuals' egotistical wants, needs and desires represented a supreme example of how the dominant ideology creates false consciousness. As Marx will suggest in his later writings, subsumption does not create unity and pacification but antagonism and class struggle.[35]

In Marx's account, through the rational subsumptive operations of the Prussian state, Hegel makes a sort of Fukuyama-like claim about the end of history. As Fine puts it: 'Marx identifies Hegel with the transmutation of social relation into timeless logical categories, whilst he recognises the transitory character of capitalist social relations'.[36] Thus, while for Hegel such subsumption represents the means and manifestation of the teleological end of history, for Marx it is its beginning, at least as far as critical inquiry is concerned:

> Rationality does not consist in the reason of the actual person achieving actuality, but in the moments of the abstract concept achieving it. It is evident that the true method is turned upside down. What is most simple is made most complex and vice versa. What should be the point of departure becomes the mystical result, and what should be the rational result becomes the mystical point of departure.[37]

While in both thinkers subsumption has strong political implications, for Hegel subsumption is the realisation of truth or de-mystification of human (in-)dividual fragmented reality, whereas for Marx subsumption is the realisation of mystification, the condition that both presupposes and posits the formal equality of capital and labour in the market place, as well as the violent abstraction of concrete labour into abstract labour and form-giving function that turns non-capitalist social relations into relations adequate to capital. This is how Fine explains it:

> The value of reading Hegel's *Philosophy of Right* for Marx lay in the mirror of reality it offered – not just in Hegel's description of the institutions of the modern state but also in Hegel's inversion of subject and predicate

---

35   Marx 1973.
36   Fine 2009, p. 109.
37   Marx 1992, p. 99.

which mirrored the actual inversion of subject and predicate in bourgeois society: '*uncritical mysticism* is the key both to the riddle of modern constitutions ... the state is transformed into the semblance of an earthly divinity, Hegel's speculative philosophy not only rationalises this upside-down reality, but it also reveals it.[38]

Fine observes how Marx's rhetorical criticism of Hegel tends to be constantly built on the rhetorical figure of chiasmus. It is actually a specific kind of chiasmus defined as anti-metabole, because this rhetorical figure involves both reversal of structure and repetition of words, as exemplified by Marx in the following cases: Hegel's true interest is not in 'the logic of the subject-matter but the subject-matter of logic';[39] it is 'not to discover the truth of empirical existence but to discover the empirical existence of the truth';[40] Hegel 'does not provide us with the logic of the body politic' but 'provides his logic with a political body';[41] Hegel 'does not say that the will of the monarch is the final decision, but that the final decision of the will is – the monarch'.[42]

For Marx, the problem is both logical and political. Hegel does distinguish between reality and how thought understands reality, which represents, as he will claim in the *Grundrisse*, the movement from the simplified reality of the 'abstract' to the complexity of the concrete, which is the result of many determinations.[43] In this sense, subsumption in Marx's thinking also means mystification because it tends to reduce the complexity of the concrete (such as labour) to the simplification of abstraction. Thus, Marx also criticises this understanding of subsumption as a method of inquiry because it is based on the incorrect understanding of abstract and concrete and incorrect movement from the latter to the former:

> Of course, the mode of presentation must differ in form from that of inquiry. The latter has to appropriate the material in detail, to analyse its different forms of development and to track down their inner connection. Only after this work has been done, can the real movement be appropriately presented. If this is done successfully, if the life of the subject matter

---

38   Fine 2009, p. 106.
39   Marx 1992, p. 73.
40   Marx 1992, p. 98.
41   Marx 1992, p. 109.
42   Marx 1992, p. 82.
43   Marx 1973, p. 101.

is now reflected in the ideas, then it may *appear as if* we have before us an *a priori* construction.⁴⁴

Marx's break with Hegel and the Young Hegelian circle consisted in a double movement: from rational philosophical ideal to the real, that is, actual, and historically constituted; instead of subsuming reality under speculative logic, Marx scrutinised the value of rationality in relation to the real life of people, thus subsuming rationality under social and historical conditions. Accordingly, the category subsumption, as a functional/dysfunctional link between state and civil society, became a component of an argument in favour of the critical deconstruction of the state, confuting an idealist understanding of the social process, but also problematising a philosophy of history propelled by abstractions instead of by human beings' praxis.

When discussing the relationship of Hegel and Marx through the lens of subsumption, Sáenz de Sicilia, describing how Marx was trying to go beyond the idealist conception, claims that 'the task demanded of a practical standpoint was not only to identify and criticise its irrational elements but also, crucially, to supersede them through real (that is, non-theoretical) action'.⁴⁵ Again, as noticed before, it seems to be crucial to specify how real action is always reflective action, mediated by thought and ideas. The transformative nature of action cannot be defined in opposition to thought or concept, but only in conjunction, that is, through praxis. In other words, I think it is important to avoid here the trap of pure and crude idealism versus pure and crude materialism. Thus, praxis is understood here as a combination of theory and action, reflective action and practical consciousness:

> Marx's discourse therefore breaks with the underlying structural antithesis between an active ideal-subjectivity (exemplified by Hegelian absolute spirit) and a passive material-objectivity (the immediacy of external, intuited otherness) that supports the seemingly counterpoised theoretical perspectives of idealism and 'traditional' materialism.⁴⁶

While this discussion may appear to be disconnected from subsumption, it actually touches a fundamental issue when it comes to the very much related notion of abstract labour, which is supposed to be a by-product of subsump-

---

44 Marx 1973, p. 102.
45 Sáenz de Sicilia 2016, p. 79.
46 Sáenz de Sicilia 2016, p. 85.

tion. For instance, Screpanti[47] insists on the importance of understanding abstract labour as an historically determined substance. In this sense, in the next section, as a way to start exploring in more systematic ways how Marx understands subsumption, we can start by considering the link between 'primitive accumulation' and subsumption.

4   Systemic Dispossession and Systemic Subsumption

Depending on how we understand subsumption, or which aspects we emphasise, primitive accumulation[48] – that is, the pre-history of capitalism or the accumulation preceding capitalist accumulation that describes the historical process of privatising the means of production – and subsumption seem to be logically connected. After all, there must have been a process that progressively incorporated the productive elements into the newly emerging capitalist totality, when people and resources were subsumed under capital. So, if primitive accumulation consists of 'the historical process of divorcing the producer from the means of production',[49] this represents the precondition for formal subsumption, when deprived small landowners moving into the city had to sell their labour-power to make a living. This historical process of ending feudalism and transitioning to capitalism represents, from the point of view of power relations and organisation, the subsumption of 'blood and fire'[50] into a new kind of violence and coercion inside the capital legal framework.

The historical and logical conditions of possibility for the establishment of capitalist subsumptive relations (at least according to what we will define as formal subsumption) can be synthetically described as the establishment of a particular kind of relation between labour and capital, which implied the emergence and diffusion of wage-labour, that is the process of subsumption of labour under exchange-value, that is the commodification of labour, which turns labour capacity into labour-power that can be sold and purchased. This particular subsumption establishes a reciprocal existential relationship between capital and labour.

---

47   Screpanti 2019, p. 16.
48   Harvey defines more specifically as 'entailed taking land, say, enclosing it, and expelling a resident population to create a landless proletariat, and then releasing the land into the privatised mainstream of capital accumulation': Harvey 2005, p. 149.
49   Marx 1990, p. 875.
50   Marx 1990, p. 875.

In this sense, Ellen Meiksins Wood[51] argues that the mutual presupposition of capital and labour has influenced Marxist historiography by a circular logic, which avoided explaining the actual origin of the relationship in question. She argues that the condition of labour subsumption under exchange-value is not to be found in the liberalisation of the job market but in fundamental changes in production and property relations. Wood problematises the view of capitalism as a necessary development from within the structure of trade, urbanisation and original accumulation of capital that could be reinvested. Significant for Wood's account is a narrative in which the mythical anthropology of the capitalist man, characterised by 'freedom and opportunities', 'individual industriousness' and 'diligent stockpiling' was replaced by the coercive pressure of market imperatives; 'it was unfixed, variable rents responsive to market imperatives that in England stimulated the development of commodity production, the improvement of productivity and self-sustaining economic development'.[52]

Wood ultimately points out how it was agrarian capitalism that turned unsuccessful market tenants into a dispossessed mass, who were forced to sell their labour-power for a wage. Such a mass of people also constituted a consumer market for the cheap everyday goods (food, textiles) that drove industrialisation in England:

> So, as competitive market forces established themselves, less productive farmers lost their property. Market forces were, no doubt, assisted by direct coercive intervention to evict tenants or to extinguish their customary rights … The famous triad of landlord, capitalist tenant and wage-labourers was the result, and with the growth of wage-labour the pressures to improve labour-productivity also increased. The same process created a highly productive agriculture capable of sustaining a large population not engaged in agricultural production, but also an increasing propertyless mass that would constitute both a large wage-labour force and a domestic market for cheap consumer goods – a type of market with no historical precedent. This is the background to the formation of English industrial capitalism[53]

While Wood qualifies the validity of Marx's argument in providing an explanation about England's expropriations due to enclosure, she nevertheless agrees

---

51   Wood 2002.
52   Wood 2002, p. 102.
53   Wood 2002, p. 63.

with him about the outcomes: a mass of people liberated both from feudal obligations as well as from their means of subsistence. However, their 'liberation' was followed by bloody and coercive laws directed against the dispossessed peasantry, who through coercion and physical violence were forcibly reshaped into wage workers.

As Tomba[54] notices, coercion of labour has always represented a constitutive trait of capitalism. Thus, even if occurring in different epochs or in different societies in different forms, such subsumption is not tied to some kind of 'original sin' – as the link to an expression such as 'primitive accumulation' suggests – but keeps on taking place in order to reproduce accumulation. If accumulation then is not the only system that needs to be sustained, how is subsumption of labour under exchange-value reproduced over time? The question can be answered by looking at the historical contingencies of a given country or, by abstraction, by looking at logical and conceptual presuppositions.

Conceptually, the compelling condition that reproduces wage-labour is not the free exchange of labour-power but must be found in the (im)possibility for the worker materially and bodily to subsist within a given class structure, including its associated power relations of command and subordination. The capability to build leadership, that is, the imposition of one class's interests inside the labour process, derives from a pre-existing position of power of both buyer and seller of labour-power. And historically, the prerequisite of power relations must be contextualised for every society. Not surprisingly though, the most exemplary historical case is the one where capitalism emerged first, England.

While, as Wood urged, we need to look seriously at the original condition of the emergence of capitalism, and at how the dispossession and separation mentioned above created two classes distinguishable by property relations and property content that can be used for exchange, the preconditions for sustaining such subsumption can also be found in another subsumptive process, that of use-values under exchange-values and the necessary mediation of money:

> When the formation of capital had reached a certain level, monetary wealth could place itself as mediator between the objective conditions of life, thus liberated, and the liberated but also *homeless* and *empty-handed* labour-powers, and buy the latter with the former.[55]

---

54 Tomba 2012.
55 Marx 1973, p. 509.

Returning to the logical argument discussed above, once labour is subsumed under the commodity/exchange-value, in other words, when it turns into wage-labour, the wage becomes a capitalist form that allows labour to be subsumed under capital as a whole. That is because, 'Through the exchange with the worker, capital has appropriated labour itself; labour has become one of its moments, which now acts as a fructifying vitality upon its merely existent and hence dead objectivity'.[56] Not by accident, labour becomes capital, that is, variable capital, due to the form-determining power of subsumption. Thus, capital operates as a unifying and totalising force: '*Capital proper does nothing but bring together the mass of hands and instruments that it finds on hand. It agglomerates them under its command*'.[57]

In regard to the argument of this book, Luxemburg[58] and Harvey's[59] claims about ongoing accumulation provide an important component of my claim about the need to reproduce subsumptive relations consistently. In fact, the need to maintain and reproduce 'primitive accumulation' through force – and not merely the 'mute compulsion' of material necessity – is in my view the basis for how subsumptive power relations are equally consistently reproduced. Thus, when Harvey points to the persistent predatory aspects of neoliberal capital, he also implies the consistent need to reproduce subsumptive power relations, so that dispossession allows for accumulation by allowing subsumptive power relations, therefore control and leadership of the system that produces absolute and relative surplus-value.[60] Fuchs, commenting on the ongoing need for primitive accumulation, draws a direct link to subsumption by claiming that:

> Subsumption does not necessarily operate only 'by brute force' (as in warfare), although physical violence can also be involved. Other methods used can include the law, illegal practices tolerated by the state, corruption, the neoliberal ideology of entrepreneurship, ideologies that create and reproduce capitalist hegemony, financial markets and other forms of violence ... Primitive accumulation and formal/real subsumption are both suited means for the Marxian explanation of the role of domination in capitalism and the relationship of class and domination.[61]

---

56   Marx 1973, p. 298.
57   Marx 1973, p. 508.
58   Luxemburg 1951, Chap. 26.
59   Harvey 2003.
60   Harvey 2003, p. 144.
61   Fuchs 2018, pp. 461–2.

Fuchs' account anticipates the key perspective of subsumption as a substantial social force that I will elaborate on in Chapter 3. We now inaugurate our exploration of how Marx himself understood subsumption by posing a problematic question that has motivated me, among other scholars, to look more closely into subsumption.

5   The Marginal Centrality of Subsumption in Marx

By the trope 'marginal centrality', I try to tackle the paradox between the objective marginality of subsumption as category utilised by Marx in his *opus operatum* as well as the potential such a category has to illuminate and interconnect many aspects of Marxian theory. For this reason, in this book I combine my own interpretation of the notion with one that springs from a symptomatic reading of Marx. Discussing this matter, Patrick Murray argues that the category of subsumption overall remains at the margins of Marxian reflections and Marxist debates:

> Marx's ideas about the subsumption of labour under capital went largely unrecognised until recent decades. When noticed, they have often been misunderstood, and they still remain on the margins of Marxian theory and studies of Marx. There are conceptual and textual reasons why this is the case. The conceptual reason is that Marx's rubric of subsumption forces the topic of specific social forms into the open since subsumption refers to subsumption under specific social forms. Because Marx was widely interpreted, by friend and foe, as a radical political economist rather than a radical critic of political economy, the topic of social form was not on the radar. ... If capital is not conceived of as a specific social form, in fact the mainspring of capitalist modernity, then the very idea of subsuming labour under capital makes no sense.[62]

Murray points to a form of theory-informed materialism that necessarily tries to synthesise the history of class struggle with the ratio of capitalism as a concrete abstraction that totalises social life by form-giving. While Murray is right, and I will elaborate on the importance of social forms when it comes to subsumption at various points in this book, his interpretation may explain why subsumption was not among the most popular Marxist notions without yet

---

62   Murray 2009, pp. 12–13.

necessarily explaining why it was not central to Marx's own repertoire. So why such marginal centrality? Let us try to answer this question.

The term subsumption features in much of the preparatory work toward the first volume of *Capital*, first omitted and then reinstated as an appendix with the title of 'The Results of Immediate Process of Production'. Its reprinting in the 1960s in German and then French, Italian and English, provided, along with the publication of the *Grundrisse*, new material through which much of Continental Marxism found new energy and perspectives that allowed for an expansion of Marx's political economy into the sphere of social life beyond the direct context of production.

The most substantial passages on subsumption were originally planned to be part of the sixth chapter of the first volume of *Capital*. As Skillman[63] notices, indeed in the actual Chapter 10 on 'The Working Day' and Chapter 15 on 'Machinery and Large-Scale Industry', subsumption as a category hinges on a theoretical argument about surplus-value (absolute and relative) and an historical argument about the coming of age of industrial capitalism. In fact, the periodisation is chronological in the sense that while it makes reference to historical events about the struggle for the length of the working day in England, it also presents an aspect of a logical and more abstract sequence. For Skillman, by incorporating subsumption into the chapters of 'The Production of Absolute Surplus Value' and 'The Production of Relative Surplus Value', Marx was ultimately privileging the logical over the historical argument: from a condition of formal subsumption that produces absolute surplus-value by lengthening of the working day, the capitalists move to real subsumption, with its machine-driven reorganisation of production based on division of labour – a process of cooperation that overcomes the limits that eventually governments set for the working day, by increasing productivity.

While Levine concentrates on reconstructing the original reasons for Marx to adopt subsumption – arguing that Marx wanted to use categories of a Hegelian logic such as subsumption to explain how an 'organic process of production',[64] founded on the interconnection of concrete working abilities and needs, was superseded by one motivated by surplus-value – he does not really explain why he then makes so little subsequent use of the category.

Again, according to Skillman, prominent Marxian scholars[65] have investigated the omission of the 'Results' from *Capital* without reaching compelling explanations. In fact, Murray defines the issue as an 'unresolved mys-

---

63   Skillman 2013.
64   Levine 2021, p. 85.
65   See Mandel 1976; Dussel 2001; Murray 2009.

tery'.⁶⁶ Three authors⁶⁷ have raised the more specific question as to why Marx elected to truncate so severely his extensive discussion of the concepts of formal and real subsumption in the second and third drafts. While their studies of Marx's treatment of the concept of subsumption are insightful on other grounds, neither White nor Arthur articulate a specific explanation as to why Marx chose to make such a fundamental change to the structural logic of his critique. Roberts does speak to this question directly, suggesting that Marx was prompted to drop most of his account of subsumption from the first volume of *Capital* due to the difficulty he encountered in maintaining a consistent distinction between formal and real subsumption. He contends, however, that it is possible to deduce such a distinction from the systemic effects of increasing capitalist control.

With somewhat a different approach, Szadkowski⁶⁸ maintains that the concept of subsumption was not regarded by Marx as a tool the reader could use to explain his project for a critique of political economy, but rather as a concept for his personal use, allowing him to navigate within the maze of his own theoretical system. In this sense, Szadkowsky, referring to the well-known distinction made by Marx in the afterword of *Capital*'s second edition, argues that subsumption pertains more to Marx's own inquiry and less to the order of presentation. He does not really justify such an interpretation, which remains highly subjective.

In my view, Skillman⁶⁹ is the author who has dealt with the question most explicitly and directly. He tries to explain why 'The Results of Immediate Process of Production', arguably a chapter of the first volume of *Capital*, was finally deleted. Elaborating on the question, he claims that for Marx it was increasingly difficult to maintain a coherent distinction between formal and real subsumption. For Skillman the issue runs deep, raising an even more general theoretical question: that of the relation between the logical explanation of the economic base of surplus-value, based on commodity exchange, and the historical account based on contingent conditions of production, that is, regardless of the specific operation of commodity prices and values. The latter account comprises two analytically related narratives, one concerning the ability of capitalists to appropriate surplus-value in the absence of any direct control over the production process – a scenario corresponding primarily to certain commercial transactions prior to the era of industrial capitalism – and the other

---

66   Murray 2009, p. 164.
67   White 1994; Arthur 2009; Roberts 2009.
68   Szadkowski 2016.
69   Skillman 2013.

regarding the ability of capitalists to extract surplus-value when they do control the labour process.

For Skillman, subsumption, understood as 'Marx's analysis of the systemic conditions underlying capitalists' appropriation of *surplus-value*',[70] was significantly downplayed because of its incompatibility with another line of argument in the first volume of *Capital*. He claims that Marx carries on two distinct lines of arguments, a *value-theoretic* and an *historical* account of surplus-value. The value-theoretic provides an economic explanation for how surplus-value gets produced and reproduced based on labour theory of value and commodity exchange. The historical argument aims at providing a longitudinal account of how capitalism was able, both with direct and indirect control of the production process, to extract surplus-value *vis-à-vis* labour, without touching on the link between commodities, price and values.

In my view, the value theoretical and the historical argument are also reflective of another tension Marx finds in capital without necessarily completely resolving it, namely the tension between capital as an historical dynamic and capital as a logical abstraction. In this sense, the process of subsumption reveals how capital passes from the abstract to the concrete through its form-determining function, which produces forms of representation such as money for value or profit for surplus-value. At the same time, the materialisation of capital requires an abstraction of the subsumed element, which loses the manifold determinations of concrete, to become something more abstract, as in the exemplary case of concrete and abstract labour.

In this sense, Sáenz de Sicilia claims that 'the "repressive abstraction" of the value-form and its expanded reproduction is the defining aspect of capitalist power'.[71] With respect to that, and with a view to further advancing his argument, in this work I contend that such power would be better defined as hegemonic rather than repressive – therefore repressive, consensual and, to a degree, negotiated – thus emphasising its instability, openness and indeterminacy.

6 Marx's Multiple Subsumptions: Formal, Real, Hybrid and Ideal

Marx first introduces the notion of subsumption in the *Economic Manuscripts of 1861–63*, describing how labour is absorbed within the capital reproductive system:

---

70 Skillman 2013, p. 476.
71 Sáenz de Sicilia 2016, p. 125.

> Historically, in fact, at the start of its formation, we see capital take under its control (subsume under itself) not only the labour process in general but the specific actual labour processes as it finds them available in the existing technology, and in the form in which they have developed on the basis of non-capitalist relations of production. It finds in existence the actual production process – the particular mode of production – and at the beginning it only subsumes it formally, without making any changes in its specific technological character. Only in the course of its development does capital not only formally subsume the labour process but transform it, give the very mode of production a new shape and thus first create the mode of production peculiar to it. ... This formal subsumption of the labour process, the assumption of control over it by capital, consists in the worker's subjection as worker to the supervision and the command of capital or the capitalist. Capital becomes command over labour.[72]

In this passage, he describes subsumption as an historical account of how capitalism opportunistically starts controlling non-capitalist labour processes and relations of production on the basis of property relations formally established by the law. Subsumption is described as the assumption of control, command and supervision of the labour process so as to transform it. It is interesting to notice how in this first account the process of subsumption does not entail specific social forms, in other words, as Marx puts it, 'capitalism subsumes under itself'.

While in the excerpt above, Marx already hints at the point, 'The Results of the Direct Production Process' involves a more explicit and articulate distinction between the formal and real subsumption of labour under capital:

> The general features of the formal subsumption remain, viz, the direct subordination of the labour process to capital, irrespective of the state of its technological development. But on this foundation there now arises a technologically and otherwise specific mode of production – capitalist production – which transforms the nature of the labour process and its actual conditions. Only when that happens do we witness the real subsumption of labour under capital. ... The real subsumption of labour under capital is developed in all the forms evolved by relative, as opposed to absolute surplus-value. With the real subsumption of labour under capital a complete (and constantly repeated) revolution takes place in the

---

72 Marx and Engels 1867, pp. 30, 92–3.

mode of production, in the productivity of the workers and in the relations between workers and capitalists.[73]

Another important difference between the 'Results of the Direct Production Process', compared to the first usage of the term in the *Economic Manuscript*, is that in the later text Marx also ties subsumption to surplus-value and the corresponding distinction between absolute and relative surplus-value.

It is also interesting to notice that in the 'Results of the Direct Production Process' and the *Economic Manuscript of 1861–63*, Marx develops the notions of 'subordination' and 'subsumption'. Sometimes he uses the two words as synonyms, sometimes as distinct terms. In this book I assert the necessity of keeping them distinct and of understanding the differences in their meanings. While 'subordination' describes an asymmetrical power relation between the capitalist and the worker in the sphere of production, 'subsumption' refers to the arrangement whereby the productive power of labour becomes a productive power of capital; in other words, it describes a richer and more complex power relation. The capitalist needs to exercise her control over the labour process because labour-power, the commodification of people's labour capacity, does not deliver up its use value in a systematic and consistent fashion. Thus, control and supervision entail making sure that capital can employ such a commodity in ways adequate to the stable and predictable extraction of surplus labour from workers. I will argue that this is achieved through a combination of coercion and consent.

The company is the legal embodiment of capital, and the productive forces deployed in the production process pertain to it, even though labour activities are executed by the workers. The firm's ownership of a worker's productive force originates from the 'subordination to capital of the labour process':

> The production process, considered as the unity of the labour process and the value creating process, is the process of production of commodities; considered as the unity of the labour process and the valorisation process, it is the capitalist process of production, or the capitalist form of the production of commodities.[74]

Subsumptive control is aimed at guaranteeing not just the valorisation process but the production of surplus-value; accordingly, '[i]f the production of

---

73   Marx 1990, pp. 1034–5.
74   Marx 1990 p. 304.

absolute surplus-value was the material expression of the formal subsumption of labour under capital, then the production of relative surplus-value may be viewed as its real subsumption'.[75] From this point of view, for Marx, the power relations linked to subsumption constitute the coercive condition through which capitalists can create value by unpaid labour executed by wage workers, which is appropriated without compensation and in a general condition of exploitation:

> First, workers are separated from the means with which production is carried on and can gain access to them only by selling their labour-power to others. Second, workers are freed of legal constraints, such as serfdom or slavery, that prevent them from disposing of their own labour-power. Third, the purpose of the employment of the worker becomes the expansion of a unit of capital belonging to the employer, who is thus functioning as a capitalist. The labour process therefore begins with a contract or agreement governing the conditions of the sale of labour-power by the worker and its purchase by the employer.[76]

The surplus-value represents the fundamental motivation for reproducing relations of production and class relations. Thus, subsumption plays a decisive role in the 'miraculous' process that produces unequal exchange between worker and capitalist (because of unpaid labour) on the basis of an apparent exchange of equivalents, that is, of wages for labour-power: 'Surplus-value is nothing but the excess amount of labour the worker gives over, above the amount of materialised labour that he receives in his own wages as the value of his labour-power'.[77] In other words, surplus-value expresses the difference between the value that living labour creates in production and value paid by the capitalist to the worker in the form of wages. Surplus-value, appropriated through exploitative practices, is for Marx the material foundation of profit, but it is not identical to profit because the surplus-value is realised in circulation and only produced at the moment of production. This represents one of the reasons why in the next chapter I will maintain that subsumption is always necessarily social subsumption, that is, expanding in a totalising fashion outside the limited context of the labour process.

Surplus-value presupposes exploitation and exploitation presupposes particular systemic production relations, which in turn correspond to class rela-

---

75 Marx and Engels 1867, 34, p. 429.
76 Braverman 1974, p. 36.
77 Marx and Engels 1867, 47, pp. 190–1.

tions, that is, relations based on unequal access to the means of production and the coercive situations in which workers must enter into exchange relations with a capitalist in order to access the conditions of their own physical reproduction, i.e., the wage. In the 'Results of the Direct Production Process', Marx explains that one of the conditions that define a capitalist is the class relation with the worker:

> The capitalist, who exists only as a potential purchaser of labour, becomes a real capitalist only when the worker, who can be turned into a wage-labourer only through the sale of his capacity for labour, really does submit to the commands of capital. The functions fulfilled by the capitalist are no more than the functions of capital – viz the valorisation of value by absorbing living labour – executed consciously and willingly. The capitalist functions only as personified capital, capital as a person, just as the worker is no more than labour personified.[78]

Furthermore, since the main implication of this subordinated relationship is that the worker becomes instrumental for the capitalist's specific interest, this power relation changes the ontological status of the worker in relation to the whole productive process: both the means of labour and the raw material for production seem to subsume the worker rather than the other way around. As in other fetishistic situations, things acquire a reason of 'being' and instrumentalise the work, which descends into the status of a passive instrumentalised object.[79]

6.1 Surplus Values

The link between the need for control and how capital is valorised during the production process is of course connected to how capitalists extract surplus-value. According to Marx's theory, the working day is divided into two portions. The first portion is dedicated to necessary labour, that is, the time needed to replace the value of the commodity labour-power, that is, the basket of goods that allow workers to sustain themselves and their families. The second portion is dedicated to surplus labour, which is in effect unpaid labour used to produce surplus-value. The two portions are analytically distinguishable but in practice

---

78 Marx and Engels 1867, 47, pp. 989–90.
79 In this sense, reading Marx against Marx, all kinds of subsumptions reshape the labour process by re-articulating that reciprocal co-constitution that Marx defines as the labour process; on this basis the form-giving purposive activity, that is, the labour process, changes the object, the working subjects and the labour process itself.

and, most importantly, in the experience of the worker, one cannot say when the first one ends and the second begins.

The second portion is evidently significant. In fact, if necessary labour were to equal the whole length of the working day, then no surplus-value and no profit would be possible, which is to say that, under conditions of perfect equivalence between wage-labour and the wage, no one would be motivated to start a capitalist enterprise. Conversely, the capitalist is motivated to initiate a working day only if she can get a 'plus' out of such a process, a plus on top of socially necessary labour. Central to the question of where control and supervision become crucial is that the capitalist does not only aim at producing surplus-value but also to increase such production, due not simply to greed but to the coercive law of competition with other capitalists.

Given the historical social conditions needed to establish wage-labour – that is, separation of workers from their means of subsistence – in order to increase surplus-value, the capitalist can choose between three routes: 1) keep necessary labour constant and increase surplus labour, thus lengthening the working day, which corresponds to absolute surplus-value production; 2) keep the length of working day constant but increase surplus labour at the cost of necessary labour by decreasing the value of the bundle of commodities needed to sustain labour-power, thus cheapening labour-power, which corresponds to relative surplus-value production (i.e., increasing productivity); or 3) increase both the length of working day and the tendency to reduce the cost of labour, in other words, combine the first two solutions. Historically, capitalists alternate between solutions according to the specific context. For instance, in periods of technological dynamism, if they can afford it, they would probably invest in technology that increases productivity. In contexts in which the legal framework allows for it, or in hybrid situations in which capitalism mixes with another mode of production, the capitalist may choose to lengthen the working day.

Solution number one is about lengthening the working day by increasing the surplus labour-time, that is, extracting absolute surplus-value. It does not require any changes in production methods. Marx[80] claims that the production of absolute surplus-value depends on two strategies: length of the working day and the intensity of labour. The individual capitalist, *vis-à-vis* the worker:

> ... will strive as hard as possible to raise output above this minimum and to extract as much work from him as possible in a given time. For every

---

80   Marx 1990, p. 305.

intensification of work above the average rate creates surplus-value for him. Furthermore, he will attempt to extend the labour process as far as possible beyond the limits which must be worked to make good the value of the variable capital invested ... Where the intensity of the labour process is given, he will seek to increase its duration, and conversely, where the duration is fixed, he will strive to increase its intensity. The capitalist forces the worker where possible to exceed the normal rate of intensity, and he forces him as best he can to extend the process of labour beyond the time necessary to replace the amount laid out in wages.[81]

Such an expansion by means of working hours and intensity requires supervision, because, in a context of formal subsumption, with no real improvement of the productive social and technological organisation, the capitalist can obtain absolute surplus-value only by 'pushing the worker harder', and therefore aggravating the class antagonism:

> ... if the value of constant capital is not to be eroded, it must as far as possible be consumed productively and not squandered ... it is here that the supervisory responsibility of the capitalist enters. (He secures his position here through piecework, deductions from wages, etc.) He must also see to it that the work is performed in an orderly and methodical fashion and that the use-value he has in mind actually emerges successfully at the end of the process. At this point to the capitalist's ability to supervise and enforce discipline is vital.[82]

So, subordination is not enough, the capitalist (or the supervisor on her behalf) must monitor labour's intensity, or, as in current-day circumstances, acquire technological or ideological means for automated monitoring or even self-monitoring.

Solution number two implies intensifying the working day by increasing productivity and the extraction of relative surplus-value, which reduces the value of labour-power – the basket of goods necessary to reproduce labour-power becomes cheaper – so that necessary labour-time decreases at the gain of surplus labour-time. This is a fix to the temporal and physiological limits of the working day and absolute surplus-value extraction; in fact, both legally and health-wise workers cannot extend forever the length of the working day. For

---

81   Marx 1990, p. 987.
82   Marx 1990, p. 895.

instance, legal provisions in the UK such as the 1847 Factories Act established limits on the number of workable hours per day. The labour intensification and increase in productivity can be achieved through a social and technological change in the organisation of labour.

Compared to the context of absolute surplus-value, the process of extraction of relative surplus-value describes a situation when the individual capitalist operates more explicitly in competition with others. I say more explicitly, because in reality pushing the workers harder in order to increase surplus-value even in absolute ways is not just motivated by subjective 'greediness' but is also based on the necessity to stay in business.

Relative surplus-value production imposes social and technological constraints at the level of organisation, which significantly reduces workers' discretion in the work process. As we shall see later in more detail, both socially coordinating mechanisms such as cooperation and division of labour as well as machinery imply a lengthening of the working day and a higher intensity of work. Second, the displacement of labour-intensive by capital-intensive production implies a rearrangement of the demand and supply of the labour force, entailing losses for labour *vis-a-vis* capital. That is because such a displacement tends to create a labour reserve army:

> It is not enough that the conditions of labour are concentrated at one pole of society in the shape of capital, while at the other pole are grouped masses of men who have nothing to sell but their labour-power. Nor is it enough that they are compelled to sell themselves voluntarily ... The constant generation of a relative surplus population keeps the law of the supply and demand of labour, and therefore wages, within narrow limits which correspond to capital's valorisation requirements. The silent compulsion of economic relations sets the seal on the domination of the capitalist over the worker. Direct extra-economic force is still of course used, but only in exceptional cases. In the ordinary run of things, the worker can be left to the 'nature allows of production', that is, it is possible to rely on his dependence on capital, which springs from the conditions of production themselves, and is guaranteed in perpetuity by them.[83]

Marx suggests how the compulsive aspect in the context of production of relative surplus-value increases because workers are now also under the threat of unemployment.

---

83   Marx 1990, p. 899.

So, from this point of view, subsumption indicates the social arrangement needed in order to extract surplus-value. However, the openness of the process has to do with the fact that, first of all, adequate arrangements may never be found or can change drastically over time, thus becoming inadequate. That is why in this book, as I will explain in more detail later on, I understand subsumption always to exist in conjunction with the possibility of its dialectical negation, supersumption. Accordingly, subsumption will be linked to uneven capitalist development and crises.

So far, I have considered Marxian subsumption from the perspective of different strategies of extracting surplus-value. The reason why I have decided to separate surplus-value extraction and subsumption is twofold. First of all, as I will elaborate more in the next chapters, while logically necessarily linked and most of the time indissolubly combined, I think it is important to analytically distinguish between surplus-value extraction and the specific socio-political arrangements, that is, class relations, which I tend to more closely link with the notion of subsumption. The extraction of surplus-value is, when compared to the class relations between capital and worker, rather more ephemeral, and the arrangements that are put in place to obtain it are frequently tactical. Conversely, class relations, because mediated by several factors beyond the labour process, are more inertial – thus they can be said to belong to a strategic perspective.

Secondly, relations of forces and extraction of surplus-value do not actually always coincide. This is the case with hybrid and ideal subsumption, as I will explain later on. This holds especially if we think of the broader perspective of what in the next chapter I will define as subsumptive relations located beyond the labour process. As Harvey observes,[84] for instance, when it comes to interclass relations between production and merchant capital – where capitalists engaged in production are responsible for the production of surplus-value – in many cases (for example, Walmart, Ikea, Apple) it is today merchant capital that receives the biggest share of surplus-value. Thirdly, in the context of the production of subjectivity moving inside an established hegemonic system such as neoliberalism, sometimes coercion is almost entirely replaced by self-activation and the deep internalisation of neoliberal values. This is especially true for knowledge workers of various kinds.

Next, I will look at subsumption from the point of view of the power relations inside the labour process. As I have already suggested in the section on primitive accumulation, the transition from feudal to capitalist society also

---

84   Harvey 2013.

constitutes a transition towards a modern conception and proceduralisation of power, which no longer limits itself to violent extortion of surplus labour but establishes via formal subsumption both a commodity exchange of labour-power between alleged peers and impersonal and mediating money relationships. In Chapter 3, I will discuss in more detail this aspect when dealing with subsumptive relations as relations of power. I will link subsumption to this 'modern' impersonal structural force.

6.2 *Formal Subsumption*

In nuce, formal subsumption describes how capitalism takes command of the labour process and economic activities originating outside capitalist relations of production. Such subsumption takes place under the social form of the wage.

In many ways, formal subsumption is based on and perpetuates the dispossession process, because the wage relation tends to deprive previously independent and self-organised workers of their means of subsistence and makes them dependent on capital. In other words, the crucial compulsive power relation that establishes asymmetry in terms of class relations is reinforced rather than originally established by subsumption. That is because, while, as we shall see, labour contracts establish a relation of force between sellers and buyers of labour-power, the very fact that most of us must sell our labour-power is based on the compulsive situation of not having another alternative in acquiring the means necessary materially to sustain our lives.

It is indeed a preexisting condition of need created by dispossession that allows the general rearrangement of labour into wage-labour by means of formal subsumption. In fact, such a reorganisation of work under conditions dictated by formal subsumption, even when considered sectorially, eventually leads to a social reorganisation on an increasingly broad social scale.

Seen from a broader perspective and thinking of Europe in the particular context of the so-called Industrial Revolution, historically the emergence of formal subsumption reflects that epochal change signalled by sociologists like Tönnies, Durkheim and Simmel,[85] who described the transition from a community of interpersonal relations to a society whose social intercourse was mediated by the abstraction of money, legal contract, and by institutions like the market and the state bureaucracy. Those are the fundamental preconditions that allow one to enter the job market in a theoretical 'peer to peer' relationship and trade between money and labour-power. Labourers and capitalists engage with each other not by established relations of serfdom or domination but by operating as different economic functions.

---

85   See Tönnies 2001; Durkheim 1997; Simmel 1971.

The fact that the compulsive social situation preceding people entering the job market, that is, removal from workers of their own means of production, is rendered opaque by the superimposition of an apparent regime of equality and freedom, makes formal subsumption a powerful example of the capability of capital to dominate by mystification, which is in turn built on abstraction: that is, instrumentally distorting (mystifying) and impoverishing (abstracting) reality. The power of this status of forms and formality itself constitutes in my view a great example of a non-idealist account of ideology: the non-equality preceding and preconditioning the relationship between workers and capitalists is obscured under the liberal ideology of freedom, equality guaranteed by a supposedly rational framework of legality, which then justifies as consensual the non-equivalence implied by the extraction of surplus-value.

It is in fact an objective regime of subordination of labour under capital that allows the latter to extend working time and increase work intensity, which in turn produces unpaid labour and surplus-value. The production of absolute surplus-value allows an overall expansion of the production process both in terms of the amount of capital and the number of workers involved.

The notion of formal subsumption designates a change in the relationship between economic agents involved in a given productive activity, between the exploiter and the exploited, and between buyer and seller of labour-power. It constitutes a component of class formation and class relations that is not strategically determined by the individuals involved or by the state, the church or any established political structure. Formal subsumption indicates how class relations systemically emerge from 'free' transactions in the labour market by turning 'free' independent workers into wage-labourers. In fact, the length of the day represents one of the first struggles where one contending party, the worker, fights for necessary and paid labour-time, and the other, the capitalist fight for surplus and unpaid labour-time:

> In the history of capitalist production, the determination of what is a working day presents itself as the result of a struggle, a struggle between collective capital, that is, the class of capitalists, and collective labour, that is, the working class.[86]

The formal aspect of this kind of subsumption is complex and ambiguous. First of all, 'formally' refers to a social form legally designated so as to recognise

---

86 Marx 1990 p. 243.

the equality and liberty of workers in dealing with the prospective buyer of their labour power; by the same token, the worker can freely dispose of their earned income. However, such liberty depends on the subjection the worker experiences in the labour process. In fact, through formal subsumption capital gains controls over labour; labour then becomes alienated labour. The relation between the two economic agents is purely monetary – and it is this relation that constitutes the most important source of subordination. Both parties are brought together in exchange by economic need, and not through pre-existing relations of lordship and servitude:

> Something implied by the first relation – for otherwise the worker would not have to sell his labour capacity – namely the fact that the objective conditions of his labour (the means of production) and the subjective conditions of his labour (the means of subsistence) confront him as capital.[87]

Again, the formal aspect of this kind of subsumption is multiple: it is a form-giving process of reshaping free-independent labour into wage-labour, but also it is the legal/formal condition of being free. A condition that is formal and ideological in this sense reproduces a particular experience of freedom: 'the consciousness (or rather the idea) of free self-determination, of freedom'; this renders them 'much better workers'.[88]

In other words, formality in this context does not de-materialise the experience of freedom, but it certainly highly qualifies it: while the worker does indeed believe themselves to a certain degree to be free, and therefore tends to accept the labour contract with a degree of consent, his/her freedom is only to submit, to choose who is going to be the master of his/her labour. Commenting on the apparent freedom as a precondition of formal subsumption, Screpanti claims that:

> ... workers are 'free' to submit to the power of their exploiters. The paradox of the employment contract is that it sanctions the formally free choice of workers to surrender their real freedom for a certain number of hours. The material condition of this paradox resides in the fact that the workers are 'free' of any wealth: that is, they do not own the means of production and subsistence that would enable them to choose autonomously how to

---

87   Marx 1990, p. 430.
88   Marx 1990, p. 435.

earn a living. Once the contract is signed, workers enter the factory, where their freedom of choice is in principle nil and labour activity is 'imposed' on them.[89]

The workers are not really free to decide how to work, when to work, what commodities to produce, how to relate to other workers, and how to use the technology at their disposal. For this reason, Screpanti describes the establishment of the formal subsumptive relationship as a non-reciprocal exchange: from the worker's point of view, it appears as the exchange of their labour-power for a wage; but for the capitalist it is not a real exchange because he/she receives more value than what the worker receives as a wage.

So, 'formal' in formal subsumption constitutes for Marx an incomplete process because it does not realise its ultimate purpose; it is an abstraction of the act of exchange and the concrete identities of the parties involved.[90] In this context, individuals are dealt with only insofar as they are the personifications of economic categories, bearers of particular class relations and interests.[91] As we will treat in more detail later on, another important aspect of the form-giving of this kind of subsumption is the transformation of concrete individuals into character masks of relations or the personifications of economic relations. When Marx says that individuals are dealt with only as bearers of particular class relations and interests, he expresses both the necessities implied by a method of inquiry and by a method of representation, in other words the deconstruction of capitalism through abstraction and its depiction as operating through abstractions. When it comes to people, this implies transforming empirical embodied subjects into personas. Through this perspective on human agents, subsumption can be defined as the process that simultaneously personifies economic categories and abstract subjective categories.

As we shall see, formal subsumption already reshapes the labour process in a significant way. For instance, E.P. Thompson[92] has pointed out that formal subsumption introduces a salient time relation in the production process, namely the division of the working day into two parts: that in which necessary labour (for the reproduction of the labourer) is performed and that in which surplus labour (for the benefit of the capitalist) is performed. In relation to that, real subsumption adds both a temporal and spatial reconfiguration of the labour process, thus completely re-signifying the experience of working.

---

89   Screpanti 2019, pp. 18–19.
90   Benhabib 2012.
91   Marx 1973, p. 92.
92   Thompson 1963.

DEFINING A LEGACY   73

The formally subsumed labour process indeed operates as a general establishment of an exploitative economic system and class structure, mediated by commodity exchange and value. Labour in a formally subsumed environment is limited in its ability to increase the quantity of value. This is why the subsumption of the labour process under the valorisation process consists of a superimposition of value over use-values. Thus, the specificity of concrete labour is reduced to an abstract crystallisation of labour-time. As Sáenz de Sicilia[93] observes, formal subsumption, with its goal of lengthening the part of labour-time dedicated to the production of surplus-value, introduces a time dimension in the production process:

> The fact that half a day's labour is necessary to keep the worker alive for 24 hours does not in any way prevent him from working a whole day. Therefore, the value of labour-power, and the value which that labour-power valorises [*verwertet*] in the labour-process, are two entirely different magnitudes; and this difference was what the capitalist had in mind when he was purchasing the labour-power.[94]

The already mentioned struggle over the length of the working day described by Marx and the laws introduced by the British state to limit the working day exemplify how a time-driven form of value established by formal subsumption becomes one fundamental terrain of class confrontation.

In the condition of formal subsumption, we can see how, on the one hand, capitalists – aggregated and coordinated in action as a class not by explicit alliance but most frequently by the coercive law of competition – try quantitatively to extend the production of absolute surplus-value as much as they can; on the other, the workers strive to reduce work to the minimum necessary for their reproduction. This configuration of class struggle is not contained by the power relations of subsumption, it is rather reproduced through it. By this, I want to already anticipate how the class tensions over the length of working day and the production of absolute surplus-value are subject to these turbulent relations, so that subsumption, by establishing conditions of class struggle, also produces the condition for its negation and permanent instability.

This perspective of more fluid power relations necessarily qualifies the Marxian assumption that formal subsumption does not alter the labour process. For instance, the search for more (absolute) surplus-value is not just

---

93   Sáenz de Sicilia 2016.
94   Marx 1990, p. 300.

implemented by lengthening the working day but also, for instance, by exerting more control and the pressure of a disciplinary apparatus to control labourers while working. Thus, the distance between formal and real subsumption appears to be more quantitative than qualitative; after all, both dynamics designate how capitalism reinterprets, rearranges and produces *ex-novo* social relations adequate to its reproduction and expansion. In other words, the distinction between *real* and *formal* is not about the *essence* and its *form* of appearance.

As I will show in the next section, formal and real reshape pre-existing relations and create new instrumental ones. After all, the process of abstraction of concrete tasks and individuals and the incorporation of time and value as a social necessity *de facto* 'realise' subsumption even at its formal level.

6.3   Real Subsumption

According to Marx[95] real subsumption describes how a given productive activity has become distinctly capitalist, in the sense that its labour process has been purposively reshaped in order to meet capital objectives. For Marx, real subsumption represents a qualitative change springing out of a quantitative increase in the condition of formal subsumption. Marx claims that the growing scale of production leads to differentiation and mutations in the labour process due to more capital and more labour involved.[96]

Real subsumption does not simply aim at accumulating more surplus-value but also at beating the competition with other capitalists by lowering production costs; this can lead both to the extraction of more gain from sales made at the same price or increased sales due to reduced prices. This is why Marx defined the production of surplus-value under real subsumption as 'relative': the increment of surplus-value becomes relative to total value-production rather than in absolute terms. The effect of lowering the value of commodities in general is to also lower the value of the bundle of commodities needed by workers to survive; therefore this subsumptive process leads to lower wages.

As Szadkowski[97] observes, real subsumption raises yet further the level of mystification of the social relations mediating labour and capital. Such a relationship in fact becomes mediated by the social and technological organisation, which removes even further the embodied subject of the capitalist in his/her function of supervision and control. Thus, the conscious employment of science and new forms of social (for example, cooperation and division of

---

95   Marx 1990, p. 1019.
96   Marx 1990, p. 1022.
97   Szadkowski 2016.

labour) and technological (for example, machinery) organisation, tend, in the context of real subsumption, to de-personalise and abstract power.[98]

While I have already claimed that, from several points of view, the distance between formal and real subsumption is more quantitative than qualitative, there is a distinctive aspect tied to real subsumption: its totalising tendency. On the one hand, Marx claims that:

> In all forms of society there is one specific kind of production which predominates over the rest, whose relations thus assign rank and influence on the others. It is a general illumination which bathes all the other colours and modifies their particularity. It is a particular ether which determines the specific gravity of every being which has materialised within it.[99]

It is through real subsumption under the historically specific categories of (re)production that the determinate forms and 'logic' of social being proper to society are generated. Subsumption under conceptual categories is thus supplanted within Marx's materialism by a far broader and more dynamic theory of subsumption under social categories. This can be considered as a totalising tendency because the restructured labour process under real subsumption becomes a social laboratory not simply for production but also social production, its social and technological arrangements increasingly establishing themselves as archetypes for ideas, practices and institutions outside the labour process.[100]

While, as we have already mentioned, formal subsumption indeed reconfigures production, with real subsumption – with capital as the articulatory agent that brings all the elements of production together in a material as well as economic sense – we also see a transformation of time. Capital coordinates all the different temporalities produced by the division of labour but also compresses time in order to increase productivity and the production of relative surplus-value. Time here is understood both as a temporal measure of the production of value but also in the broader sense of perennial historical development:

---

98 Again, even in this sense, formal and real could be seen in the continuum of the evolution of modern power, in which the latter ceases to be immediate, pure coercion and crude violence and becomes increasingly mediated and therefore less detectable.

99 Marx 1973, pp. 106–7.

100 According to Dan Schiller, the consolidation of the structural functionalist paradigm in sociology is a reflection of an instrumentalist way of thinking about society, explaining how political economic interests of the military industrial complex affect broader views on society: Schiller 2013. Similarly, for Marcuse, a proceduralist way of thinking and speaking derives from the rationalisation of industrial production: Marcuse 1964.

> Real subsumption implies that a complete (and constantly continued and repeated) revolution takes place in the mode of production, in the productivity of the workers and in the relation between workers and capitalists.[101]

Even in this sense, I see more of a quantitative variation than a qualitative one. Time in conditions of real subsumption is further fragmented in two main ways: through multiple temporalities, for instance produced by the incorporations of technology that reduce turnover times; and, linked to this, through intensification, in which seconds and fractions of seconds become significant margin of improvements.

For Marx, there is indeed a substantial qualitative difference, because with real subsumption the real nature and full force of capitalism become manifest only with real subsumption, when capital development becomes necessary and seemingly unavoidable:

> Production for production's sake – production as an end in itself – does indeed come on to the scene with the formal subsumption of labour under capital. It makes its appearance as soon as the immediate purpose of production is to produce as much and as many surplus-value as possible, as soon as the exchange-value of the product becomes the deciding factor. But this inherent tendency of the capital relation does not become adequately realised – it does not become indispensable, and that also means technologically indispensable – until the specific capitalist mode of production and hence the real subsumption of labour under capital has developed.[102]

Murray[103] adds to this by claiming that, with real subsumption, qualitative changes take place: the law of valorisation comes into its own, we see economies of scale, collective productive power is created, the labour force becomes more efficient, and the speed, scale and space of production all increase. Let us examine those changes in detail. First of all, value reaches maturity, it becomes a self-referential process. As Fred Moseley explains:

> Value cannot be defined in the simple sense of either a substance pre-existing exchange or as a mere phenomenal relation, but only as a mo-

---

101 Marx 1990 p. 1035.
102 Marx 1990, p. 103.
103 Murray 2004.

ment of a totalising process of development of internally related forms of a complex whole. Capital is the most complex value form; indeed, in a sense it is the value form, because only at this level of development of the concept of value can we grasp that value is a real substance, instead of a vanishing mediator in exchange ... A methodological consequence of this understanding is that the concept of capital itself (as the most highly mediated) requires, not a definition, whether nominal or real, ostensive or stipulative, but a dialectical exposition of its inner self-development.[104]

Secondly, the collective usage of the means of production may lower the costs of constant capital. Furthermore, as the number of workers increases, their average productivity increases as well. With real subsumption, as we shall see, while the introduction of machinery implies large capital investment upfront, cooperation and division of labour practically cost nothing. In this sense, real subsumption is about the development of the power of social labour, which when it is organised by workers themselves does not accord with capital's own needs.

Thirdly, Marx identifies three main forms in which real subsumption is implemented: cooperation, division of labour and manufacture, and machinery and large-scale industry. By cooperation, workers' individual differences such as age, skills, strength, motivation and personal idiosyncrasies are flattened and reduced to a regular, ideally predictable and quantifiable middle ground, thus pushed closer to the general average intensity and productivity. In the *Manuscripts of 1861–63* Marx discusses this as follows:

> Their own association in labour – cooperation – is in fact a power alien to them; it is the power of capital which confronts the isolated workers. In so far as they have a relation to the capitalist as independent persons, as sellers, it is the relation of isolated, mutually independent workers, who stand in a relation to the capitalist but not to each other.[105]

Collective cooperation for Marx constitutes a new productive power that capitalises on people's sociality, which is itself a 'free gift' from (social) nature. In this sense, cooperation confirms my reading of subsumption as a totalising force in action which, when considered beyond production – for example from the per-

---

104   Moseley 2015, p. 301.
105   Marx and Engels 1867 30, pp. 261–2.

spective of logistic-driven capitalism, cooperation and coordination – appears as a glue that joins individuals, their spaces and their temporalities into a functional ensemble. As I will elaborate in more detail later on, it is a hegemonic totality also because 'non-subsumed labour cannot be realised competitively, is unable to carry on independently and will therefore perish unless it is incorporated into the capitalist production process'.[106]

Cooperation represents another socially substantial aspect of abstract labour, because establishing a cooperative organisation of production means creating a compulsive system that levels out natural differences among workers, thus *de facto* imposing with no force the necessity of socially necessary labour-time.

The second implementation strategy described by Marx is the division of labour and manufacture. Simultaneous to the process of levelling out difference among workers, capital can also develop differentiation in productive tasks and partial operations. Each worker specialises in one particular isolated function so that he/she can increase their efficiency. The traditional process of production is decomposed and mechanically recomposed in order to increase productivity. The worker is alienated and separated from the overall productive goal (that is, production of a complete object). In this sense, division of labour appears as a sophistication of simple cooperation.

The subsumption of specialised workers under the social organisation that divides their labour brings along with it alienation, monotony, intensified labour, deskilling and the dispossession of knowledge and understanding of the whole process. It is also a spectacular incrementation of labour abstraction, since the labour task is sometimes so compartmentalised that a given quantum of labour-power can be indifferently performed by worker A or worker B:

> Knowledge judgement and will … are faculties now required only for the workshop as a whole, whilst for the worker himself no combination of activities takes place. The combination is rather a combination of the one-sided functions under which every worker or number of workers is subsumed, group by group. His function is one-sided, abstract, partial. The totality which is formed from this is based precisely on his merely partial existence and isolation in his separate function. It is therefore a combination of which he forms apart, but it depends on the fact that his labour is not combined.[107]

---

106 Roberts 2022.
107 Marx 1990, p. 470.

With the division of labour, the power relationship established by subsumption becomes more abstract; this is because, while control and supervision may still be needed, it is mostly the manufacturing process itself that operates as a disciplinary machine.

Finally, the third strategy to implement real subsumption is defined by Marx as machinery and large-scale industry. As Sáenz de Sicilia points out:

> The material inversion, separation and integration characteristic of real subsumption – that proceeds on the basis the social relations introduced with labour's formal subsumption and develops through the stages of cooperation and manufacture – achieve their apotheosis in large-scale industry based on machinery, the technical from of production most adequate to the valorisation of capital.[108]

Technology has always been employed in the labour process, but what characterised this context is '*an automatic system of machinery*'[109] that is liberated from the limits of human labour: faster, more precise consistent, it becomes the real 'virtuoso'.[110] Machinery surpasses by far the increase of productivity generated through simple cooperation and division of labour. In fact, machinery subsumes the division of labour and cooperation under a mechanised and automatised organisation of production. The application of science and rational instrumentality to machines materialises the abstract nature of capital most emphatically:

> Like every other instrument for increasing the productivity of labour, machinery is intended to cheapen commodities and, by shortening the part of the working day in which the worker works for himself, to lengthen the other part, the part he gives to the capitalist for nothing. The machine is a means for producing surplus-value.[111]

The new productive *modus operandi* powered by machines – with their temporalities and speed of operation not limited by human bodies – pushes towards the production of absolute value as well. The working day and its extraction of dead labour may then become endless. Furthermore, the indifference to the human body means that women and children can increasingly be em-

---

108   Sáenz de Sicilia 2016, p. 174.
109   Marx 1973, p. 692.
110   Marx 1973, p. 693.
111   Marx 1990, p. 494.

ployed to work in machinery and large-scale industry. Just as with the division of labour and cooperation, control and supervision are still needed, but are also built into the machines themselves, with which workers must strive to keep pace. Machines become weapons of class struggle, disciplining, exploiting and isolating workers.

As mentioned earlier, the dynamic driving real subsumption must be understood as simultaneously functioning across individual capitals operating in specific economic sectors as well as at the level of the total social capital. That is because, once the whole labour process becomes available to restructuration, capital automatically spills out towards any social sphere linked to it or functional to production. Thus, after subjugating all production, capital also subjugates new contexts: from means of circulation, transport and communication to workers' subjectivities. This is what Negri and many Operaist thinkers would define as social subsumption,[112] and this is what I meant by the totalising tendency of real subsumption. To be sure, an important assumption of this book is that all subsumptive social arrangements tend to be totalising because securing surplus-value means not only securing its production but also its realisation, as well as the reproduction of its conditions of production. However, such a tendency in the context of real subsumption becomes more poignant.

The totality emerging from real subsumption processes is not just the result of one process of colonisation that expands, that is, capital in centrifugal motion, but also of the integration and consolidation of internal relations. Thus, the three strategies mentioned by Marx through which real subsumption manifests itself indicate how science and technology are subsumed under capital; then, as Marx describes in the *Grundrisse*, 'the entire production process appears as not subsumed under the immediate skilfulness of the worker, but rather as the technological application of science'.[113] In turn, and simultaneously, the scientific-technological organisation subsumes workers:

> The accumulation of knowledge and of skill, of the general productive forces of the social brain, is thus absorbed into capital, as opposed to labour, and hence appears as an attribute of capital, and more specifically of *fixed capital* in so far as it enters into the production process as a means of production proper.[114]

---

112   Negri 1996.
113   Marx 1973, p. 699.
114   Marx 1973, p. 694.

DEFINING A LEGACY   81

The power-knowledge objectified into machinery turns into the power of what Marx defined as fixed capital, a combination of 'the use of science, this general product of social development, in the immediate process of production'.[115] Fixed capital is both objectified labour and the objectified capitalist because fixed capital as a means of production, is also a 'means of controlling and exploiting living labour, [and] appears as something utterly appropriate to them ... as inseparable from them'.[116] Fixed capital becomes an effective representative for all the agents and agencies originally involved in production:

> In machinery, objectified labour materially confronts living labour as a ruling power and as an active subsumption of the latter under itself, not only by appropriating it, but in the real production process itself; the relation of capital as value that appropriates value-creating activity is, in fixed capital existing as machinery, posited at the same time as the relation of the use-value of capital to the use-value of labour capacity; further, the value objectified in the machinery appears as a presupposition against which the value-creating power of the individual labour capacity is an infinitesimal, vanishing magnitude ...[117]

The conceptual displacement involving fixed capital and living labour is of course also hierarchical: the machinist, the worker, becomes a machined tool, 'cast merely as its conscious linkages', overseeing operations as 'watchman and regulator' rather than 'chief actor'. With real subsumption, fetishism materialises beyond any metaphorical level: dead labour acquires movements, life and energy, while living labour is deprived of creative energy and social life. Dead and living labour unite in a machinic assemblage and exchange features, but they also exchange ontological conditions: the subject becomes the object, and the object becomes the subject.

Subsumption also implies alienation from form-giving. While in traditional artisanal forms of work, the worker was the Demiurge of shapes and forms, when the role of technology and machinery becomes preponderant, these replace workers as form givers. By the same logic, capital becomes the master key, the matrix of all forms which have to be reshaped so as to become adequate for capital.

Fourthly, the reason why Marx claims that real subsumption necessarily follows formal subsumption is that legal and physical limits to the lengthening of

---

115   Marx and Engels, 2010, 34, p. 1024.
116   Marx and Engels, 2010, 34, pp. 988–9.
117   Marx 1973, pp. 693–4.

the working day push capitalism to adopt another strategy so as to increase surplus-value, reshaping the labour process in order to intensify labour and increased productivity: that is, real subsumption. In this respect, the division of labour, cooperation and the introduction of machinery all represent ways to go beyond the limits of absolute value production. As I will argue in more detail later on, the limits posed by class struggle, physical constraints and state/legal intervention can be seen as moments in dialectical movement that, by constraining subsumption, often drive it strongly ahead. Fifthly, as Marx puts it, 'instead of the scale of production being controlled by existing needs, the quantity of products made is determined by the constantly increasing scale of production dictated by the mode of production itself'.[118]

Finally, the displacement entailed by real subsumption is also spatial, in physical and conceptual ways. In larger-scale industry, the worker is decentred as the fulcrum of production and physically displaced by machinery, which tends to occupy more and more space. Workers tend to be spatially separated by tasks, by machines, and from audible relations, because the machines tend to dominate the acoustic spectrum.

Spatial relations, as we shall see in Chapter 6, are fundamental. Real subsumption does not simply control production but reshapes the production process of the space of production so that more surplus-value is produced. While, practically speaking, the turning of independent labour into wage-labour would not be possible without actual material revision of the labour process, the degree of material transformation is often (but not always) qualitatively on a different scale. For instance, the social reorganisation implied by what Marx defines as cooperation and a more sophisticated division of labour entails a spatial and temporal reconfiguration of the workplace.

Sáenz de Sicilia[119] claims that the combination of formal and real subsumption represents the way in which capital subsumes living labour and reshapes human praxis both quantitively and qualitatively, so as to manipulate and reshape – *ergo* to give form – to nature at its core; in fact, the metabolic link between people and nature, which used to be based fairly direct on the nexus of production and consumption, is now mediated by the imperative to accumulate capital. In this sense, we mentioned earlier that formal subsumption introduced the crucially necessary time dimension; real subsumption adds to this a spatial reconfiguration. For instance, the increased number of workers operating in the same labour process may indeed change the space of pro-

---

118   Marx and Engels 2010, 34, pp. 1037–8.
119   Sáenz de Sicilia 2016.

duction – it could expand in the case of building infrastructures, or it could compress, as in the case of the transition from extensive to intensive land cultivation.[120]

As I will elaborate in much more detail in Chapter 6, space is fundamental to understanding subsumption but also fundamental to understanding how subsumption affects class composition and decomposition to the degree that it facilitates or creates obstacles to social alienation, communication among workers, and collective identity formation. That is because the individual worker becomes a partial 'incomplete' worker in so far as she loses the capability to grasp the whole production process. Thus, the partial works become complete only in the collective social worker, which is the social organisation of workers, or when integrated into the cybernetic system of machinery. However, the worker still receives her individual wage, so most of the benefits of the collective worker are translated into relative surplus-value.

Summing up what has been said so far, subsumption operates in Marx to integrate heterogeneous elements into the social totality of capital by giving them a form adequate to capital, but also to configure those elements (such as labour under capital) according to power relations. While real subsumption shows how, both logically and historically, a capitalist totality emerges, such a totality is always incomplete, heterogeneous, unstable and contradictory, and riddled by class antagonism. It is indeed always totalising but never totalised. Thus, through the dialectical perspective that I will later convey using the notion of determinate supersumption, I want to show how all those strategies to secure and increase the production of surplus-value also become 'real' opportunities for de-valorisation.

While theorists such as Jacques Camatte and Carlo Vercellone[121] tend to conceptualise the relation of formal and real subsumption as linear progress towards a more capitalist mode of production, in this book I try to define a more open path: for example, real can revert to formal, formal can transition to less formal, or, as I will discuss in a moment, into 'hybrid' or 'ideal' forms. The trajectory taken by capital in a given sector may be conditioned by numerous factors, such as crisis, class struggle, and state intervention. For example, the employment of fixed capital, that is, orienting of production towards more

---

120 This leads to an important ramification that I do not have space here adequately to develop. The massive incorporation of technology in terms of both means of communication and transportation leads, in the context defined by Harvey as postmodernity, to a double spatial movement under real subsumption: space and time compression in terms of the circulation of capital; and space and time expansion in absolute terms of distances.

121 Camatte 1988; Vercellone 2007.

capital-intensive rather than labour-intensive strategies, may trigger a tendency for the rate of profit to fall and therefore eventually push capital to look for fixes, such as new sectors to colonise, where profits may be higher due to the formal subsumption of those sectors:

> It is precisely the productivity of labour, the mass of production, of population and of surplus population created by this mode of production that constantly calls new branches of industry into being once labour and capital have been set free.[122]

Thus, the expansive tendency already noticed in the context of formal subsumption is supported and reinvigorated by both real subsumption and its search after 'fixes', which can lead to a switch back to formal subsumption.

It is important to point out, as per many other aspects of Marxian thought, that subsumption in the *Grundrisse* is dealt with via a slightly different approach. The most significant passage can be found in the so-called 'Fragment on Machines'. The Italian Marxist tradition of workerism has developed its conceptualisation of subsumption alongside a discussion of other categories that are present in the same fragment, such as fixed capital and general intellect. These are all inserted into a general narrative of the grand immanent contradiction and limit to capital:

> Capital itself is the moving contradiction, in that it presses to reduce labour-time to a minimum, while it posits labour-time, on the other side, as sole measure, and source of wealth. Hence it diminishes labour-time in the necessary form so as to increase it in the superfluous form; hence posits the superfluous in growing measure as a condition – question of life or death – for the necessary.[123]

This is the 'moving contradiction', wherein capital's accumulation is premised entirely on the appropriation of surplus-value from workers, while the inescapable competition for greater productivity per worker necessarily renders an ever-greater portion of labour superfluous over the long run. Thus, correspondingly, an increasing proportion of workers, the very source of accumulation, is expelled from the production process in favour of machines: 'it is the machine which possesses skill and strength in place of the worker, is itself the virtuoso,

---

122   Marx 1990, p. 1035.
123   Marx 1973, p. 706.

with a soul of its own in the mechanical laws acting through it'. Labour increasingly appears as collective consciousness, 'subsumed under the total process of the machinery itself', while for the labourer it is 'the living (active) machinery, which confronts his individual, insignificant doings as a mighty organism'.[124]

The machine becomes an artificial form of life, a poltergeist replacing the agency of living labour. Not by accident in this fragment, subsumption is described as 'active subsumption': the transformation of the means of labour into machinery is the realisation of this tendency. By the employment of machinery, objectified labour materially confronts living labour as a ruling power and as active subsumption of the latter under itself. Machinery, by appropriating the worker's agency, alienates the worker's labour and then 'in so far as the *means of labour*, as a physical thing, loses its direct form, becomes *fixed capital*, and confronts the worker physically as *capital*. In machinery, knowledge appears as alien, external to him; and living labour as subsumed under self-activating objectified labour'.[125]

Real subsumption also gives rise to a fetish force with a life of its own, which is objectified in the machinery that is gradually expanding its control not simply over labour-power but also people's productive capacity in general:

> In this transformation, it is neither the direct human labour he himself performs, nor the time during which he works, but rather the appropriation of his own general productive power, his understanding of nature and his mastery over it by virtue of his presence as a social body – it is, in a word, the development of the social individual which appears as the great foundation-stone of production and of wealth. The *theft of alien labour-time, on which the present wealth is based*, appears a miserable foundation in face of this new one, created by large-scale industry itself. As soon as labour in the direct form has ceased to be the great well-spring of wealth, labour-time ceases and must cease to be its measure, and hence exchange-value [must cease to be the measure] of use-value. The *surplus labour of the mass* has ceased to be the condition for the development of general wealth, just as the *non-labour of the few*, for the development of the general powers of the human head.[126]

Subsumption becomes social: beyond technical and technological organisation, it comes to affect social organisation and social, cultural and symbolic

---

124   Marx 1973, p. 694.
125   Marx 1973, pp. 694, 696.
126   Marx 1973, p. 705.

wealth constricted by the general intellect. It is in the *Grundrisse* that subsumption reveals in the most explicit language its totalising power, where it is situated at the centre of the production of 'the whole ensemble of sciences, languages, knowledge, activities and skills that circulate through society'.[127]

Similarly, for Murray,[128] subsumption under a specific social form, such as a commodity, capital or abstract labour, describes how capitalism shapes the history of a given social formation and its production of surplus-value. In this respect, in this section I examine in more detail the different forms capitalist subsumption can take, based on Marx and a symptomatic reading of his writings. It is important here to remark how the next section on 'hybrid and ideal' subsumptions are the result of symptomatic readings such as Murray's.

In the case of ideal subsumption, as I will detail later on, surplus-value is not necessarily produced, but important conditions for its possibility are prepared for, such as adequate forms of practical consciousness, that is, adequate ideological practices. In the case of hybrid subsumption, things get more fluid. Again, as I will elaborate in a moment, hybrid social forms describe circumstances in which surplus labour-time is not extracted by direct control, as the producer is not yet formally subordinated to capital. Historically, in sectors such as artisanship and some agricultural activities, hybrid forms may emerge and reproduce. However, as I will review in Chapters 5 and 6 in the case of gig and platform work, subcontracting to formally self-employed workers represents a way to extract surplus-value without direct subordination.

Skillman,[129] while not really accepting the notion of hybrid subsumption, observes how capitalist control is not a *sine qua non* condition for extracting surplus-value. He argues that the capability to exert influence deriving from ownership of financial merchant capital gives business the chance to appropriate a part of surplus-value without managing the labour process.

6.4 Hybrid Subsumption and Ideal Subsumption

Subsumption mediates people's metabolic relation to nature by controlling and reshaping the labour process, it mediates the exchange-value (logical) and use-value (historical) dimensions and interpretation of capitalism and it mediates the particular manifestation with the general totality. If capitalism is engaged in a never-ending expansion, it necessarily touches grey liminal areas where subsumption mediates the 'internal' and the 'external' of the capitalist totality.

---

127   Thoburn 2001, p. 81.
128   Murray 2009.
129   Skillman 2015.

This brings us to interstitial dimensions, which in my view justify the possibility of liminal informal or incompletely realised forms of subsumption. This is the case with ideal and hybrid subsumption, and in his fragmented examination of subsumption, Marx seems to hint at the existence of forms of subsumption that take place outside and beyond formal and real subsumption.

The very interesting aspect of this liminal world is that it tends to separate what would be considered constitutive and necessary aspects of subsumption: a power relation mostly, but not limited to, subordination and the production of surplus-value. For instance, while in the case of hybrid subsumption, the surplus-value may be produced without direct compulsion (more characteristic of formal and real subsumption), in the case of ideal subsumption, there is certainly a level of ideological power in place, possibly spanning across the continuum of persuasion and compulsion, but not necessarily the production of surplus-value.

While theorists like Murray and Tomba[130] explicitly talk about hybrid and ideal forms of subsumption, others like Skillman reject the idea of alternative forms of subsumption and claim that what some call hybrids are in fact phenomena that can be grouped (not to say subsumed ...) under either formal or real subsumption, or that should be considered more as 'hybrid forms of social production'. I tend to align with the first two, because treating them as social production limits the broader implications those notions may have vis-à-vis capitalist totality and also qualifies the compactness of the labour process.

In the *Economic Manuscripts of 1861–1863* Marx describes hybrid subsumption as a situation in which capital, while not exercising direct control, or not having yet become the purchaser of labour, can take advantage of particular productive activities. This is a form of subsumption that, according to such a definition, could also be renamed 'informal subsumption', because it does not involve direct control of the labour process but rather indirect control implemented by contracts. In the 'Results of the Direct Production Process',[131] Marx cites the example of Indian usurers advancing capital for raw material and tools to the producer, which involves *de facto* extraction via interest on the loan, that is, surplus-value from the producer. More recently, examining the agricultural economic sector in India, Das[132] claims that hybrid subsumption represents an ongoing form that coexists with other capitalist relations. It is a sleight of

---

130   Murray 2004; Tomba 2012.
131   Marx 1990, p. 989.
132   Das 2012.

hand made use of by 'formal' capitalism in order to address contingent problems. Those hybrid forms, Das continues, can be understood in the context of uneven development of global capitalism as a way to incorporate a portion of the reserve army of labour into the economy.

According to Murray,[133] hybrid subsumption may comprise two forms: transitional hybrid subsumption, that is, what precedes a more traditional form of subsumption; and/or coexistence with proper capitalist production, that is, a kind of accompanying hybrid subsumption. Synthetically put, hybrid subsumption describes a situation when capital gains surplus-value indirectly, in other words, when capital does not directly command the labour process.

Ideal Subsumption: According to Szadkowski,[134] ideal subsumption is even more implicitly formulated by Marx and mostly utilised by him as an argumentative tool against bourgeois political economists when they incorrectly consider a realm of production as capitalist. I think its employment is much broader than that, even though never made explicit. When earlier I referred to the mystification implied by both formal and real subsumption as ideological, I meant to lay the ground for the discussion of ideal subsumption here as the 'most' ideological form of subsumption, and in many ways its most dynamic form. As material social practices such as communication and signification of social reality well illustrate, idealisation and materialisation processes feed each other and are indissolubly connected. Thus, for instance, the various forms of representation of value, such as money, commodities and labour, are not free-floating signifiers – they become food for thought:

> Some of the labour which produces commodities in capitalist production is performed in a manner which belongs to *earlier modes of production*, where the *relation of capital and wage-labour* does not yet exist in practice, and therefore the category of *productive and unproductive* labour, which corresponds to the capitalist standpoint, is entirely inapplicable. But in accordance with the ruling mode of production even those relations which have not yet been subsumed under it in fact are subsumed under it notionally.[135]

Like in Debord's theory of the Spectacle,[136] when capitalism becomes the productive structure in dominance, it becomes a cognitive framework for the

---

133 Murray 2004.
134 Szadkowski 2016.
135 Marx 1990, p. 1042.
136 Debord 1995.

whole society, thus excluding the possibility of non-capitalist realms. 'It is a general illumination which bathes all the other colours and modifies their particularity'.

Furthermore, in *The German Ideology*, Marx and Engels seem to hint at a sort of ideal subsumption. The basis for ideal subsumption:

> For [the bourgeois] only one relation is valid on its own account the relation of exploitation; all other relations have validity for him only insofar as he can subsume them under this one relation; and even where he encounters relations which cannot be directly subordinated to the relation of exploitation, he subordinates them to it at least in his imagination.[137]

The idea of treating non-capitalist relations using terms like value and profit reveals the hegemony of capitalist imagery and discourse. Accordingly, especially with the emergence of neoliberal subjectivity, the categories of 'self-employed' or 'contactor' come to rationalise those non-wage form categories that were ideally subsumed under wage-labour.

Murray describes 'ideal subsumption' that involves 'treating labour that is not actually subsumed under capital (whether formally or in a hybrid manner)' as if it were.[138] He also distinguishes between a) ideal subsumption of pre-capitalist economic formations under capital imagery; b) ideal subsumption of non-capitalist production processes under capital imagery; and c) ideal subsumption that takes place within a capitalist firm.

In my view, ideal subsumption is fundamental in the construction of subjectivities that are adequate to capital and which, through a myriad of different activities such as education, games, social media practices and affective labour, are socialised so as to effectively train the individual in a particular 'extractive-instrumental' perspective on social life. The body of literature documenting such a dynamic describes the kind of exploitation of affective relations made use of by social media users to gain social capital, showing that many users do this as if it were almost a social duty.[139] As Jason Read[140] argues, especially when we consider it in the continuum of coercion and consent, subsumption must somehow be capable of developing subjection as subordination and also as constitution of subjectivities.

---

137   Marx and Engels 1998, p. 434.
138   Murray 2004, pp. 265–6.
139   See for instance Muelenbach 2012.
140   Read 2013.

To sum up, subsumption in Marx comprises at least two components, a power relation (that is, a class relation) and an orientation towards surplus-value. In this sense, the examination of the multiple sub-forms of subsumption can show that the relationship between the two aspects may change, and their relative weight may vary as well, to the point that one of the two elements may even disappear. I do not think it is possible to conceive subsumption without some presence of at least one of the two aspects, since otherwise, as with hybrid or ideal subsumption, either surplus-value or the relation of subordination seems to disappear. Thus, at a given period of time, one aspect may be much more visible than the other because one may operate as short-term tactic and the other as long-term strategy. While not perfectly matching, this complex rapport between the class relation and surplus-value informs the two main ways in which more recent Marxist literature has understood subsumption.

7   Selective Traditions of Subsumptions: Two Main Narratives of Totalisations

Joshua Clover[141] argues that the renewed interest in the notion of subsumption that began during the 1970s can be historically understood in a context characterised by two conjunctures. First, a prolonged period of crisis after a long economic boom, which prompted critical questions concerning both periodisation and the uneven development of capitalism. Second, the copresence in the 1970s – in both Europe and North America – of a period of strong labour organisation and a decline in profitability, which led to a capital-intensive kind of production, characterised by massive incorporation of information and communication technology, as well as an ideological offensive aimed at reshaping the labourer's subjectivity. In other words, starting in the mid-1970s, the capitalist offensive against labour that for Harvey[142] inaugurates Neoliberalism as a class project brought about a new wave of real subsumption.

As already mentioned, this renewed interest tended to develop along the lines of two already established main narratives that have influenced how subsumption has been received in the Marxist literature: as a synchronic self-referential and self-reproducing perspective on capital on the one hand, and as a progressivist diachronic perspective, on the other. Drawing from the conceptual distinctions advanced by Marxist interpreters,[143] I could define those

---

141   Clover 2006.
142   Harvey 2005.
143   See Russell 2015; Skillman 2013; Arthur 2009.

strands as reflective – even if the correspondence is not perfect – of two different grand narratives about Marx's interpretation of capital: systematic and historical dialectic. I am fully aware that those categorisations greatly oversimplified the interpretation of the authors I examine here, which *de facto* constantly overlap the systematic and the historical, and/or even go beyond those categories. However, the reason to continue to work with such a distinction and its forceful polarisation is that it sheds light on the productive tension characterising subsumption, between surplus-value and the class relations perspective.

7.1   *Subsumption: Systematic Dialectic and Historical Dialectic*

For several authors, subsumption has been reconsidered as a theoretical framework in order to periodise capitalism, according to a somewhat linear progression of stages: primitive accumulation – formal subsumption – real subsumption (and even total subsumption). However, the progression is not simply historical, but chrono-*logical*. Marxist theorists such as Murray and Arthur – particularly interested in reconstructing the logic of *Capital* via its affinity with the Hegelian legacy, systematic dialectic, and capitalist forms theory – see subsumption more as a conceptual than an historical category. On the one hand, Arthur considers that while the distinction between formal and real subsumption can be understood as the historically grounded attempt by capital to overcome all barriers to its accumulation, such a development has been intrinsic to capital since its emergence.[144] On the other hand, Murray argues that the terms 'formal subsumption' and 'real subsumption' refer first to concepts of subsumption and only secondarily – if at all – to historical stages of subsumption. Murray argues that Marx considers the possibility of a distinct historical stage of merely formal subsumption, but finds no evidence of one.[145]

So, then what is the rationale behind using subsumption to periodise capitalism? Rob Lucas and Nicholas Grey of the Endnotes collective, while problematising subsumption as a narrative characterised by linear historical evolution for either production or class relations, provide us with a very qualified justification for this approach:

> ... according to Marx, though formal subsumption must precede real subsumption, real subsumption in one branch can also be the basis for further formal subsumption in other areas. If the categories of subsumption

---

144   Arthur 2002, p. 76.
145   Murray 2004, p. 202.

are applicable to history at all, this can therefore only be in a 'nonlinear' fashion: they cannot apply simplistically or unidirectionally to the historical development of the class relation.[146]

On the other hand, they recognise the thrust provided by competition and technological dynamism always to revolutionise the production process and the social context that surrounds it. In this sense, the multiple attempts to use subsumption to periodise capitalism are not simply motivated by the need to establish a chronology of capitalism but rather to produce a time-driven framework that allows us to grasp the distinctness of a given stage, primarily the present, and possibly to predict aspects of future developments and how those stages affect class relations.

Furthermore, Endnotes argue that, while not always tenable, the merit of historicisations of subsumption offered by authors such as Camatte, Negri, Théorie Communiste and Vercellone is to try to extend the application of subsumption 'beyond the immediate process of production'.[147] The general presupposition is that once capitalism has reached real subsumption, it has already entered a state of a constant revolutionising driven by high technological and competition dynamism; this would in turn radically change its broader social context. I think this is an important point that should be incorporated into a broader understanding of subsumption. In my case, as I have already discussed on several occasions, subsumption is, both logically and historically, to some degree, social subsumption.

Among the first continental authors who re-energised the interest in subsumption is Jacques Camatte, who tried to provide a fresh reading of Marx through the insights of his recently published 'Results of the Direct Production Process' and *The Grundrisse*. In his most known publication, *Capital and Community*,[148] Camatte defines the notion of subsumption as follows:

> Subsumption means rather more than just submission. *Subsumieren* really means 'to include in something', 'to subordinate', 'to implicate', so it seems that Marx wanted to indicate that capital makes its own substance out of labour, that capital incorporates labour inside itself and makes it into capital.[149]

---

146 Endnotes 2010.
147 Vercellone 2007, p. 4.
148 Camatte 1988.
149 Camatte 1988, p. 106.

For Camatte, subsumption functions in two united but distinct ways: absorbing non-capitalist elements, and secondly, reforming them, giving them a capitalist form. According to this interpretation, he theorises 'the different periods of the capitalist form' via the two forms of subsumption, transposing them into periods of 'formal domination' and 'real domination' of capital. For Camatte, the crucial feature of real subsumption is the domination of dead labour – embodied in the means of production – over living labour. He argues that the superimposition of technology and machinery over workers represents the condition for an expansion of subsumption outside the sphere of production, and towards society as a whole.

Real subsumption implies the expansion of the *ratio* of constant capital over variable capital and both the reduction of necessary labour-time and its intensification. As the title of Camatte's book suggests, he claims that the community, understood as the main sphere of socialisation for people, is replaced by capital that becomes the new material community. For Camatte, the community is more than sociality, it is a lifeworld sphere that remains uncolonised by capital; thus its replacement with capital indicates the completion of real subsumption, or what he called total subsumption under capital.[150] Capital does not simply subsume the social relations that glue a given community together but also its imagery, the new material community becomes people's ideality as well: 'The material community has developed and tends to preserve its existence, to fix the social relations, which become increasingly reified'.[151]

With its tripartite distinction between formal, real and total subsumption, Camatte significantly contributes to the perspective on subsumption as a means of longitudinally tracking capitalist development. He highlights how the replacement of the 'human community' by the community of capital starts from the ontological inversion pushed by real subsumption: dead labour becomes the supervisor of living labour.

Like Camatte's definition of subsumption cited above, Negri, in his essay 'Twenty Theses on Marx, Interpretation of the Class Situation Today',[152] offers an interpretation of subsumption that goes beyond subordination and implies social integration. He provides the following periodisation: a manufacturing stage of capitalism linked to formal subsumption, two phases of large-scale industry linked to real subsumption, and the current phase of immaterial post-industrial production linked to social subsumption.

---

150   Camatte 1988, p. 15.
151   Camatte 1988, p. 155.
152   Negri 1996.

Negri describes those phases in terms of class composition/decomposition, through the process of socialisation of the worker inside an increasingly expanded production sphere; he also considers how this shapes its identity. Accordingly, the first stage of large-scale industry was characterised by professional craft workers; the second stage by the Fordist mass worker, and finally the current phase is characterised by what he calls the 'socialised worker'. Thus, according to Negri, after 1968 there began a new phase of political history, characterised by what he terms the 'subsumption of the entire society under capital in the process of capitalist accumulation';[153] this, argues Negri, marks the 'end of the centrality of the factory working class as the site of the emergence of revolutionary subjectivity'.[154]

Negri thus echoes Tronti's earlier 'social factory' thesis, in arguing that in the present period the capitalist process of production encompasses even the smallest fraction of social production. Production is no longer limited to the sphere of industrial production, but rather is diffuse and occurs across society as capitalist production.

Negri's approach to subsumption focuses much needed attention on the worker's subjectivity and a class that pushes back against a tendency to privilege 'objective' social relations. While several commentators noticed that many thinkers working within the parameters of Operaismo have fallen into the subjectivist trap,[155] thinkers like Negri possibly avoided some of those risks by connecting worker subjectivity with the broader-scale dimension of class composition and the multitude. Arguably this alternative point of view allows Negri to identify new dynamics of control and subordination that extend their grip to bodies and minds associated with both the utilisation of ICTs inside the labour process and outside of it, thus connecting work and leisure time. Together with Hardt, Negri summarises this account as follows:

> Postmodern capitalism should be understood first, or as a first approximation, in terms of what Marx called the phase of the real subsumption of society under capital. In the previous phase (that of the formal subsumption), capital operated an hegemony over social production, but there still remained numerous production processes that originated outside of capital as leftovers from the pre-capitalist era. Capital subsumes these foreign processes formally, bringing them under the reign of capitalist relations. In the phase of the real subsumption, capital no longer has an outside in

---

153 Negri 1996, p. 149.
154 Negri 1996, p. 149.
155 Wright 2002.

the sense that these foreign processes of production have disappeared. All productive processes arise within capital itself and thus the production and reproduction of the entire social world take place within capital. The specifically capitalist rules of productive relations and capitalist exploitation that were developed in the factory have now seeped outside the factory walls to permeate and define all social relations – this is the sense in which we insist that contemporary society should now be recognised as a factory-society.[156]

As they will then articulate in more detail in *Empire*,[157] Negri and Hardt claim that social subsumption has led capitalism to establish a bio-political regime that aims at extracting value from all spheres of social life in its entirety.

Like Negri, the collective Théorie Communiste uses subsumption not just to periodise capitalism but to track longitudinally the historic process of production and reproduction of the proletariat and its relationship with capital: 'real subsumption', they argue, brings into play the reproduction of the proletariat. ... Real subsumption establishes the systematic and historical interconnection between the reproduction of the proletariat and the reproduction of capital'.[158]

Furthermore, as with Negri, Théorie Communiste is interested in understanding subsumption outside the labour process, studying class struggle over time. Accordingly, different kinds of subsumptions indicate different phases of struggle. The collective identifies formal subsumption and two phases inside real subsumption. Phase 1 (1913–18 to 1960s) is characterised by self-affirmation and composition of the proletariat. Especially after World War II, the US and much of Western Europe experienced Fordism, during which, according to Heinrich,[159] both the rate of exploitation associated with the extraction of relative surplus-value and the material wealth of workers increased at the same time. Conversely, Phase 2 (1968–73 to the present), characterised by capital as a social relation and by the decomposition of the proletariat.

For Théorie Communiste, absolute and relative surplus-value are conceptual determinations of capital, while formal and real subsumption are historical configurations of capital. In this connection, the group establishes a crucial conceptual distinction between formal subsumption and real subsumption in terms of their extension: formal subsumption affects only the immediate labour-process, while it is argued that real subsumption extends beyond the

---

156 Hardt and Negri 1994, p. 15.
157 Hardt and Negri 2000.
158 Théorie Communiste 2003, p. 145.
159 Heinrich 2012.

sphere of production to society as a whole. Real subsumption thus establishes the systematic and historical interconnection between the reproduction of the proletariat and the reproduction of capital.

While not matching Théorie Communiste's periodisation, Vercellone[160] also identifies three stages of subsumption. The first is formal subsumption, which develops between the beginning of the sixteenth and the end of the eighteenth century. In this stage, the relation of capital/labour is marked by the hegemony of the knowledge of craftsmen and of workers with a trade, and by the pre-eminence of the mechanisms of accumulation of a mercantile and financial type. Then, the second stage is marked by real subsumption, which starts with the first industrial revolution. The division of labour is characterised by a process of polarisation of knowledge, which is expressed in the parcelling out and disqualification of the labour of execution and in the overqualification of a minoritarian component of labour-power, destined for intellectual functions. Finally, the third stage indicates cognitive capitalism, which begins with the social crisis of Fordism and of the division of labour. The relation of capital to labour is marked by the hegemony of knowledge, a diffuse intellectuality, and by the driving role of the production of knowledge by means of knowledge connected to the increasingly immaterial and cognitive character of labour. This new phase of the division of labour is accompanied by the crisis of the labour theory of value and by the strong return of mercantile and financial mechanisms of accumulation.

The principal elements of this new configuration of capitalism and of the conflicts that derive from it are, in large measure, anticipated by Marx's notion of the general intellect. Vercellone develops a perspective that I think is crucial when it comes to the link between subsumption and fixed capital: linking fixed capital to the general intellect means providing a critical view of what currently a machine really looks like – that is, something much less physically tangible than in the past, made up of scientific- and culturally-based practices that capital is able to take over from people's lives and submit to its own valorisation processes.

Compared to the literature so far reviewed, Adorno shares the tendency to link subsumption to a *telos* of capitalism's overwhelming domination. However, he is much less preoccupied with historical phases of class struggle and more oriented towards a more theoretical analysis of subsumption as abstraction. In turn, he treats abstraction, identity thinking and alienation as a general impoverishment of individual subjectivity. Capitalism for Adorno turns

---

160   Vercellone 2007.

into an autonomous system that shapes subjectivities under conditions of real subsumption. Adorno provides valuable insights about the link between subsumption and abstraction, pointing out how capitalism takes on a life on its own, independent from its embodied economic agents, a kind of automaton, echoing Marx when he claims, 'those who consider the automation of value as a mere abstraction forget that the movement of industrial capital is this abstraction in action'.[161] In this sense, a fundamental aspect of 'power' under real subsumption is that it works as repressive abstraction, because abstracted from the will and praxis of individuals, therefore automated and systemic; but it is also abstracted from the genuine interests and needs of people.

Adorno's notion of total administration[162] can be considered similar to Camatte's idea of total subsumption and Negri's social subsumption, which we have already discussed. Like Camatte and Negri, by subsumption Adorno emphasises the totalising dynamic of capitalism that treats people as 'objects of administration'[163] moved by a necessary force. In Adorno's view, subjects are exposed to the power of the culture industry to create consciousness: means of communication and representation that while pursuing particular commercial interests operate as one homogenous industry capable of saturating people's consciousness, which becomes a platform through which the cultural industry can create artificial wants, needs and desires. In the exchange principle, as a real abstraction, Adorno finds the primary source of abstraction: people become personifications of economic dynamics, and so they, as well as their relations, get subsumed under the exchange principle. Thus their use-value turns into exchange-value.

Adorno's take on subsumption goes beyond the sphere of production and expands towards consumption, but his definition makes it into a quality and a function of the totalising capitalist whole that takes place at the expense of individual subjectivities. Influenced by Lukács, he privileges the moment of subsumption under the commodity over capital or the value form. In *Minima Moralia*, Adorno claims:

> Here it is precisely subjectivity itself, knowledge, temperament and powers of expression that are reduced to an abstract mechanism, functioning autonomously and divorced both from the personality of their 'owner' and from the material and concrete nature of the subject-matter in hand.[164]

---

161   Marx 1996, p. 185.
162   Adorno 1987.
163   Horkheimer and Adorno 1944, p. 30.
164   Adorno 2005, p. 38.

Similarly, Marcuse in *One Dimensional Man*[165] links subsumption to damaged and alienated subjectivities subordinated to capital. Like Adorno, Marcuse sees the false identity between the individual and the social whole dominated by late capitalism as the outcome of real subsumption. In sum, the general take of the Frankfurt school can be synthesised in the subsumption of social life under the exchange principle, which also becomes the dominant form of social mediation, limiting all social intercourse,[166] while critical thinking itself is subsumed under procedural thought.

In many ways, with his theory of the spectacle, Debord combines the Frankfurt school lines of arguments with the Italian Operaist idea of the social factory. First of all, in his *Society of the Spectacle*[167] he claims that reality subsumed under capitalism becomes its mere representation. The spectacle seems to represent the overwhelming power of a perfect combination of ideal and real subsumption, in other words, it is a social and technological organisation perfectly interiorised in the practical consciousness of people:

> The spectacle presents itself simultaneously as society itself, as a part of society, and as a means of unification. As a part of society, it is ostensibly the focal point of all vision and all consciousness: But due to the very fact that this sector is separate, it is in reality the domain of delusion and false consciousness: the unification it achieves is nothing but an official language of universal separation.[168]

Like Adorno, following Lukács' theoretical legacy, Debord suggests that the most important subsuming capitalist form is the commodity. It is the immense accumulation of commodities that have subsumed reality: 'In societies where modern conditions of production prevail, life is presented as an immense accumulation of spectacles. Everything that was directly lived has receded into a representation'.[169] What is lost is a less mediated and more genuine sense of reality, but individual critical consciousness and individual reality are both repressed by the spectacle.

At the same time, all individual reality, being directly dependent on social power and completely shaped by that power, has assumed a social character. Indeed, it is only insofar as individual reality is not truly individual that it is

---

165 Marcuse 1968.
166 Marcuse 1968, p. 121.
167 Debord 1995.
168 Debord 1995, §3.
169 Debord 1995, §1.

allowed to appear. The spectacle then becomes, among other things, a way of understanding the truth of capital's mutation in this epoch: the social becomes economic, and the economic becomes social. Society in its length and breadth becomes capital's faithful portrait. It is as if the great factory of the industrial revolution had been aerosolised.

Finally, the Marxist feminist tradition provides an alternative perspective on subsumption. Several of its thinkers, influenced by Italian Operaismo, claimed that housework constitutes a necessary condition for the reproduction of labour and an important exemplification of social productivity and social subsumption. This perspective problematises the distinction between productive and unproductive labour and the (in)capacity to produce surplus-value. For instance, Fortunati claims that one of the issues in failing to recognise value creation in housework is the failure to recognise both the necessary condition of social reproduction and how the intimate sphere has been subsumed by capital:

> Thus, the real difference between production and reproduction is not that of value/non-value, but that while production both is and appears as the creation of value, reproduction is the creation of value but appears otherwise ... It is the positing of reproduction as non-value that enables both production and reproduction to function as the production of value.[170]

She suggests that domestic labour is exposed to the power relation established by both formal and real subsumption. Thus, if it is true that the worker being subsumed can be exploited, then women's reproductive labour implies non-recognition and exploitation in the same way. As Clover points out:

> The Marxist feminist account provides a vital hinge as well in the subsumption narrative. It suggests that the concept is itself gendered: a woman in the conventional family was always already formally subsumed under capital in just this sense, secretly productive without resembling the industrial revolution's model of labour. Moments of real subsumption might be seen in the vacuum cleaner, dishwasher and other such domestic productivity tools.[171]

This home-driven political economy of reproductive labour is funded by the opacity of wage-labour, therefore informal formal subsumption. The wage in

---

170 Fortunati 1995, p. 9.
171 Clover 2010, p. 1578.

fact hides the actual length of people's working day, which clearly extends into their time spent at home, a darker, more obscure source of surplus-value production. This is a formidable example of the notion of the social factory and in general reveals the principle that, as Silvia Federici has maintained, capitalism rests on an enormous amount of unpaid labour, that is to say, labour that is included but not accounted for in contractual relations, and that, in the case of housework, is overlooked altogether:

> It was discovering that unpaid labour is not extracted by the capitalist class only from the waged workday, but that it is also extracted from the workday of millions of unwaged houseworkers as well as many other unpaid and unfree labourers. It was redefining the capitalist function of the wage as a creator of labour hierarchies, and an instrument serving to naturalise exploitative social relations and to delegate to wage-workers power over the unwaged. It was unmasking the socio-economic function of the creation of a fictional private sphere, and thereby re-politicising family life, sexuality, procreation.[172]

As we shall see later in Chapter 9, the Marxist feminist perspective helps us to understand how the intimate private sphere of the household becomes a platform where capital production and reproduction circulate in multiple ways.

What can we learn from this brief review? First of all, we notice that most authors tend to understand subsumption in a broader (sometimes much broader) frame of reference compared to Marx, who mostly tends to treat subsumption as something internal to the labour process. Accordingly, the great majority of authors treat subsumption as an analytic category that articulates a general feature of capitalism, namely its character as a totalising process, as a totality, as a process of expansion and development both in terms of social space and social time. As we will show in more detail in Chapter 4, in this book I try to scale down the explanatory power of subsumption to the concrete level of relations and the practices of individuals by examining the so-called molecular level, which is my contribution to moving subsumption beyond the idealist realm and expanding its horizon of meanings.

---

172   Federici 2019, p. 1.

CHAPTER 3

From Subsumption to Subsumptive Relations

> ... the revolution that the bourgeois class has brought into the conception of law, and hence into the function of the state, consists especially in the will of conformism (hence ethnicity of the law and of the state). The previous ruling classes were essentially conservative in the sense that they did not tend to construct an organic passage from the other classes into their own, that is, to enlarge their class sphere 'technically' and ideologically: their conception was that of a closed class. The bourgeois class poses itself as an organism in continuous movement, capable of absorbing the entire society, assimilating it to its own cultural and economic level. The entire function of the state has been transformed; the state has become an 'educator'.[1]

∴

In the 'Results of the Direct Production Process', Marx observes that in the context of (formal) subsumption, 'the formal relation of buyer and seller, at least ideally, displaces all other politically or socially fixed relations of domination and subordination'.[2] Formal subsumption does not eliminate the power relation but replaces it by incorporating it into a highly mediated ensemble of economic and social relations. This is the issue to which this chapter and Chapter 4 are dedicated; I will try to explore some of the main social mediations that make subsumption a contradictory ensemble of subsumptive relations at different scales.

The main thesis explored here is that subsumption is best understood not as a category, a solidified state, or an established condition, but as a fluid bundle of power relations instrumental to both surplus-value production and the reproduction of 'adequate' class relations. In this sense, in order deconstruct the received understanding of subsumption, I claim that for each subsumptive

---

1 Gramsci 1975, Q 8, § 2.
2 Marx 1990, p. 1022.

relation we study we must consider the subsuming agent acting upon a subsumed element or objectified subject, under historic-specific capitalist forms, and through a specific kind of power relation such as subordination, incorporation, mediation, and negotiation. Most of all, we must attend to how those positions change over time.

However, as Murray points out,[3] while subsumption tends conceptually to privilege abstractions, such as exchangeability and universality, the process of subsuming an element/process/action can be described as an integration under specific social forms, that is, the fairly stable arrangement that a given set of social relations form, which consistently informs social practices.[4] This is to say that understanding subsumptive relations means systematically addressing the tension between motion and fixity, transformation and reproduction. Subsumptive relations constitute an attempt with no guarantee to secure the systematic extortion of unpaid labour, that is, surplus-value. And again, achieving this over time, in a regime of competition and class antagonism, means constant modulations in the manner of approach.

I will also define those relations as hegemonic. They are not just exploitative relations but also prototypical hegemonic relations; their coercive force is rarely overt, frequently nuanced by consensual aspects and frequently built into the very structures – such as the legal framework and the market – that legitimise the private ownership of the means of production and project a veil of freedom onto the coercive forces that undergird work contracts.

Thus, subsumptive relations rest on what Jeffrey Reiman[5] defines as 'structural force'. By that, I understand the coercive component of subsumption as mostly structural in the sense that it is based on generalised, diffused and synergetic leverage that allows for the reproduction of the condition of dispossession and the removal from a given class of its means of production. It thus does not only operate inside the sphere of production but also requires lawyers, landlords, bankers, police officers and teachers. However, as I will argue here in terms of openness and what I will define in the next chapter as determinate supersumption, between the structural force of subsumptive relations and their effects, there is always a margin of manoeuvre and indeterminacy.

---

3 Murray 2004.
4 Thus, for instance, in the process of subsuming a given element or a social practice under the commodity form, it is not just about subordinating the element/practice to commodity exchange (or the commodity fetish) but also a matter of reshaping the constitutive social relations of the 'object' of subsumption, on the basis of the morphology of the commodity itself.
5 Reiman 1987, p. 8.

Subsumptive relations consistently combine what in Marx are two connected but distinct aspects, primitive accumulation and subsumption. While the former has been mostly described as a forceful and frequently violent divorcing of the producers from their means of production, the latter represents a rejoinder, with the means of production frequently mediated by 'softer' power, and therefore defined by specific exploitative conditions. The former mostly implies coercion, the latter also implies formal and ideological consent. The combination produces a hegemonic state of right. The state in fact operates as a contradictory mediator, so that sometimes the state acts as a de-commodifier and subsumption reverser, as in the case of the welfare state as understood by Gøsta Esping-Andersen.[6] In this sense, subsumption (and its dialectical other) sheds light on a more ambiguous reality, in which separation and integration coexist.

Subsumptive relations are also economic and extra-economic relations of power: they inscribe workers within a social context in which subsumption under capitalist forms is reproduced materially by ongoing accumulation by dispossession as well as ideologically, by the fiction of the marketplace and a legal framework that hides class difference and class struggle behind a thick veil – what Marx calls equality, freedom and Bentham. Material dispossession, class decomposition and re-composition are all necessary aspects of subsumptive relations. Subsumptive relations do much more than offer flat commands to workers about how to ensure their bodily and social reproduction; instead, they turn such necessity into (apparent) freedom, coercion into consent, and objective relation into subjective identities.

When Marx claims in the *Grundrisse* that 'individuals are now ruled by abstractions, whereas earlier they depended on one another',[7] he describes the qualitative transition in the form of political subordination brought about by capitalist relations that I previously defined as a structural force. However, political subordination is not abstract, since class warfare depends on subsumption. Such subordination is not just violent and coercive but also relies on consent and even a mix of functional and dysfunctional dissent, which I will define as determinate supersumption. The hegemonic reconfiguration of power relations entails a reconfiguration of how class politics can be performed.

In fact, all forms of subsumption addressed by Marx represent a displacement of the political process and class warfare at a different level: overt violence

---

6 Esping-Andersen 1990.
7 Marx 1973, p. 123.

is frequently eliminated, defused or effectively masked, which signals the establishment of a modern kind of power that replaces crude coercion and violence with governmentality, biopolitics, administrative regulation and the fictions of fairness of rational power conveyed by institutions such as the marketplace and its processes of 'fair exchange'. The hegemonic attempt to build an integrated total system is both a class project – as per the definition of Neoliberalism offered by Harvey[8] – but also a systemic outcome of subsumptive processes. In fact, especially under the conditions of real subsumption, the subsumption of capital under the valorisation process constitutes a dynamic that concerns the whole circulatory system of capitalist production/reproduction and that gradually attempts to colonise all spheres of life. Real subsumption constitutes a totalising organisation whose aim is to produce adequate institutions, adequate workers, adequate consumers and adequate commodities. In many ways, this social subsumption would in theory try to even produce 'adequate-to-capital' antagonism.

Based on the literature review provided above, subsumption is both a process of abstractive homogenisation, as well as a way of creating new differences, relating to hierarchical orders, spaces, needs, wants and desires. One important aim of this study is to try not to overplay either one of the two sides, falling neither on the side of the 'systematic' nor the 'historic' dialectical narrative but instead using subsumption as a way to mediate the two; this reflects the intellectual project of a critical political economy that strives to balance the risks of crude materialism and crude idealism:

> The crude materialism of the economists who regard as the *natural properties* of things what are social relations of production among people, and qualities which things obtain because they are subsumed under these relations, is at the same time just as crude an idealism, even fetishism, since it imputes social relations to things as inherent characteristics, and thus mystifies them.[9]

In my view, reframing subsumption as subsumptive relations constitutes a significant step in that direction: it makes subsumption a social process in which the logical/systematic agency of subsumption as a means of determining form – for instance, turning labour into wage-labour, commodity, or circulation – and of transforming people into social categories, encounters its own inverse,

---

8 Harvey 2005.
9 Marx 1973, p. 687.

namely the process through which social categories become – or better put, come once again to be considered as – people, bodies, specific subjectivities. Thus, subsumption becomes a social process of production and valorisation, a social relation, and a concrete praxis.

Similarly to how Michael Burawoy[10] understands the labour process, I argue that all capitalist production contexts involve an economic dimension (that is, production of goods and services), a political dimension (that is, production of effective social relations), and an ideological dimension (production of an experience of these relations). Those three inseparable dimensions form the subjects who experience and operate by means of those relations and are synthesised through subsumption, which ultimately recognises the indeterminacy that characterises labour-capital relations.

The expansive move I want to convey using a perspective defined by 'subsumptive relations' is not simply tied to the already mentioned notion of the social factory and social production, but is also linked to the recognition that subsumption constitutes a dialectical process based on power relations that requires constant maintenance and reproduction. Its relational nature implies that those kinds of relations are systemically produced but not in a serial fashion, so that they may develop in different ways, involving different combination of coercion and consent, different combinations of autonomy and dependence and subordination, different combinations of the production of surplus-value. Subsumption requires constant maintenance because those relations are exerted over a mutable component, which is embodied living labour. As we shall see, embodied labour subsumed under exchange-value also has profound implications in terms of race and gender, since when capitalists 'buy' 'labour-power' what they purchase is a power of command over workers' bodies and their persons.[11]

As I will elaborate in more detail in the next chapter on the notion of determinate supersumption, this constant effort to preserve a given balance and given trajectory for a given set of power relations makes subsumptive relations, like any kind of power relations, vulnerable and unstable; the process can vary in intensity, stop, stall, reverse and evolve.

---

10   Burawoy 1979.
11   Banaji 2003, p. 70.

1 The Terrain of Class Struggle Relations

Subsumptive relations find their dialectical negation both in their inner process of development, caused by internal contradictory dynamics, as well as in the way they engage embodied workers. This means that they present both 'objective' and 'subjective' dimensions, and a variable degree of active politics of antagonisation from both sides, capital and work. Thus, in many ways, while subsumptive politics are frequently less overt and frontal compared to politics at other levels, they still raise the debate between spontaneity and conscious control – and especially for the subordinate class. Spontaneity represents the *relatively* immediate and subjective response from the worker to the objectiveness of relations of production, and therefore including subsumptive relations.

As I will articulate more fully in Chapter 4, what I call 'conscious control' is not simply strategic collective action but also concerns the attainment of a critical consciousness, which involves pushing back against the fetish resulting from subsumption: once subsumed, living labour perceives capital to be the productive agent and not labour itself. Thus, for instance, part of waging class struggle is not simply about antagonising capital but also about composing out of heterogeneity a common class experience, and more importantly, a common line of mobilisation.

It is also relative, because in a complex social organisation of production the determining force of the structural and the subjective moment are engaged in a continuous dialectic: 'the concrete moments of the struggle, which cannot but be the results of opposing forces in continuous movement'.[12] Gramsci argues that assessing the potential for transformative politics entails analysing the 'correct relation' between the organic and conjunctural moments, finding the correct equilibrium between economic mechanical causes and voluntaristic ones. This means that envisioning a politics of subsumption from the perspective of labour means articulating a vision that combines the determinate supersumptive conditions both at the objective and subjective levels: from both economic and ideological perspectives.

Gramsci observes how spontaneity tends to define subaltern political struggles. While spontaneity represents a fundamental indicator of discontent, the instinctual rejection of unacceptable conditions rarely succeeds without conscious direction and leadership:

---

12   Gramsci 1971, p. 438.

> ... a 'multiplicity' of elements of 'conscious leadership', but none of them predominates or goes beyond the level of the 'popular science' – the 'common sense', that is, the [traditional] conception of the world – of a given social stratum.[13]

In other words, seen from the perspective of class relations as defined by Gramsci, subsumptive politics always appear as the combination of objective and subjective, organic and conjunctural, spontaneous and conscious leadership elements:

> It must be stressed that 'pure' spontaneity does not exist in history: it would come to the same thing as 'pure' mechanicity. In the 'most spontaneous' movement it is simply the case that the elements of 'conscious leadership' cannot be checked, have left no reliable document. It may be said that spontaneity is therefore characteristic of the 'history of the subaltern classes', and indeed of their most marginal and peripheral elements ... Hence in such movements there exist multiple elements of 'conscious leadership' but no one of them is predominant or transcends the level of a given social stratum's 'popular science' – its 'common sense' or traditional conception of the world.[14]

For Gramsci, every political movement contains elements of both, a mixture of approaches spanning from common sense to a more systematic good sense. For him, the factory council of Turin and Milan in 1919–20 represented an invaluable experience for self-organisation and prefigurative subsumptive politics, a way radically to redefine the subsumptive power relations that emerged in the workplace. The experience of the factory councils entailed an internal commission which stood against both capital and the union. The councils demanded to be recognised in terms of bargaining contracts and general wage demands. Looking back, he reflected on the experience of *L'Ordine Nuovo* in 1919–20:

> This unity between 'spontaneity' and 'conscious leadership' or 'discipline' is precisely the real political action of the subaltern classes, insofar as this is mass politics and not merely an adventure by groups claiming to represent the masses.[15]

---

13   Gramsci 1975, N 3, § 48.
14   Gramsci 1971, pp. 196–7.
15   Gramsci 1971, p. 198.

While in Gramsci's view there is still a degree of exteriority involved in so-called conscious leadership, the Italian Marxist tradition of Workerism represents one of the few schools of thought that explicitly incorporated subsumption as a central category. Mario Tronti,[16] for example, was particularly interested in two aspects of subsumption: firstly, the historical struggle over the length of the working day discussed under a regime of formal subsumption by Marx in the first volume of *Capital*, which in his view demonstrated the active role assumed by the proletariat in terms of class struggle; and secondly, how the generalisation of real subsumption and the production of relative surplus-value was affecting capitalist societies like Italy, where the drive for social technological innovation was particularly intense during the 1970s. Could a more technologically savvy worker problematise the typical assumption *à la* Braverman about an intensified labour process de-skilling and disabling workers?

Both perspectives indicate how subsumption was understood as a class struggle in terms of class composition and decomposition tendencies, and that was a reciprocal dynamic that affected the composition of both classes. As Wright maintains:

> ... such a dialectic had continued after the introduction of a 'normal' working day. If working-class pressure forced 'the incessant development of the productive forces' upon capital, this process simultaneously entailed 'the incessant development of the greatest productive force, the working class as revolutionary class'. Here, too, capital faced the necessity of reorganising production, since 'it is only within labour that [capital] can disintegrate the collective worker in order to then integrate the individual worker'. Even if successful, however, each attack upon labour ultimately displaced the class antagonism to a higher, more socialised level, so that 'production relations become increasingly identified with the social relation of the factory, and the latter acquires an increasingly direct political content'.[17]

In Tronti's view, the turn to real subsumption involves a transition from extending the length of the day to speed up, and spatial extension beyond the manufacturing plant: the factory absorbs the entire society. The socialisation of production means that all social relations tend to become relations of produc-

---

16   Tronti 1972.
17   Wright 2002, p. 54.

tion. Industrial society, once decomposed by capitalism, now gets recomposed and re-articulated by it. By a 'generalised' or a 'social subsumption', Tronti refers to the process that takes place under different exchange-value forms such as wage-labour and commodification processes, but also within the circulation process.

For Tronti, labour must be seen as labour-power, in other words, the commodification of the capacity to labour is the most important antagonism and terrain of struggle. Individual workers would unify as a class through such antagonisms. Trying to avoid a too subjectivist perspective, the great insight that can be extrapolated from Tronti concerns the coexistence within subsumptive relations of both subjection as objectification as well as subjection as subjective collective resistance to it.

In this sense, the primordial reason to reframe subsumption as subsumptive relations is to re-humanise what frequently remains a category that fails to relate itself to social and material experience, even in the case of productive activities already subsumed under capital. This in turn partly problematises Sáenz de Sicilia's interpretation, namely that subsumption has logical priority over the social-life process.

Subsumptive relations are the social preconditions for exploitation, alienation and production of surplus-value. Those aspects most frequently go together. As Braverman's study of labour[18] claims, for instance, Taylor's system was not a method for elaborating effective methods of work, but rather a system for increasing the rate of exploitation of alienated labour and, one should add, counteracting worker resistance. Braverman observes how the disciplinary aspect of the power relation characterising subsumptive relations is due to the uncertainty and variability that labour-power entails for the capitalist, an inevitable consequence of the fact that it is controlled by the subjective state of the workers.[19] If the production of surplus-value tends to expand, this means that the capitalist often must tighten control over the workers' indeterminate labour capacity, which in turn fuels class antagonism.

Thus, for Braverman, management tries to reduce such uncertainty by gaining control over workers through class decomposition. It pursues this aim via real subsumption, by separating tasks, for example into separate elements of conception and execution, and by deskilling workers by reducing the imaginative aspect of work. Mental, imaginative work was regarded as a source of uncertainty for management and of prefigurative initiative against capital.

---

18   Braverman 1974.
19   Braverman 1974, p. 57.

This process of emptying the mental/imaginative/creative aspect of work is implemented by both managers and automated machinery. However, if subsumptive relations try to secure the production of surplus-value by exploitation and rational control of the worker's uncertain labour capacity, they also tend to create the conditions for what I will describe later on as determinate supersumption, an incentive to resist control and exploitation, thus potentially exacerbating class struggle.

Thus, subsumptive relations are ultimately class relations in the perpetual process of production and reproduction, composition and decomposition. Looking at the labour process as subsumptive relations produced and producing class antagonism represents a way of re-populating the abstract development of economic categories with people whose relations are mediated by conflicting economic interests and reified forms of representation of their social relations, such as money, wages and interest rates.

The Workerist tradition understood class composition as comprising two elements: technical and political composition. The notion of 'technical' refers to the material organisation of workers into a collective articulated by social relations of work in which aspects of the labour process such as division of labour, cooperation, technology and management shape the larger entity, the class. The second aspect is defined as political composition, the organising tendency of the working class, which establishes the working environment as a terrain of class confrontation through determinate supersumptive relations such as resistance and workers' organisation. In my perspective, technical and political composition are both aspects of subsumptive relations. Those dynamics provide the decisive bases for the struggle for hegemony.

I align with the collective Notes from Below's position in arguing that class composition does not only take place in the subsumption of work under exchange-value, at the point at which people sell their work:

> Social composition combines with technical composition before the leap into political composition. Social composition is the specific material organisation of workers into a class society through the social relations of consumption and reproduction. This general formula of working-class reproduction allows us to understand the boundaries between forms of composition. … It involves factors like: where workers live and in what kind of housing, the gendered division of labour, patterns of migration, racism, community infrastructure, and so on. The ongoing dispossession, ideological state apparati, the process of shaping subjectifies and how those subjectivities may or may not form collective identities, all constitute the terrain of political class based struggle beyond the strictly

speaking and traditionally considered as working/production environment. That is true especially when, as in many current contexts, the very space of working has changed and has expanded beyond traditional work places.[20]

Social composition represents a way to understand how what we do when we are not technically working affects the structuring process that determines class belonging. The social composition of class, from the perspective conveyed in this book, crucially affects and is crucially affected by the power relations through which subsumption is implemented.

The concept of class composition points to what I will define in the next chapter (Chapter 4) as active supersumptive politics, a 'political leap'[21] of collective organising of workers against subsumptive domination and its goal to absorb work only as individual and fragmented labour-power, where the 'working class affirms itself as an independent class-for-itself only through struggles which rupture capital's self-reproduction'.[22]

2   Subsumptive Relations and Hegemony

Subsumptive relations, as power relations, cannot be equated with traditional forms of 'subordination by domination'. In my view the 'formal' aspect to which Marx refers points to a broader issue, namely ideological mediation. The already mentioned Marxian trope of 'freedom, equality and Bentham' represents how the market formally provides a level of consent and 'rhetoric of choice' that, while mostly working as a mystification, is nevertheless objectively present and significantly shapes the way those relations are understood and acted upon.[23]

For this reason, I claim that subsumptive relations, as expansive social relations, are also hegemonic relations. While subsumptive relations are relational, interactional, open and multidirectional, it is true that most of the time they are characterised by asymmetric power relations; in this sense, within the general Gramscian framework of hegemony, subsumptive relations can be interpreted – again, frequently but not always – as 'passive revolution', a revolution from

---

20   Notes from Below 2018.
21   Tronti 1966, p. 202.
22   Cleaver 1979, p. 66.
23   Read 2013.

above. Accordingly, capitalists tend to instigate transformation from above.[24] The reason why I carefully qualify this dynamic is that workers can indeed lead the transformation of subsumptive relations, for instance in a period of mobilisation or in moments of capital–labour negotiations.

The idea of framing subsumptive relations as hegemonic relations is that it allows them to be seen in terms of reversibility, in connection with social and cultural processes that affect the productive sphere at large, therefore beyond the manufacturing/work environment. In the chapter 'Americanism and Fordism' in his *Prison Notebooks*, Gramsci describes how the Fordist labour process was trying both to exert control and to acquire consent over moral issues and social practices such as leisure, drinking and sexuality, which were all seen as a waste of physical and cognitive resources. The idea was to forge a 'new man'.[25]

In a society where capitalism is hegemonic, body politics is worker body politics, and we know that subsumption functions most frequently with the principle that every limit is just a barrier to be overcome. The body represents the most crucial materialisation of excess and indeterminacy, motivating the obsessively subordinating and controlling aspects of capital. The aim, as Gramsci understood very well in his famous writing on 'Americanism and Fordism', was obviously not to replace the body with machines but to forge a capitalist anthropology: the systematic shaping of bodies and subjectivities adequate to capital, via measures such as the prevention of alcoholism, sexual promiscuity and abortion. These requirements certainly change over time. For instance, Taylorism aimed at conserving and effectively employing the workers' psycho-physical energies inside the factory. When, as in the case I will discuss in Chapter 6, our own home becomes a privileged space for production and consumption, those requirements change. The question of course is about adequate biopolitics. Thus, my understanding of subsumptive relations enriches the idea of subsumption as social-form-giving, because it sheds light on the labour process as an anthropological project based on the disciplinary microphysics of power: the biopolitics of controlling bodies and its impulses.[26]

---

24   Morton 2007.
25   Gramsci 1975, N 22, § 2 p. 2146.
26   By biopolitics, I refer to the one adequate to capital, thus understanding capital as bio-capitalist enterprise. By a capitalist biopolitics I refer to the process of valorisation associated with human bodies and their commodification. According to Fumagalli and Morini, in a context of bio-capitalism, 'the value of labour at the basis of bio-capitalistic accumulation is also the value of knowledge, of affects, and of relationships; it is the value of the imaginary and the symbolic': Fumagalli and Morini 2012, p. 236. Capitalist biopolitics represents an extractive attack against both mental and physical resources of people, as Marazzi eloquently observes:

An hegemonic project requires coordinated action at all social scales, from the individual to the fundamental institution of civil and political society. In this sense, a fundamental element in Gramsci's political theory is the 'expanded conception of the state'.[27] As is known, the Gramscian state is not just the whole system of public agencies but also 'a political balance between Political society (or dictatorship, or coercive apparatus aimed at bringing the mass of people according to the type of production and economy of a given time) with Civil society (or hegemony of a social group over the entire national society exercised through the so-called private organisations)'.[28]

Linking subsumptive relations to hegemony may seem counterintuitive unless some clarifications about the latter are not presented first. On the one hand, I reframe subsumption in terms of relations in order to highlight its processual way of constructing hegemonic power relations. In this sense, the problem is that, in order to make sense of the interpretation of subsumptive relations as hegemonic relations, not just subsumption but both notions must be understood in anti-reductionist ways.

Thus, first of all, I need briefly to clarify my understanding of hegemony. As Raymond Williams puts it, hegemony is useful to make sense of the connection between domination and determination:

> The key question is the degree to which the 'objective' conditions are seen as external. Since, by definition, within Marxism, the objective conditions are and can only be the result of human actions in the material world, the real distinction can be only between historical objectivity – the conditions into which, at any particular point in time, men find themselves born, thus the 'accessible' conditions into which they 'enter' – and abstract objectivity, in which the 'determining' process is 'independent of

---

The metamorphosis toward the capitalist anthropogenetic model or, if you prefer, the 'biopolitical turning point' of the economy, has a precise amount reflected in the evolution of employment of the labour force. Over the past decade the secular decline of the manufacturing sector compared to the service sector accelerates. This is not only a decrease in the number of industrial activity for increases in population (a phenomenon that has been going on since the beginning of the 1900), but also a decline in absolute terms, since 1996, which in United States, England and Japan is equivalent to a reduction of one-fifth of jobs and, in Europe, at an average net loss of five per cent. The difficulties, which we encounter in analysing these trends in the labour market, indirectly confirm that the emerging model is an anthropogenetic paradigm, a model in which growth factors are in fact directly attributable to human activity, to his communication, relational, creative, and innovative skills. – Marazzi 2005, p. 112.

27 Buci-Glucksmann 1980.
28 Gramsci 1971, pp. 458–599.

their will' not in the historical sense that they have inherited it but in the absolute sense that they cannot control it; they can seek only to understand it and guide their actions accordingly.[29]

Williams here makes explicit the combination of a structural force with a class project, which is effectively synthesised by the well-known definition he provides of social determination as 'setting the limits and exerting pressure'.[30]

Linking hegemony to subsumption really seems to escalate the level of overdetermined confusion, since hegemony has been interpreted and misinterpreted across a wide range of ideologically informed agendas: from a Leninist take to a Eurocommunist project, from a rescue of the 'superstructures' to the manifesto of totality, from a liberal Crocean position to Hegelian Marxism, from revolution to reformation, from radical democracy to totalitarian regimes.

Hegemony is processual, always incomplete, but a totalising process. It is the struggle to produce a contained – rather than controlled – environment for social relations marked by power, co-development and asymmetric reciprocity. Hegemony shapes subjectivities by a practical pedagogy, that is, through 'show rather than tell', which means *ex-ducere* to lead the subject towards a specific desired position by means of open conformism and controlled spontaneity at the level of production and implementation of ideas, practices, behaviour. I am not referring only to education in its strict sense, but to the capabilities of hegemonic apparati such as labour processes, media, families, and cultural institutions that constitute subjects through internalisation of a dominant world view.

Hegemony negotiates with the dynamism of the molecular level of individuals, classes and class fractions, state and civil society, and the fixity of 'fortified trenches', which move and resist movement with a considerable level of inertia. Thus, attacking hegemony does not equate to breaching the walls of a castle but rather entails entering a territory shaped by trenches, fortresses and bunkers both systematically and unsystematically placed across the land.

Reading subsumptive relations through a hegemonic lens means recognising the relations of production as broader social relations of power and the class struggle that derives from its role played inside the economy[31] as extending to the whole society by way of a higher synthesis of its elements. Subsumptive relations, in their insatiability – as the result both of class struggle and the inherent tensions of the capitalist system – can move across a wide spectrum of hegemonic configurations, searching for an always moving optimum

---

29   Williams 1977, p. 85.
30   Williams 1977, p. 34.
31   Gramsci 1975.

between coercion and consent, which is to say between absorption in decision-making processes and passive revolution and the crisis of hegemony, where force and violence may prevail.

While hegemony is a social cement, that is, an articulatory dynamic of the social whole, subsumptive relations constitute one of its most formidable apparati. Their homology across different scales is achieved through the form determination of social relations. Both hegemony and subsumptive relations aim at integrating a 'lower-level specificity' into a relatively more general degree of social order.

By hegemony, I do not refer to the dominant ideology. While ideology constitutes the most dynamic apparatus of hegemony, it remains only an aspect of a holistic power-induced configuration of a given society; when a class becomes hegemonic, it leads and dominates:

> 'Society' is never only the 'dead husk' which limits social and individual fulfilment. It is always also a constitutive process with very powerful pressures which are both expressed in political, economic and cultural formations, and, to take the full weight of 'constitutive', are internalised and become 'individual wills'. Determination of this whole kind – this complex and interrelated process of events and pressures – is in the whole social process itself and nowhere else.[32]

Hegemony is about praxis, a combination of ideas and practices. My understanding of hegemony aligns with what Peter Thomas identifies as the broadest Gramscian interpretation of hegemony as a category utilised for a 'differential analysis of the structures of bourgeois power in the West'.[33]

Like Thomas, I do not follow Anderson's popular assumptions about hegemony:

> ... it denotes a strategy aiming at the production of consent, as opposed to coercion; the terrain of its efficacy is civil society, rather than the state; its field of operation is 'the West', the proper terrain of war of position, in its distinction from 'the East', suited to a war of movement; and, finally, it can be applied equally to bourgeois and proletarian leadership strategies, because it is *in nuce* a generic and formal theory of social power.[34]

---

32 Williams 1977, p. 87.
33 Thomas 2007, p. 160.
34 Thomas 2007, p. 160.

I characterise it instead as a dialectical unity of coercion and consent, exerting its influence at the combined level of the integral state, comprising both offensives of position and of manoeuvre. I do not refer to a generic social power, but one attained by a dominant class in a capitalist society, which implies a permanent struggle to maintain and sustain:

> In practice, then, hegemony can never be singular. Its internal structures are highly complex, as can readily be seen in any concrete analysis. ... It has continually to be renewed, recreated, defended and modified. It is also continually resisted, limited, altered, challenged by pressures not at all its own. We have then to add to the concept of hegemony the concepts of counter-hegemony and alternative hegemony, which are real and persistent elements of practice.[35]

Along the same line, Negri and Hardt[36] describe subsumption as a process that does not work 'by brute force' (as in warfare) – although physical violence can also be involved – but also through the law, corruption, and the neoliberal ideology of entrepreneurship, ideologies that create and reproduce both capitalist hegemony and capitalist financial markets.

Hardt and Negri claim that contemporary capitalism produces a new configuration of the organic composition of capital, that is, a change of the productive forces and relations of production, a transformation that moves away from the productive criteria of large-scale industry. Living labour productivity has been intensified through the increase in labour cooperation via enhancement of means and practices of communication.

The role of the legal system in subsumptive relations is ultimately a reflection on (one of) the role of the state in reproducing subsumption both as surplus-value production and as power relations. It is Gramsci's notion of the integral state that here produces useful results: 'By the State should be understood not merely the governmental apparatus, but also the "private" apparatus of hegemony or civil society'.[37] Gramsci posited a dialectical unity of political and civil society, and not their identity or fusion. While, as Marxist legal scholars have suggested,[38] there is an important homology between the legal form and the commodity form, there are also important divergences; likewise, state

---

35 Williams 1977, pp. 112–13.
36 Negri and Hardt, 2000.
37 Gramsci 1975, Q 6, § 137.
38 See Balbus 1977.

and civil society and the 'inner' and 'outer' realms of production are far from being identical, even when shaped by a unitary ensemble of subsumptive relations.

The second characteristic of my understanding of hegemony as a model of power relations, is the combination of coercive and consensual elements. Hegemony is understood here not as the 'antitheses of domination', as Anderson claimed;[39] on the contrary, Gramsci explicitly argues that 'leadership' – in other words, following Lenin's synonymous usage, hegemony – constitutes a moment of domination, one of the concrete forms in which it is practiced:

> Another point which needs to be defined and developed is the 'dual perspective' in political action and in the life of the State. The dual perspective can present itself on various levels, from the most elementary to the most complex; but these can all theoretically be reduced to two fundamental levels, corresponding to the dual nature of Machiavelli's Centaur – half-animal and half-human. They are the levels of force and of consent, authority and hegemony, violence and civilisation, of the individual moment and of the universal moment ('Church' and 'State'), of agitation and of propaganda, of tactics and of strategy, etc. Some have reduced the theory of the 'dual perspective' to something petty and banal, to nothing but two forms of 'immediacy' which succeed each other mechanically in time, with greater or less 'proximity'. In actual fact, it often happens that the more the first 'perspective' is 'immediate' and elementary, the more the second has to be 'distant' (not in time, but as a dialectical relation), complex and elevated. In other words, it may happen as in human life, that the more an individual is compelled to defend his own immediate physical existence, the more will he uphold and identify with the complex and most noble values of civilisation and of humanity.[40]

Thus, if subsumptive relations are essentially a particular materialisation of class relations, Gramsci's conceptualisation of class struggle reproduces the level of complexity at which confrontation, antagonism and subordination in (but not limited to) the labour process are understood as non-linear complex relations of forces in which subsumptive dynamic are engaged, resisted and even pushed back, thus frequently necessitating additional mediations.

---

39   Anderson 1976.
40   Gramsci 1975, Q 13, § 14.

In my analysis, subsumptive relations are the intransitive process where those forces do not find their 'stable' or necessary position, but where they continuously measure each other.

Reading subsumptive processes through Gramsci provides a trajectory of power that never reaches the status of *telos*: from corporate domination of the ruling class to a hegemonic one, which entails an expansion of the sphere of influence of subsumptive relations as well as an expansion of the degree of class consciousness and political organisation associated with such power:

> The primitive economic moment in which the consciousness of a group's own professional interests are expressed but not as yet their interests as a social class; the political economic moment which is the one in which the consciousness of class interests is expressed, but only at an economic level; the third moment is that of hegemony, 'in which one becomes aware that one's own corporate interests, in their present and future development, transcend the corporate limits of the purely economic class, and can and must also become the interests of other subordinate groups'.[41]

In my view, the role of class confrontation inside subsumption, thus with its determinate negations, constitutes a powerful force that may – not always, not automatically – push the capitalist class to reproduce and renegotiate those power relations, but that also may push capital to develop into a new phase. Gramsci helps us to see more clearly where the politics of subsumption are situated and become manifest. Subsumption becomes, not just a terrain for the production of surplus-value, but also a fluid power relation, combining an ideological struggle with a dynamic of class composition and decomposition and producing a unity between economic and political objectives. Thus, it ultimately aims at what Gramsci describes as the intellectual and moral dimension of hegemony.[42]

Subsumptive relations are wholly socially reproductive relations at several levels: they reproduce capital accumulation by extracting surplus-value, they integrate a given activity into the capitalist productive system, and they reduce heterogeneity to homogeneity by abstraction of quality into quantity, thus reproducing the consistency of the social totality. Those relations assume a form, a mode of existence of capitalist relations. The form, as a mode of existence and a mode of representation, is inherently relational; as with the case of money, value, wages and capital, we are dealing with social relations with their

---

41   Gramsci 191, pp. 180–3.
42   Gramsci 1975.

own internal consistency and social morphism. Due to the very nature of the social relations of embodied subjects, these forms are necessarily always more than economic, as well as more than strictly productive.

The link between subsumptive relations and hegemony is indicative of the tensions created by such instability and of the ways in which capital responds to it. In this sense, Burawoy[43] pushes further Braverman's seminal analysis of the labour process by accounting for the element of consent. Drawing on Gramsci, Burawoy argues that consent does not eliminate subordination, but reveals instead a sphere of negotiation that deifies/problematises subordination as a constant and necessary dominating element. Instead of understanding capitalistic control as purely repressive and 'de-skilling', Burawoy observes a more hegemonic approach involving co-optation and subtle coercion, which neither Marx nor Braverman really acknowledged. Burawoy observes how workers frequently embrace significant principles of capitalism, despite these being the very basis of the constraints and exploitation they experience. In his ethnographic examination of changes in the labour process over 30 years at Allied Corporation (1945–75), he observed how consent was produced by promoting individualism in the organisation of work, through relaxed labour control and inspections, through more bargaining, and a piece-rate that emphasised individual performance rather than collective work.

Burawoy did not really equate consent and freedom because such consent was based on a rhetorical 'illusion of choice',[44] propelled by the goal of 'manufacturing consent' through a variety of strategies. First, in the machine shop, the piece-rate system created the illusion of labour as a game. Workers competed to 'make out' and surpass their expected production quotas. Over time, job satisfaction came from mastering the intricate and often devious strategies to 'make out' under various production conditions. Those more skilful in 'playing all the angles' garnered the most respect and prestige. The 'making out' game divided workers and obscured the fact that management was gaining productivity with only minor increases in wages. The act of playing the game generated consent for its rules, while providing a challenging diversion from the general boredom of repetitive labour.[45]

Furthermore, increasing job mobility within the company allowed management to reduce conflict and increase the illusion that workers had a choice. Potential labour conflicts could be avoided by separating workers. Burawoy also concluded that the collective bargaining between unions and management

---

43   Burawoy 1979.
44   Burawoy 1979, p. 8.
45   Burawoy 1979.

was yet another 'game', one that gave labour the illusion of participation and choice. Therefore, instead of alienating workers, modern capitalism has succeeded in coopting workers into embracing capitalism as its preferred ideology (despite the fundamental differences between capital and labour). Burawoy anticipates what for Read will be a constitutive aspect of subjective subsumption, a worker's will to participate in her exploitation, by a sort of internalised vocation, a new kind of Weberian calling to self-fulfilment through hard work, which is also at the basis of heteronormativity.[46]

In this context, subsumptive relations constitute a hegemonic apparatus, not hegemony at large. Again, as Buci-Glucksmann argues:

> The hegemonic apparatus qualifies the concept of hegemony and gives it greater precision, hegemony being understood as the political and cultural hegemony of the dominant classes. As a complex set of institutions, ideologies, practices and agents (including the 'intellectuals'), the hegemonic apparatus only finds its unity when the expansion of a class is under analysis. Hegemony is only unified into an apparatus by reference to the class that constitutes itself in and by the mediation of various subsystems.[47]

Accordingly, to frame them as hegemonic apparatus means also recognising subsumptive relations as a field of class confrontation. Thus, if hegemony comprises the large field of the integral state (that is, the combination of state and civil society), subsumptive relations concern the field of an integrated production, which is 'social', *à la* Tronti and Negri, and embodied, as Thomas points out. 'Gramsci's concept of a hegemonic apparatus', he writes, 'can be comprehended as a realistic translation of the themes that have more recently been proposed under the thesis of *biopower* and *biopolitics*'.[48]

Summing up, subsumptive relations are necessarily asymmetric power relations insofar as they secure the production of surplus-value, value is always tied to power, and power to the control of social outcomes. Value is not simply social labour that we do for others but is social labour we must do for others and sometimes are willing to do for others. 'Necessary' labour-time involves various levels of dependency, coercion and consent, as well as of constitution and self-activation.[49]

---

46 Ekbia and Nardi 2017.
47 Buci-Glucksmann 1980.
48 Thomas 2007, p. 225.
49 When value is defined as social necessary labour-time, the 'necessity' is a unitary com-

3   Integral and Welfare State

The state is a powerful mediator of subsumptive relations, especially in its hegemonic agency as integral state and welfare state, thus effectively mediating and defusing class antagonism, by, for instance, regulating the length and the arrangement of the normal working day. In the third volume of *Capital*, Marx describes the state as a determinate re-elaboration of a historically specific mode of production:

> The specific economic form, in which unpaid surplus-labour is pumped out of direct producers determines the relationship of domination and servitude, as this grows directly out of production itself and reacts back upon it in turn as a determinant. On this is based the entire configuration of the economic community arising from the actual relations of production, and hence also its specific political form. It is in each case the direct relationship of the owners of the conditions of production to the immediate producers – a relationship whose particular form naturally corresponds always to a certain level of development of the type and manner of labour, and hence to its social productive power – in which we find the innermost secret, the hidden basis of the entire social edifice, and hence also the political form of the relationship of sovereignty and dependence, in short, the specific form of the state in each case. This does not prevent the same economic basis – the same in its major conditions – from displaying endless variations of innumerable different empirical circumstances, natural conditions, racial relations, historical influences acting outside, etc. and these can only be understood by analysing these empirically given conditions.[50]

Marx thus contests the Hegelian conceptualisation of a state capable of sublimating particularisms into a universal base, the state is not only a 'particularism'

---

bination of various necessities: the working time needed to produce a use value under the normal conditions of production, and with an average degree of skill and intensity of labour in a given society. The normality of conditions of production, the prevalence of a given degree of skill and intensity are not produced in a vacuum but are an outcome of sustained pressure. The fact that I take 72 hours to make a pizza, which is way longer than an average pizza-maker today, does not mean that I earn more money compared to those who make a pizza in the average amount of time, rather the opposite. Thus, under the pressure to bake faster and cheaper, most workers are pushed to conform to the socially necessary labour-time to make a pizza.

50   Marx 1996, pp. 927–28.

in itself but also a mediated expression of the dominant social relations, therefore also expressing the interests of the dominant class.

In my view, in the optic of subsumptive relations, the notion of the integral state illuminates the tight link between a mode of production that in order to reproduce itself needs to integrate and coordinate both civil and political society. Marx and Engels defined the historically contingent development of a specifically bourgeois civil society as follows:

> Civil society embraces the whole material intercourse of individuals within a definite stage of the development of productive forces. It embraces the whole commercial and industrial life of a given stage and, insofar, transcends the state and the nation, though, on the other hand again, it must assert itself in its external relations as nationality and internally must organise itself as state. The word 'civil society' [*bürgerliche Gesellschaft*] emerged in the eighteenth century, when property relations had already extricated themselves from the ancient and medieval community. Civil society as such only develops with the bourgeoisie; the social organisation evolving directly out of production and intercourse, which in all ages forms the basis of the state and of the rest of the idealistic superstructure, has, however, always been designated by the same name.[51]

In this sense, the two thinkers agree with Hegel that the state appeared to exist above all classes and separate from the sphere of production and the market. For Marx, the idea of a political society separated from civil society was a modern abstraction and a mystification. That is because, as Lucio Colletti[52] claims, the abstraction is alienation: social power operating in civil society appears at the level of the state as a neutral legitimate power hovering over all citizens.

Compared to Marx, Gramsci provides a more developed conceptualisation of the relationship between civil society and political society. As with many other of his concepts, due to the fragmentary and open nature of his writings, Gramsci's notion of the integral state has spurred a lively debate over its definition. Anderson[53] provided three main formulations of the relationship between civil and political society: 1) while political society organises coercion, hegemony is organised within civil society; 2) both regions involve an element of coercion and hegemony; 3) political and civil society are co-extensive and hegemony covers both regions. My interpretation tends to align with Thomas'

---

51   Marx and Engels 1998, p. 98.
52   Colletti, 1973.
53   Anderson 1976.

leaning toward the third 'option'.⁵⁴ Thomas defines Gramsci's integral state as 'a network of social relations to produce consent, for the integration of the subaltern classes into the expansive project of the historical development of the leading social group'.⁵⁵ According to such a definition, the integral state operates based on the hegemonic apparatus that tries to harmonise different spatialities and temporalities.⁵⁶

I see the integral state as a materialisation of social subsumption in its totalising tendencies; as a hegemonic apparatus, then, but one also with open tendencies, consistently negotiating – and also failing to negotiate – between conflicting interests and antagonistic social forces. Thus, while the integral state is a hegemonic apparatus trying to cement social relations, it remains unstable and open. Indeed, Gramsci's political project is to look for adequate conditions for the construction of proletarian hegemony; in this sense he thought of the bourgeois integral state as the main overall structure in which dominant class hegemony was situated. The state appears for a moment within the overall larger unity. Thomas explains as follows:

> Far from being opposed to the state, civil society in this image appears as the state's complement, tending towards and reflecting the rational organisation, system of rights and juridical equality that distinguish the modern state. Civil society's primary role was to act as a mediating instance or moment of 'organic passage' for the subaltern classes towards the state of the ruling classes: a school of modern 'statehood'.⁵⁷

In this sense, subsumptive power relations are enforced both inside and outside the sphere of production by the state, through its legal apparatus, its police, its military and other state institutions oriented toward moral and cultural leadership rather than crude domination. However, the state's agency goes far beyond that, as the state constitutes a powerful mediation of both subsumptive and supersumptive dynamics. It operates in the terrain where different class-based political and economic interests confront each other.

Especially through a Gramscian informed optic of hegemony, the state is understood in its broadest sense, as the integral state, being the integration of what Gramsci defines as political and civil society, as well as of consensus (mostly located in the marketplace and public sphere) and coercion (located

---

54   Thomas 2007, p. 142.
55   Thomas 2007, p. 143.
56   Tomba 2012.
57   Thomas 2007, pp. 143–144.

in the state). The integral state constitutes the hegemonic apparatus par excellence, where the dominant class finds most of the resources it needs in order to rule with force and persuasion, 'State = political society + civil society, that is, armoured hegemony of coercion'.[58] The integration implemented by the integral state of political society and civil society rests on a dialectical relationship, which is characterised by the tension between unity and difference.[59] The interpenetration of private institutions within 'political society' – the state in a narrow sense – and public state-driven institutions within civil society tends to create a robust hegemonic structure that guarantees the stability and the conditions for production and reproduction of subsumptive relations, as Gramsci describes in this well-known passage:

> In the East, the State was everything, civil society was primitive and gelatinous; in the West there was a fair relationship between the State and civil society, and by oscillating the State one could immediately recognise a robust structure of civil society.[60]

The robustness of civil society, especially in respect of power relations involved in managing the production of surplus-value through labour exploitation, is not simply provided by the legal framework enforced by the state, but also by the moral and intellectual leadership that the integral state is capable of exerting, for instance by establishing and reinforcing values such as 'legalism', 'civic sense', 'citizenship', 'collective interests'.

According to this conceptualisation, civil society represents the terrain of confrontation for class hegemony, which then gets armoured by the state. In fact, for Gramsci, different spaces of civil and political society can describe how a subordinate but emerging class can lead in the sphere of civil society but not be dominant in the sense of controlling political society as well. And a given class, before becoming hegemonic, must exert leadership in civil society and then become dominant in the political society.

The integral state for Gramsci reaches out well beyond the apparatus of government as he understands it, creating links between civil society organisations and the basic structure given by the capitalist mode of production.[61] Thus, both political society and civil society, in the 'formula' of the integral state, are dialectically related to the economic structure:

---

58   Gramsci 1975, C 7, §16.
59   Liguori 2015.
60   Gramsci 1975, N 7, §16.
61   Gramsci 1975, N 6, §137.

> The formulation of the free-trade movement is based on a theoretical error whose practical origin is not difficult to identify, that is, it is based on the distinction between political society and civil society, which from methodological distinction is transformed and presented as organic distinction. Thus, it is said that economic activity belongs to civil society and that the State should not intervene in its regulation. But given that civil society and the State identify themselves in the reality of the facts, it must be established that liberalism is also a 'regulation' of a state character, introduced and maintained by legislative and coercive means: it is a fact of conscious will of its own ends, and not the spontaneous, automatic expression of the economic fact. Therefore, liberalism is a political programme designed to modify, when it triumphs, the leaders of a State and the economic programme of the State itself, that is, to modify the distribution of national income.[62]

My understanding of civil society inside the integral state reaffirms the material productive core of the civil society, against readings such as Norberto Bobbio's,[63] who claims that civil society is the locus of the ideological superstructure *par excellence*. It is from the same synergetic perspective that I see the integral state functioning in connection to subsumptive relations. The state is not just the legal framework for subsumptive relations, not just the enforcer, but also performs as an educator by conveying a particularly ideologically shaped sense of order, civilisation and legitimacy:

> ... every State is ethical in that one of its most important functions is to raise the great mass of the population to a certain cultural and moral level, a level (or type) that corresponds to the development needs of the productive forces and, therefore, to the interests of the ruling classes.[64]

A work ethic plus a moral-legal ethic form for Gramsci 'a technical-moral unitary social organism',[65] active when a whole (or most of) society is assimilated by hegemonic power.

The combination of a technical apparatus with a particular Victorian and paternalistic morality produces a welfare state, another name for the integration of state and civil society. As we shall see in the second part of the chapter

---

62   Gramsci 1975, N 13, § 18.
63   Bobbio 1979.
64   Gramsci 1975, C 8, § 179.
65   Gramsci 1975 C 8, § 179.

specifically dealing with the state as a legal framework, the welfare state operates as a critical mediator of class struggle, trying to defuse its basic antagonism but also mitigating subsumption by acting as a commodifier,[66] something which reveals its complex relation with subsumption in both its subsumptive and supersumptive aspects. The integral state acts as a welfare state by providing social resources, health and education. Furthermore, it defuses capitalist social contradictions by eradicating poverty, unemployment and complete wage dependency.

Peter Flora and Jens Alber[67] claim that the welfare state replaces older social institutions destroyed by capitalism with an organisation designed to mediate capitalist–labour relations. In this sense, Richard Titmuss[68] distinguished between welfare and different kinds of interventions: for example, a state that assumes reasonability only when the market fails, thus in effect becoming the actually hidden hand of the market. This is different from a state that remains permanently interventionist in key areas and in the broader social domain. In turn, the introduction of modern social rights implies a loosening of the process of commodification of social life.

De-commodification occurs when a service is rendered as a matter of right, and when a person can maintain a livelihood without reliance on the market. The welfare state as de-commodifying agent directly operates at the roots of the power relations on which subsumption rests, by emancipating citizens/worker – to a degree – from their dependency on the market and therefore diminishing the material prequisites for their formal subsumption under the form of wage-labour.

All in all, the welfare state is not a pure negation of subsumption; rather it operates as a terrain of class struggle. The organisational features of the welfare state help determine the articulation of social solidarity, divisions of class, and status differentiation. In this sense, it is important to notice, as a good deal of Marxist literature typically argues, that even the advanced welfare state merely reproduces (and perhaps even nurtures) existing class society.[69]

Moving on, we must explore how different aspects of social relations intersect each other in the polymorphous space of subsumption: legal/contract relations, power relations (lordship and bondage, hegemony, passive revolution), the fluid continuous space between coercion and consent, subordination

---

66   Esping-Andersen 1990.
67   Flora and Alber 1981.
68   Titmuss 1958.
69   See Offe 2020.

and independence, as well as the fact that economic agents may inhabit different positionalities in different moments of the social process of production and reproduction of a given social formation (for example, as seller of labour-power, buyer of labour-power, buyer of commodities ...).

4   The Legal Hegemonic Apparatus

Linking subsumption to the legal form constitutes in my view a way to tie hegemonic subsumptive relations to the legal system, a disciplinary and moral framework of the state, or more precisely, of the integral state and its interpenetrative realm that links civil society and political society. The legal is in effect a powerful platform in relation to subsumptive relations, and for a variety of reasons: it provides to labour contracts, via the semiosis of 'legality', a moral and political legitimacy; as mentioned in Chapter 2, legal subsumption is a great 'translation machine' for social meanings; and finally, it bridges political and civil society within the larger structure of the integral state.

Reading subsumption in the light of hegemony and the integral state means enriching it in order to show how, over time, leadership of the capitalist class in relation to the production of surplus-value necessarily involves a tendency to rearrange the entire society.

According to Tom Brass,[70] based on Marx's critique of Hegel's *Philosophy of Right* and *The German Ideology*, the traditional view of Marxist legal scholars tended toward an understanding of law as an archetype of the instrumentalisation of the so-called superstructures, as not just depending on the economic base but also mediating and refracting the actual determining social relations.[71] Richard Hazard summarises quite well how Marxist legal scholars wanted to demystify the innately logical, self-sufficient ontological state of legal norms and to reduce them almost to pure instrumentality:

> We find that the juridic relationship is generated by the material production relationships of human beings immediately at hand – from which it follows that an analysis of the legal relationship in its simplest form need not start from the concept of a norm as an external authoritative imperative. It is sufficient to take for a basis a juridic relationship 'whose content

---

70   Brass 2011.
71   Collins 1982.

has been provided by the economic relationship itself' (in the words of Marx) and to investigate the 'legal' form of this juridic relationship as one of the particular cases.[72]

My perspective tends to align with legal theorists such as Jacques Bidet[73] and Ben Fine,[74] who have convincingly argued that the relations of production that drive capitalism are necessarily both economic and juridic in nature. In other words, the economic and juridic are indissolubly united, and not necessarily hierarchically and ontologically stratified. Law persistently conditions the universe of possibilities that determines the degree of economic coercion, and more generally the power relations that people experience in capitalist societies.

The whole legal system is built on a fetishism: to the degree that law explains itself by its own internal dynamics, independent and autonomous from historical and material realities, it completely hides its source, nature and rationale. In this sense we can speak of legal fetishism: 'In this broader sense, legal fetishism refers to blindness, to the tension between enactment of law and its application, through a focus on the rituals of the law rather than on its efficacy'.[75] As Pashukanis claims, the theoretical task of Marxist legal studies is to treat law neither as pure epiphenomenon nor as an ideological falsity:

> The principle of legal subjectivity (which we take to mean the formal principle of freedom and equality, the autonomy of the personality, and so forth) is not only an instrument of deceit and a product of the hypocrisy of the bourgeoisie, insofar as it is used to counter the proletarian struggle to abolish classes, but is at the same time a concretely effective principle which is embodied in bourgeois society from the moment it emerges from and destroys feudal-patriarchal society. Second, they failed to take into account that the victory of this process is not only and not so much an ideological process (that is to say, a process belonging entirely to the history of ideas, persuasions and so on), but rather is an actual process, making human relations into legal relations, which accompanies the development of the economy based on the commodity and on money (in Europe this means capitalist economy), and which is associated with profound, universal changes of an objective kind. These changes include: the

---

72 Hazard 1951, p. 149.
73 Bidet 2005.
74 Fine 1984.
75 Lemaitre 2007, p. 9.

emergence and consolidation of private property; its universal expansion to every kind of object possible, as well as to subjects; the liberation of the land and the soil from the relations of domination and subservience; the transformation of all property into moveable property; the development and dominance of relations of liability; and, finally, the precipitation of a political authority as a separate power, functioning alongside the purely economic power of money, and the resulting more or less sharp differentiation between the spheres of public and private relations, public and private law.[76]

The legal form provides a false rational justification for the entire capitalist universe: everything translated by the legal norm is effectively justified in its existence. Plus, as Weber pointed out, the notion of rational-legal authority gives the state the legal monopoly over physical violence.[77]

The legal form also parallels the commodity form, in the sense that the exchange of commodities parallels the exchange of legally constituted citizens, as Isaac Balbus claims.[78] Balbus, aligning with Pashukanis, justifies this by arguing that the process of reproduction of the legal form is based on a similar dynamic to that of the commodity form: qualitatively distinct individuals with otherwise incommensurable interests enter into a formal relationship of equivalence with one another, that is, so that the qualitatively different subjects become what they are not – that is, equal. This is yet another lens through which we assess the level of articulation of subsumptive relations.

In this sense, contracts constitute the central legal premise on which all other aspects of the law are based, and the highest form of expression of the commodity-owning subject. Contracts are the necessary legal expression of commodity owners' ability to use their commodities in the market. The individual subject in both the commodity and legal form is the pure abstract form:

> The juridic subject is, therefore, the abstract goods-possessor elevated to the heavens. His will – understood in the juridic sense – has its real basis in the wish to alienate as it acquires, and to acquire as it alienates. In order for this wish to be realised, it is essential that the wishes of goods-producers go out to meet each other. This relationship is expressed juridically as a contract or accord of independent wills, and contract is

---

76   Pashukanis 1987, pp. 40–41.
77   Weber 1978.
78   Balbus 1977.

therefore one of the central concepts in the law. In more grandiloquent phraseology, it becomes a constituent part of the idea of law.[79]

In contrast to its liberal conceptualisation, Pashukanis proposes an historical materialist conception in which law represents a social practice among other historically grounded social practices:

> Law in its general definitions, law as a form, does not exist in the heads and the theories of learned jurists. It has a parallel, real history which unfolds not as a set of ideas, but as a specific set of relations which men enter into not by conscious choice, but because the relations of production compel them to do so. Man becomes a legal subject by virtue of the same necessity which transforms the product of nature into a commodity complete with the enigmatic property of value.[80]

For Pashukanis, all other forms of legal relations in capitalism spring from this. The subject of 'equal rights' substitutes for the concrete subject of needs, and the abstract legal person substitutes for the real, flesh-and-blood, socially differentiated individual. Thus, we find the same double movement from the concrete to the abstract, the same twofold abstraction of form from content, which characterises the commodity form. Law represents for Pashukanis the universal political equivalent adequate to capital. Its origin is not the social contract but a general level of subsumption of people's social action under capitalist logics. Its logic comes from the class-based dominance of capital circulation and accumulation, not reason. In the same way, the state derives from a systematic legitimation of governments controlled by capital interests.

Law's universality does not derive from pure or absolute logic, but from being universally applied. According to Pashukanis, the law cannot be understood without commodity exchange that has already subsumed the economy of a given country; in the same way, the foundation of public law must be found in private law. Pashukanis claims that both historically and logically, law requires an established commodity exchange system:

> It is only with the advent of bourgeois-capitalist society that all the necessary conditions are created for juridical factors to attain complete distinctness in social relations … A basic prerequisite for legal regulation is

---

79   Hazard 1951, p. 169.
80   Pashukanis 1978, p. 68.

the conflict of private interests. This is both the logical premise of the legal form and the actual origin of the development of the legal superstructure. Human conduct can be regulated by the most complex regulations, but the juridical factor in this regulation arises at the point when differentiation and opposition of interests begin.[81]

However, despite the way in which the economy provides the preconditions for its emergence, the law becomes vital, especially for processes of subsumption, as it provides capitalism with both the source to legitimise physical violence and overt coercion as well as to lay the basis of an ideological justification for the regime of private property and legal enforcement of contracts. Similarly, for Nielson[82] law represents the political technology that supports surplus-value extraction.

While the legal framework constantly reproduces the fiction of peer-to-peer contracting of labour-power, the bloody legislation that Marx describes in the first volume of *Capital* demonstrates the importance of overt force. Subordination for Marx's model implies coercion driven by physical survival. Not only does the legislation function in line with capitalist interests, but in his/her factory, the capitalist often operates as an autocrat, a private legislator. An example is the so-called master and servant act regulating employer and employee relations in the UK, a law whose origin can be traced back to the fourteenth-century Statute of Laborers, but which was implemented during the historic process of industrialisation.[83] The law reflected an asymmetrical power relation because while workers could bring a civil suit against the employer for failure to pay out for a wage contract, the employer could bring a criminal charge against a worker for failure to engage in a written contract, unauthorised absence, failure to complete a contract (parole or written), misconduct, or the misrepresentation of skills. In fact, Deakin and Wilkson argue that the Master and Servant laws were passed to provide employers with a means of workplace control that offered a ready form of direct coercion.[84]

The legal apparatus also operates as the discursive and logical medium that sets the rules of the game, its alleged rationality, the stage where conflicting interests translate into rights confronting each other, and most of all, where the circulation and exchange of capitalist forms such as commodities, money and value can take place. Thus, the traditional definition of law as an ideological

---

81 Beirne and Sharlet 1980, p. 58.
82 Nielson 2007.
83 Deakin and Wilkinson 2005.
84 Deakin and Wilkinson 2005.

epiphenomenon[85] is replaced by an objective legal fetishism so that both goods and humans are constructed as abstract and independent entities for the purposes of formally 'free' exchange.[86] Furthermore, the legal discourse functions as a veritable subsumption avant-garde, in other words as ideal subsumption that re-verbalises phenomena so that they are already primed for subsumptive consumption.

Thus the legal component is vital for the realisation of value, in other words, for the implementation of transactions and the stability of the underlying social relations. Finally, the employment relationship in the condition of formal subsumption is crucially mediated by law: labour-power becomes a commodity that is alienated from the worker, but since labour-power cannot be abstracted from the bodily condition of the worker, he/she remains the ultimate owner.

4.1   Legally Formal and Informal Subsumptive Relations

Working with the thesis of subsumptive relations as essentially apparati of a hegemonic framework means understanding the legal framework as an arena in which workers become engaged and are directed by both consensual and coercive dynamics. In my view, the ideological core of this approach is provided by the idea of a contract between free economic agents involved in the purchase–sale transaction of a very peculiar commodity, that is, labour-power. Thus, as I mentioned in Chapter 2, when discussing how legal theory understands the notion, subsumption operates as a translation machine.

In this case, the translation forces an equivalence where there is not one. In fact, the node that explains the peculiarity of the commodity of labour-power can be found in the ownership of a commodity that is intransitive and does not resemble any other commodity, because the seller of labour-power sells his/her commodity only partially – a consequence of the fact that it is materially attached to their own body. Bidet observes how 'this division of property is not adequately expressed by the category of "hiring" that Marx introduces (as in the comparison "just like a horse he hired for the day") which simply denotes a division of property between two owners who share its disposition'.[87] Labour-power is the commodity with a bodily based labour capacity. This peculiarity explains why capitalists require a level of subordination/domination over the worker, in order to reduce as far as possible the margin of uncertainty that such labour capacity entails – for example, because embodied people can feel sick,

---

85   Hunt 1985.
86   Fine 1984, p. 184.
87   Bidet 1997, pp. 48–49.

not motivated to work and distracted, can try to evade work, etc. Hence, the level of control implied by the labour process and therefore the adequate usage of the commodity bought as labour-power. Legally, these requirements are fulfilled by labour contracts.

Contracts, in liberal theory, represent one of the highest exemplifications of free, fruitful relations between free subjects with private conscious volition and autonomy. In fact, the very enforcing of contracts was treated ideologically as the implementation and guarantee of the freedom of the agreeing parties.[88] However, the problem is that contracts are never completely free, because they are motivated by needs, which can be mutual but never completely equivalent or symmetrical. For this reason, the absence of coercion and the plenitude of the right of the law is performed more than implemented:

> If consent is to retain its justifying power, the law must be able to distinguish when consent is real. But once the veil is pulled aside and the reality of consent is examined, all kinds of everyday economic pressure or necessity clamour for attention as potentially undermining consent. And since the law of contract has traditionally adopted an objective theory of agreement, where what counts is the appearance of agreement, it is not well equipped to begin to identify real consent. Thus, the problem that legal writers face is one of confinement: how to define pressure in a way which will allow the victim to say the consent was not real without thereby undermining doctrines which depend on a much more restrictive conception of consent, the consequence of which would be the unravelling of all manner of contracts which are common.[89]

Along the same lines, Marx, not surprisingly, carries out in the first volume of *Capital* an ideological critique of contractual law as a fictitious platform for freedom, equality, individual independence, property and labour rights. Marx wants to show how command over the individual worker does not start when he/she sells his/her labour-power but precedes the legal mystification: 'The worker sold the right to control his labour-power in exchange for the necessary means of subsistence'.[90] That is to say that the social historical and legal conditions that make somebody a proletarian subject to subsumptive power relations actually precede entry into the labour process, because a prospective worker is economically dependent on capital due to the whole social context

---

88 Dalton 1985.
89 Whightman, 1996 p. 19.
90 Marx 1990, p. 1060.

that pushes them to be hired as a worker in the first place. Thus, legal contracts are both constitutive and provide legal status and enforcement to an already existing social relation.

Therefore, wage-labour is a deceptive appearance. As Feinman and Gabel explain:

> The rise of capitalism generated a dramatic and dislocating social upheaval. How could people have been persuaded or forced to accept such massive disruptions in their lives? One vehicle of persuasion was the law of contracts, which generated a new ideological imagery that sought to give legitimacy to the new order. Contract law was one of many such forms of imagery in law, politics, religion and other representations of social experience that concealed and denied the oppressive and alienating aspects of the new social and economic relations. Contract law denied the nature of the system by creating an imagery that made the oppression and alienation appear to be the consequences of what the people themselves desired.[91]

In order to push back against such a mystification, Marx's understanding of contractual relations can be summarised by his famous line, 'Between equal rights, force decides',[92] so that instead of free choice in the sale of labour-power, we should instead talk of voluntary subjection to a stronger party. Both economic and legal coercion, as well as freedom, are necessarily linked. Economic coercion always has its source in a set of legal rights, privileges and powers that places one person in a position to force another person to choose between labour and some more disagreeable alternative to labour, just as so-called legal compulsion does. The exercise of economic power is also quite personal and direct. Consider, for instance, economic coercion exerted in the bargaining relationship between employers and employees.

What this perspective suggests is that contracts are platforms that effectively mediate on a fluid spectrum between equivalence and non-equivalence, coercion and consent, free and unfree labour, and most importantly, as a primordial condition, between possession and dispossession of the means of labour. Contracts operate in order to implement both ideal and formal subsumption. While the combinatory *ratio* between coercion and consent is overwhelmingly in favour of coercion, the consent aspect of legal contracts is not a pure ideolo-

---

91   Gabel and Feinmann 1998, p. 501.
92   Marx 1990, p. 159.

gical and rhetorical fiction either. While the legal framework is both produced and managed by the dominant class's specific interests, this indeed leaves to labour, in determinate social and historic cases, a margin of negotiation. For instance, in Chapter 2 I mentioned how *Théorie Communiste* and Negri used subsumption to make sense of how the relationship between capital and labour evolved over time; in that situation, the parenthesis between the 1930s and 1970s was defined by the strength of labour *both* constrained and enabled by the existing legal framework.

5   UnFreedom of Labour

The complexity of subsumptive relations, which makes them into a hegemonic apparatus, rests on this synthetic status of the worker as someone independent and yet subordinate at the same time. This is a combination of consent and coercion at the level of subsumption, rooted in the reality of being both the object (more than the subject) of a formal 'exchange of equivalents' and engaged simultaneously in a *de facto* exchange of 'non-equivalents'. This independence has to do with our ability to choose what activity will satisfy our dependence on wage-labour. It relates to pre-existing and ongoing divestment and dispossession, *qua* an objectifying alienated condition, that pushes us to exchange labour-power for objectified labour, that is, money. Money, moreover, that is just enough for us to keep living, with the result that we remain in a condition of dependence on the exchange between labour and objectified labour. As Skepton explains:

> Value-creating living labour is bought with objectified labour, or money as exchange-value. It is the labour-time of living labour that determines exchange-value, but when that living labour is itself commodified, objectified as a unit of duration, its exchange-value is equivalent to the objectified labour-time socially required to produce the commodities whose use-value can maintain its mere existence as living labour. This exchange of living labour for objectified 'dead' labour both maintains and rests on the poverty and lack of property of the workers.[93]

The reason I think it is important to insist on the material base of freedom and unfreedom is that it seems that several scholars discuss free and unfree labour

---

93   Skepton 2010, p. 115.

as if such a relation could be examined independently from the material preconditioning that necessarily influences our free/unfree choices.

The general ideological assumption posits that capitalist development is incompatible with unfree labour, that is, relations of productions must be understood in a context of equal rights and freedom of the economic agents to engage with them. Tom Brass[94] observes how the most committed exponents of the argument that unfree labour was economically inefficient were non-Marxists: Adam Smith in the late eighteenth century; John Stuart Mill and John Bright in the mid-nineteenth century; and Max Weber in the late-nineteenth and early twentieth century. The main, ideologically charged, narrative linking these authors suggests that each historical stage possessed its own distinctive form of social and economic organisation, as well as a distinctive labour type. Feudalism, for example, was defined in part using a particular form of labour, serfdom. When feudalism began to give way to a mercantilist version of market society, new forms of labour began to replace serfdom. In mercantilism, markets were heavily regulated, as was the wage-labour used in these markets. Over time, however, state regulation was relaxed, and by the nineteenth century, free-market society, with its characteristic labour type, free wage-labour, had triumphed almost completely. According to such a narrative, the movement from feudalism to a free-market society brought greater and greater freedoms to more and more people. Unfree serf labour gave way to regulated wage-labour and finally to free wage-labour as part of the larger historical process.

Equally significant is the fact that most of the figures mentioned above were economic liberals, and forerunners of the neoclassical economic historians who went on to question whether slavery was indeed coercive.[95] Most importantly, this perspective assumed that productivity was linked to the capacity of the individual worker to exercise 'choice' in the context of the labour process. A worker 'chose' to work hard because he/she individually benefited from this. It was also assumed that unfree labour is inefficient; it cannot undertake skilled tasks; it cannot be combined with advanced productive forces; it is too costly; it hinders market expansion; and the supply of such workers is anyway not assured.

In this sense, I tend to align with Robert Steinfeld and Christopher Tomlins[96] in their problematising of a clear distinction between free and unfree labour, which neglects the broad range of practices standing in between:

---

94 Brass 2011.
95 Steinfeld and Engerman 1997.
96 See Steinfeld 2001, Tomlins 2012.

> Rather than view compulsion in labour relations in terms of a binary opposition divided by type of pressure, it seems more plausible to think in terms of a combined scale of pressures, legal, physical, economic, social, psychological, all running along a continuum from severe to mild, rather than falling into a binary opposition.[97]

There are plenty of conditions that in today's global labour market can facilitate unfree labour: war, ecological degradation, structural adjustment policies, migration repression, all facets defining global-scale neoliberalism.[98]

In this sense, feminist political economy provides an exemplary account of the fluidity between free and unfree work, by recognising that coercive realities are at once highly opaque and also the result of patriarchal norms that apply in liminal working places such as household-sweatshops or the household.[99] What I think is very salient in this perspective is its ability to show how subsumptive power relations are exerted in spheres outside of production, by combining coercion and consent, and can provoke different forms of resistance.

Indicative of such fluidity is also Sudipta Mundle's[100] discussion of the period in which capitalism penetrated the Indian agrarian system, transforming peasants into wage workers. In several Indian regions, landowners established bonded labour rather than free labour, in order to control wages. If the core of formal subsumption is the legally formal subordination of previously autonomous workers as wage workers, the Indian case signals an interesting variant, in which the formality was provided by a caste system that dictated a rigid stratification of social and occupational positions, guaranteeing the subordination of workers. In this case 'the labourer in bondage and the free wage-labourer stands at two ends of a continuum of degrees of unfreedom'.[101] Jan Breman persuasively explains how the dispossession mechanism that consistently created landless bond-workers was not so different from the debit–credit system in the West, which, then but especially now, is responsible for the *de facto* creation of bonded labour:

> The typical story of this subjugation was something like this: a young male from a landless family began to work with a substantial landowner

---

97   Steinfeld 2009, p. 12.
98   Gordon 2019.
99   Mezzadri 2016.
100 Mundle 1979.
101 Ramachandran 1990, p. 170.

fairly early in life and helped in grazing cattle or with other odd jobs. As he grew older, and attained marriageable age, he needed money to finance his own wedding. There could also be other sources that generated the need for money, such as the wedding of a sister or any other kin, ill-health in the family, or need for construction or repair of the house. Given his economic status and near complete lack of any assets, the only way he could mobilise money was through mortgaging his labour-power to a landowner. Low wage rates and lack of any alternative sources of employment or income meant perpetual indebtedness, which in turn led to a prolonged relation of dependency and bondage, often lasting for life and beyond, to the next generation and would invariably suck in the entire family of the labourer.[102]

This case shows how all the conditions surrounding subsumption must in fact be qualified according to the historically specific case; this is why I argue in this book that it is necessary to cover all social scales of subsumption. Thus, for instance, in the Indian agricultural case above, wage-labour goes hand in hand with a system that pushes formal subsumption into the 'informal' – and what in other parts of the world would be considered the illegal – context of bonded labour. On the other hand, as we shall see is the case for many precarious workers employed in the platform economy, the process of restructuring the economy under the conditions of real subsumption entails the extensive introduction of technology and new forms of the social organisation of labour; this has the effect of pushing workers who were previously formally employed towards the informal economy, shaped by a mixture of 'informal', formal and real subsumption.

We have reached the end of this chapter and are now prepared to deal with the dialectical alter-ego of subsumption, determinate supersumption. We will do this by showing how subsumptive relations, as opposed to subsumption, require there to be a structure in place that exceeds the confined boundaries of the labour process and spills over into the integral state.

In many ways, when I claim that subsumption is always social subsumption, I refer to the fact that in order to sustain subsumptive relations, a totality must be in place. I have not explored this totality in full, but have simply showed some significant factors outside the labour process that need to be operating so as to reproduce subsumption. The most important is the state, acting as an integral and welfare state, but it is not the only one. If we consider the general

---

[102] Breman 2007, p. 29.

circuit of reproduction of capital – comprising moments of production, circulation, realisation, consumption and distribution, subsumption implies all of them. However, the bigger the system in place for sustaining subsumptive relations, the more opportunities for crisis and breaking points there will be.

Accordingly, in the next chapter I will keep exploring the ramifications of those subsumptive relations, but will also point to their impasse; and I will discuss how an impasse can produce either new crises of subsumption or incentivise the discovery of new 'fixes', or even entire new waves of subsumption. In fact, I will claim that subsumptive relations confront their crisis both in functional and dysfunctional terms. For this reason, I will claim that such a moment of negation is co-constitutive of subsumptive relations, just as it is for subsumption itself.

In fact, the next chapter *de facto* continues the exploration of subsumptive relations not just in their dialectical and less immediate side, but also in relation to subsumptive relations at what Gramsci would define as a molecular level.[103] While this chapter has expanded the sphere of subsumption to an ensemble of subsumptive relations that radiates from the labour process through to the whole general circulation of capital, and finally to crucial levels such as the integral state, the next chapter will explore the level of agency of subjects and collective subjectivities, thus presenting subsumptive relations from the point of view of their capacity to reproduce and transform the social, starting from individual and collective action.

---

103   Gramsci 1975, Q 8, § 195.

CHAPTER 4

Determinate Supersumption: Molar and Molecular

> When we consider and reflect upon nature ... we see the picture of an endless entanglement of relations and reactions in which nothing remains, what, where and as it was, but everything moves, changes, comes into being and passes away. This primitive, naïve but intrinsically correct conception of the world is that of ancient Greek philosophy, and was first clearly formulated by Heraclitus: everything is and is not, for everything is fluid, is constantly changing, constantly coming into being, and passing away.[1]

∴

Both in the Introduction and Chapter 2, I mentioned how, through the optic of subsumptive relations, production, exchange, distribution and consumption cannot be simply reduced to syllogism or identity, but should be considered as dialectically mediated. If the production of surplus-value is dialectically mediated so that it is seen as the ensemble of subsumptive relations, we see that subsumption is anything but a linear motion, or progress. Marx in the *Grundrisse* claims that

> Capital undertakes only *advantageous* undertakings, advantageous in its sense. True, it also speculates unsoundly, and, as we shall see, *must* do so. It then undertakes *investments* which do not pay, and which pay only as soon as they have become to a certain degree *devalued*. Hence the many undertakings where the first *investment* is sunk and lost, the first entrepreneurs go bankrupt – and begin to realise themselves only at second or third hand, where the invested capital has become smaller owing to *devaluation*.[2]

If there can be waves of 'undertakings', we can also assume that there could be waves of subsumption as well, since capitalist undertakings to secure a profit

---

1 Engels 1959, 25, p. 33.
2 Marx 1973, p. 531.

require the production of surplus-value (exception made for fictitious capital) and this requires a the mobilisation of subsumptive relations. Hence, as I mentioned in the Introduction, the process of subsumption should be negatively defined.

In given historic specific circumstances, such an attempt can be accelerated, made subject to multiple 'incursions', diverted, or even stopped. This is why I introduce the idea of determinate supersumption. This is admittedly a conceptual mouthful, but it aims at incorporating the idea that the enterprise of producing surplus-value in a context of antagonistic class relations is anything but a triumphant and unstoppable *Ride of the Valkyries*; rather, it represents a constant struggle to overcome obstacles and threats of devaluation, stoppage and crises of all kinds.

Therefore, 'determinately' to negate subsumption is not to reject the concept but to grasp it through a relational and dialectical logic. Determinate supersumption is the dialectical other that constitutes subsumptive relations through contradictions such as the re-infiltration of concreteness into capitalist abstractions, including abstract labour and abstract space, as we shall especially see in Chapters 6 and 7. The explanatory power of negativity consists in understanding any present subsumptive state with its concrete possibility for becoming.

The question is not about uncovering a logic of 'Aufhebung' as a developmental dynamic of surpassing and conserving, but rather about acknowledging its perpetual instability, its motion due to its own contradictions. It is important to remark here that those contradictions are indeed directly and indirectly produced by people living through social intercourse, rather than directed by some inner or transcendental logic. This is a question of political possibilism rather than of historical inevitability,[3] according to which, while the life process of definite individuals is mobilised by those individuals, they also operate in a context in which material conditions are independent of their will, and those conditions affect the outcomes of the will. There is no *a priori* logic that determines subsumptive relations, and in this respect my understanding of dialectics follows a logic similar to that of Engels in his *Anti-Dühring*.[4]

The determinate negation of subsumptive relations can therefore come both from active 'supersumptive' politics as well as from more unwanted outcomes of people's social activity. Subsumption and supersumption are produced by the never-ending combination of agent and structural causality, contingency,

---

3 Marx 1990, p. 124.
4 Arthur 2009.

necessity, intersubjectivity and trans-individuality. In this sense, Gramsci provides the conceptualisation of a level of analysis that is very useful here, the molecular level. While, as with many Gramscian terms, this notion evades easy and clear-cut definitions, the molecular indicates a middle-range scale of analysis that acknowledges the complexity of historic specifical processes by considering the level of agency of individuals and collectives, thus of a lower scale compared to the one offered by the earlier chapter.

Though it does not constitute a subjectivist approach to politics, the molecular level begins its examination with the formation of subjectivities and collective wills. As part of Gramsci's absolute historicism, the molecular indicates the level where concrete embodied subjects (in the so-called body–mind nexus) confront power relations and find concrete ways to resist. When he speaks of the molecular form, Gramsci is trying to understand how a collective will can emerge and consolidate itself with reference to specific concrete historic cases and subjects. The concept therefore refers to a finer-grain analysis of transformation, based on variations in quantity that turn into qualitative changes. Finally, the molecular level represents an optic that, together with the notion of determinate supersumption, pushes against any deterministic or automatic approach to subsumption.

This is my main militant theoretical contribution, the political component carved out of my project of 'subsuming subsumption'. Subsumption produces abstraction commanding over the manifold concrete – for instance, abstract over concrete labour, or exchange-value over use-values – and produces a powerful fetish of inversion, according to which the creative and productive powers of living labour, once subsumed, appear to be moving towards capital. In this respect, the molecular perspective stands as a rejection of abstraction and mystification by reasserting a relatively more concrete sphere of action, by analysing the ways in which the small scale, focused around individuals and groups, acts upon an established ensemble of power relations.

Homologically to the molecular, if subsumptive relations are form-determining relations, then determinate supersumption represents, indeed simultaneously, an alternative set of form-determining process as well as that which cannot be easily translated into existing capitalist forms – a kind of signifying 'noise'. Determinate supersumption is both within and without subsumption, it constitutes both an immanent and a transcendental antagonist to the process of subsumption, operating through subsumptive relations: on the one hand, it is linked to the tensions inherent in the production of the capitalist environment; on the other hand, it is a necessary external element – as with the case of the embodied worker – that in a sense enables subsumption, precisely because it is never completely subsumed.

Incorporating its dialectical negation means going beyond a semi-idealist understanding of subsumption as a pure logical category; it means historicising it and welcoming the insights it produces when, for instance (but this is only one case among many) it is concretised by embodied human practice. It is indeed in the name of concreteness as understood by Marx that we can argue that subsumption cannot be understood without its negative. In their reflection on the Hegelian legacy of Marx, Richard Norman and Sean Sayers claim that:

> Nothing concrete and real is merely positive. Everything is contradictory and contains negative as well as positive aspects within it. The dialectical notion of contradiction is that such conflicts between opposed aspects are necessary and essential. ... [The dialectic] ... is a logic in the sense that it specifies the laws of thought which must be adhered to if reality is to be grasped concretely.[5]

Accordingly, concrete subsumption is a process that incorporates the ambiguous variable of crises in its motion. Thus, if subsumption represents a condition for both the continuity and acceleration of the process of surplus-value production, subsumption understood dialectically, linked to its alter-ego determinate supersumption, warps the regularity of Hegelian bad infinity, that is, the spiral. Determinate supersumption warps the spiral, the generality of the law of motion of capital deformed by historical conjunctures and even by events approaching singularity.

Harvey, describing the reproductive logic of capital, frequently invokes Hegel's bad infinity to distinguish between Marx's simple and expanded reproduction:

> ... it is almost as if he wishes to explore the virtuous cyclical forms of reproduction that might be possible in a non-capitalist world of zero accumulation. The trouble starts with the production of surplus-value and the necessity of its perpetual expansion, which entails the shift from a cyclical virtuous infinity to a spiral of endless accumulation. It is this shift that forces the perpetual pursuit of an 'incompletable infinitude' on the part of capital.[6]

---

5 Norman and Sayers 1980, p. 181.
6 Harvey 2017, p. 173.

The representational distance between mere capital reproduction and its accumulation is depicted by the difference between the stable state of a circular dynamic and the expanding tendency of a spiral, in other words, the production of surplus-value leads to endless growth in the form of a spiral.

While capital accumulation represented in terms of the overall expansion at the aggregate level may indeed resemble, in its geometrical form, a regular spiral winding around a centre (see red spiral in Figure 1), smaller scales such as the molecular create the possibility for eccentrism, irregular shapes, even a sort of double spiral, formed by concentric shapes that both recede from and approach their centre or pole.

Thus, the pair subsumption/supersumption creates turbulences in the regularity of the shape but also a potential tangential spiral (see green spiral, Figure 1). In relation to its dialectical other, determinate supersumption thus does not describe a general counter-narrative but rather a general instability, a general qualification of the main narrative of continuous expansion, which carries within itself the possible and relatively frequent particularity of eccentrism (see blue spiral, Figure 1), including shocks and impasses and the possible singularity of a reverted and/or collapsing spiral.

Supersumption is both the determinate negation of subsumption, therefore the possible negation or interruption in the process of production of surplus-value, that is, devaluation, *as well as* the condition of possibility for future subsumptive relations and future surplus-value extraction. In fact, the instability of subsumptive relations constitutes an incentive for capital to secure them with a varying combination of coercive and consensual measures *vis-à-vis* labour, through the organisation of production mediated by technology. At the same time, the emergence of an impasse may create conditions for a 'fix', a temporary solution to the problem that moves the extractive activity to another sector.

An unevenly developed spiral indicates the constitutive connection between subsumption and crisis, which Joshua Clover[7] rightly points out represents another way to describe the dialectical and constitutive unity between subsumption and supersumption. Here, when it comes to determinate supersumption, we need to force an analytical distinction between crises that are primarily understood as systemic failures due to tensions intrinsic to capitalism – a kind of objective determinate supersumption – and crises caused directly or indirectly by an active politics that is antagonistic to subsumption, a kind of subjective determinate supersumption. In the same way, supersump-

---

7 Clover 2010.

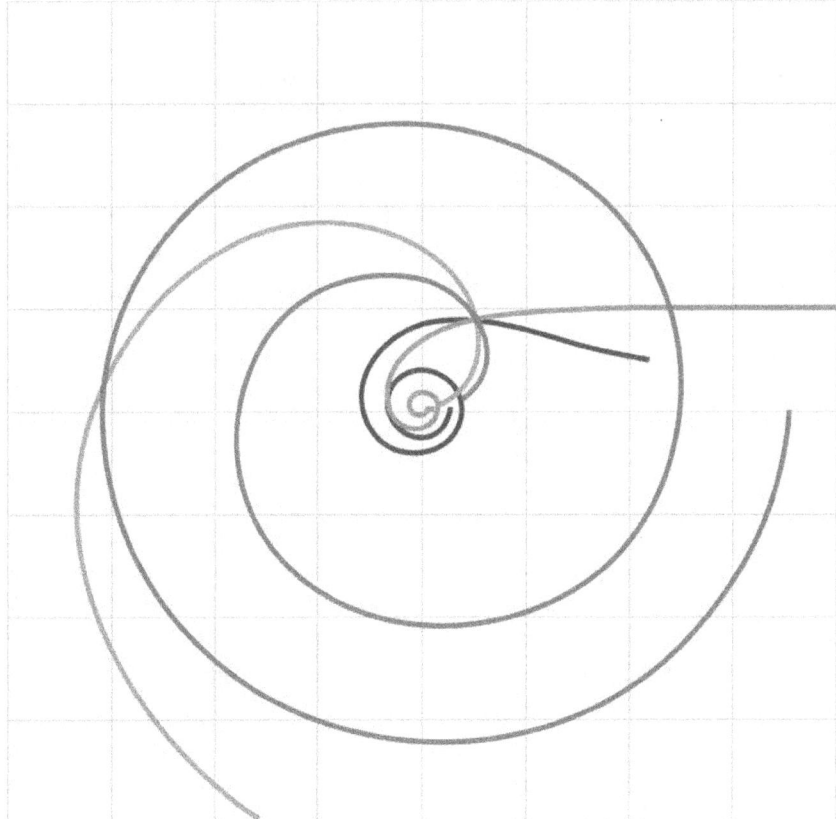

FIGURE 1   The three spirals showing how the expansion can actually end up taking different routes

tion can be examined both in an objective and subjective way, as systemic erosion of subsumptive power relations and as a strategic and tactical way in which labour resists and struggles against capitalist forms of control and coercion in the production of surplus-value.

1   Molar Determinate Supersumption

As I have just explained, the focus of this chapter is the molecular level of subsumptive dialectics, which I have defined as determinate supersumption. However, the fact that I chose to conduct my examination of subsumptive relation at this level does not necessarily mean that determinate supersumption does not happen at all levels. For instance, in relation to the previous treatment of the state, when it operates as a welfare provider, the state *de facto* enters into a contradictory relation with subsumption at the molar level.

On the one hand, by covering the social costs of production via a funded health care system, pensions funds and other fundamental social rights, the state defends both labour and capital by mediating their antagonism, as in the case of collective bargaining. It thus operates by potentially defusing class antagonism when it might be on the brink of some eruption. On the other hand, when the state extends and guarantees certain labour rights to everybody, it decommodifies them, therefore partially or completely eliminating subsumptive relations.

Subsumption is a project that when materialised can only be implemented through the establishment of adequate social relations, that is, subsumptive relations, which requires a constant effort to be reproduced despite an equally constant level of indeterminacy. I speak about indeterminacy because the relative negation of subsumptive relations can complicate the sustainability of subsumption but also offers the opportunity to develop it incrementally. This indeterminacy derives from an objective and unavoidable contradiction: in order to guarantee the consistent production of surplus-value, subsumptive relations must expand their reach, thus 'subsumption is always social subsumption'; but the solution to indeterminacy is to deal with an increasingly high level of social complexity, which in the end also elevates the potential for indeterminacy. The above represents the core assumption for what I define as objective determinate supersumption, tensions arising in social intercourse established by the project of subsumption.

If we look at the general cycle of reproduction of capital both logically and historically, crisis is not simply a possibility but a systemic event, integral to the overall dynamic, because capital itself is the moving contradiction, insofar as it presses to reduce labour-time to a minimum while it posits labour-time, on the other side, as the sole measure and source of wealth.[8] From this point of view, objective determinate supersumption is exemplified by the general tendency of the law of motion of capital to be caught in a trap of its own making. The revolutionary power of social and technological organisation carries within itself an important contradiction, because the rate of surplus-value, on which depends the overall mass of surplus-value, cannot be increased without diminishing the amount of variable capital employed, that is, the number of workers. When technology permits a reduction in labour employed, the rate of profit tends to fall.

---

8 Marx 1973, p. 705.

The tension this produces is linked to surplus-value to the degree that the capitalist wants to reduce labour costs, a consequence of the fact that value depends primordially on workers. The reason for this is that, since all new value, including surplus-value, is created solely by living labour, the less that living labour contributes to the production process, the less surplus there is available for extraction by capitalists. According to Marx, capitalists are pushed to face such a contradiction because, on the one hand, they must face the so-called coercive law of competition against other capitalists, while in the short run they try to capture transient forms of relative surplus-value based on technological innovation:

> The development of capitalist production makes it constantly necessary to keep increasing the amount of the capital laid out in a given industrial undertaking, and competition makes the immanent laws of capitalist production to be felt by each individual capitalist as external coercive laws. It compels him to keep constantly extending his capital, in order to preserve it.[9]

While classical political economists such as Smith, Ricardo and Malthus had already discussed the tendency for capitalism to slow down and even experience crisis, Marx claims that such a tendency is an immanent law rather an exogenous variable; this is the level at which determinate supersumption may be considered as an objective factor. Thus, the increase in the organic composition of capital via the replacement of workers with machines – assuming all other things unchanged – will provoke a falling rate of profit.

According to Marx, capital can produce surplus-value by consistently reproducing a differential in value and labour-time, namely, the situation where the value of a worker's labour-power is less than the value that labour produces during production, which corresponds to the time spent working, rather than the amount of work required to reproduce the worker's livelihood. Increasing surplus-value means decreasing the necessary labour-time needed to reproduce labour-power, which is accomplished by cheapening the value of the labour-power commodity itself by increasing productivity. This relative surplus-value describes a situation in which capital keeps 'revolutionising the means of production' by the technology of mechanisation and automation. This creates a situation in which the value produced might be less than the value of capital invested.

---

9 Marx 1990, p. 555.

The tendency of the rate of profit to fall can be understood as an objective force complicating the sustainability of real subsumption via social and technological innovations, which, however, dialectically enough, can be counteracted by increasing subsumption via intensification of labour exploitation and by more 'supersumption' involving a growing reserve army of labour. In many ways, the example of the falling profit rate constitutes an instance in which capital tries to overcome constraints that are internal to its own nature, regardless of the people involved. By this, I refer to the fact that the crisis created by the tendency of the rate of profit to fall is frequently caused by capital looking for a solution/fix in terms that translate into an increased incorporation of technology.

The linking of real subsumption and its material expression of relative surplus-value to a crisis, not only complicates the understanding of subsumption as a representation of the *telos* of ever-expanding capital accumulation, but also problematises the historical sequencing of formal and real subsumption. In fact, the tendency of the rate of profit to fall, as a result of the technological dynamics that characterise real subsumption, has tended to imply consecutive rounds of formal subsumption that take place in order to defer and defuse the potential crisis created by real subsumption; this is another way of speaking about David Harvey's notion of a 'fix' that occurs during moments of economic downturn. Absolute and relative surplus-values coexist as much as real and formal subsumption. Clover explains it as follows:

> The context of crisis challenges this view. While it is logically the case that formal precedes real subsumption, once the latter appears they must both be present, as real subsumption's generation of relative surplus-value finally a reallocation of absolute surplus-value derived from formal subsumption. This coexistence is classically dialectical: both mutually constitutive and antagonistic with a drive toward self-overcoming. It is real subsumption's fate to undermine the gains in absolute surplus-value gotten through formal subsumption. This in turn proposes further rounds of formal subsumption to defer crisis. As the concomitant productivity increasingly expel labour from the production process, capital must seek absolute surplus-value elsewhere: by extending the working day, enlarging the sector, or by opening new lines.[10]

---

10   Clover 2010, p. 1580.

While Clover hypothesises a dialectical relation between formal and real subsumption in order to cope with their reciprocal tendency to bring about crisis, this is true even in another, broader sense: assuming the indissoluble pair of subsumptions and determinate supersumption means incorporating the dimension of a crisis in all of its etymological richness, that is, as a constitutive and decisive moment of change. In this sense, Gerard Duménil and Dominique Levy[11] argue that together with production, Marx's analysis of labour also provides a parallel perspective, which, while underdeveloped, potentially opens up important insights on contemporary capitalism. In the conditions of real subsumption of labour, management is in charge of labour control, buying and selling of labour, coordinating the labour process, and maximising profit. Managers are first of all managers of indeterminacy by means of control and supervision, in order to maintain stable revenues.

The transformation of the labour process implied by real subsumption entails the establishment of new capitalist institutions and figures: managers, external financing (credit), and corporate economy. The salaried manager pushes the capitalist out of the labour process. This is a delegation process that tends to constitute a new managerial class mediating between capital and labour. The importance of management was already pointed out by Harry Braverman, who argued that the superintendence role implied a degradation of the labour process both in terms of workers' deskilling and labour's own ability to oppose capital. Braverman's perspective on managerialism replaces simple cooperation with management and Taylorism with modern manufacturing. He writes:

> Corresponding to the managing functions of the capitalist of the past, there is now a complex of departments. Each has taken over in greatly expanded form a single duty that a single capitalist exercised with very little assistance in the past.[12]

Close supervision, discipline and Taylor's scientific management are all aspects of real subsumption that exacerbate the division of labour between the working class and managerial class, distinguishing between execution and conception, manual and mental labour.

All in all, the molar plane of determinate supersumption shows how subsumptive relations operating at the strategic level find objective constraints that constantly call for temporary solutions, that is, fixes.

---

11   Duménil and Levy 2012.
12   Braverman 1974, p. 267.

2   Molecular Determinate Supersumption

When Marx claims that in the capitalist mode of production we are dominated by abstractions, he describes how a combination of molecular forces has turned into a combination of molar ones, so that each molecular explanation, in the combined mole, is removed, therefore abstracted, from its social-historical context. Therefore I think it is important to engage subsumption from a molecular level, because it provides a perspective inside of the 'black box' of abstractions, allowing us to understand and critique them.

Most ideally, molecular determinate supersumption culminates with an effective class struggle waged by workers, in which labour organises and enters into a particular relation of force with capital, a kind organised antagonism, a synthesis between spontaneous rebellion and conscious direction. Talking about an active antagonistic politics, Michael Lebowitz[13] argues that, because the value of labour-power is determined in the process of class struggle, an extrinsic and antagonistic logic necessarily resists the reifying power of capital. Marx also recognises that capitalists act within the labour process to try to overcome worker resistance: 'As the number of the co-operating labourers increases, so too does their resistance to the domination of capital, and with it, the necessity for capital to overcome this resistance by counter-pressure'.[14]

However, what Marx did not study systematically was the possibility that technical and social changes might occur under the capitalist mode of production in response to the contradictory or self-destructive forces created by capitalist accumulation, which is the other side of determinate supersumption, the 'negation of the negation' of subsumption. In other words, he did not address in depth how that which at first *impairs* subsumption can go on to constitute an incentive, not only to address the impasse, but to push the limits of subsumption even further. Historically, this has been the case when capital has surpassed the limits of absolute surplus-value by means of more refined socio-technical organisation. Thus, Marx did not carefully examine how contradictions are accommodated, with a view to sustaining the mode of production. The determinate supersumptive aspect of worker resistance must be seen as a force (thrown up by the basic mode of production) that affects capitalist development, rather than simply an important antagonist that may eventually result in the destruction or reproduction of the capitalist mode of production. These neglected realms – perhaps understandable

---

13   Lebowitz 2003.
14   Marx 1990, p. 313.

in the mid-nineteenth century, when Marx was writing – have become of much more concern for Marxists in the twentieth and twenty-first centuries.

2.1 Tactics and Strategies

If it is true that subsumptive relations are class relations within a framework of hegemony, an important aspect of this is the politics of oppositional and negotiated practices. As Paulsen rightly points out,[15] while the body of literature on oppositional practices is itself small, even less attention has been paid to this kind of action within the labour process. As exemplified by the seminal study published by Michel de Certeau,[16] opposition seems to be studied as a politics of consumption rather than production. This is not irrelevant, though, because if subsumption is about the necessary relations of power that enable the production of (surplus) value, then the value that is not realised is essentially no-value. Thus, in the overcall circulation of capital as represented by value, we may find in practices outside production clues about the hidden abode of production.

So, for example, the tension between strategies and tactics, repressive structures, and expressive practices seem to confirm the intractability that Dussel describes in his account of living embodied labour,[17] which we will be examining later. Let us consider de Certeau's thesis for a moment. On the one hand, he describes strategies in the same way we could describe a capitalist labour process: a highly defined and controlled, rule-governed, institutionalised environment mostly determined by economic rationality. On the other hand, tactics represent the 'living' and 'variable' side of labour, especially when it is not organised: tactics indicate practices that are opportunistic, always on the watch, and involve combining disparate elements to gain a momentary advantage.

De Certeau provides a beautiful example of walking around a typical US city. On the one hand, city planners tend to construct the city as a place instrumental to the logistics of capital circulation, with streets with names and signals that are intended to direct you as if in a controlled environment, propelled by a strategy of governmentality. Urbanisation, as Lefebvre teaches us, has this strategic component.[18] On the other, walkers approach the city tactically in the

---

15 Paulsen 2014.
16 De Certeau 1984.
17 Dussel 2001.
18 Lefebvre 1991.

everyday, by cutting across defined space, taking shortcuts, and using the rules and products that already exist in the city environment in creative ways.[19]

Paulsen defines such practices as passive resistance, because for him this represents 'symbolic and quite harmless types of resistance, or singular acts of open defiance that sooner or later are knocked down'. However, in my view, passivity would be better defined as not always purposeful; in other words, living labour may operate in a liminal space of tactics, while strategies relate simply to the practice of existing, living and interacting with the world.

Compared to de Certeau, James Scott[20] defines practices that could be understood in the middle of the tactical-strategic spectrum. He distinguishes between public transcripts – 'the open interaction between subordinates and those who dominate'[21] and hidden transcripts – 'discourse that takes place 'offstage', beyond direct observation by powerholders'.[22] Public and hidden transcripts show everyday politics of micro-power as well as the ways in which subordinate subjects negotiate with it, displaying a variable degree of resistance:

> Offstage, where subordinates may gather outside the intimidating gaze of power, a sharply dissonant political culture is possible. Slaves in the relative safety of their quarters can speak the words of anger, revenge, self-assertion that they must normally choke back when in the presence of the masters and mistresses.[23]

From the perspective of the hidden transcripts, Scotts indeed adds a strategic component that problematises those approaches to ideologies and hegemony that consider the subordinate class as either being duped or uncritically sharing the values and practices of the ruling class:

> A combination of adaptive strategic behaviour and the dialogue implicit in most power relations ensures that public action will provide a constant stream of evidence that appears to support an interpretation of ideological hegemony.[24]

---

19   The distinction, of course, has its own grey area. For instance, bike-riders in the food delivery sector, as workers, cut across 'tactical' and 'strategic' space in order to deliver their orders.
20   Scott 1990.
21   Scott 1990, p. 2.
22   Scotts 1990 p. 4.
23   Scotts 1990, p. 18.
24   Scotts 1990, p. 70.

This aspect leads us to another key aspect of subsumption, the emergence of (dys-)functional subjectivities and how they navigate subsumptive relations. We will return to de Certeau in Chapter 6, when we will be talking about workers' practices such as *la perruque*. In this sense, *la perruque* seems to represent the combination of both de Certeau and Scott: tactical and off-stage resistance, aimed at the preservation of workers' subjectivity.

In relation to subjective tactics, in the following, final portion of the chapter, I am examining the fundamental link between subsumptive relations (thus subsumption+determinate supersumption) and subject by the notion of subjection.

2.2   *Subjection and Subsumption*

For Marx, the metabolic and transformative relation people have with the world is necessarily mediated by working. Through work, people change their environment and themselves: 'Through this movement he acts upon external nature and changes it, and in this way he simultaneously changes his own nature'.[25] Because subsumptive relations intervene first at the level of the labour process, they necessarily intervene in the process of producing and reproducing subjects. Furthermore, as we shall see, a similar dynamic could be said to operate when we think of the link between the constitution of people's wants, needs and desires and consumption

So, constitutive production as well as consumption as constitutive deprivation of it. In fact, the formal process that transforms independent workers into wage-labourers via formal subsumption, that is, proletarianisation,[26] constitutes a crucial form of subjectivation that subjugates free skilled labour to increasingly de-skilled wage-labour, alienation, and social individuals who through abstract labour gain in 'socialisation' – for example, through the abstraction of their task, through cooperation – at the loss of individualisation. It shapes a social habitus[27] by leaving workers with no life prospects, most frequently in unimaginative jobs that lead to an alienated life.[28]

---

25   Marx 1990, p. 283.
26   As the reader probably has noticed, I tend to avoid the usage of the term proletariat to define a class, because, when this category is plugged into current capitalism, it seems to open up many issues and debates that I cannot address here. Still, I think the process of proletarianisation is still fundamental to understanding structured power relations based on compelling needs and subsumptive relations.
27   Bourdieu 1977.
28   The literature on proletarianisation as a process of subjection is very rich. While the term is still contested, I think that for instance the work of Ursula Huws on precarious subjectivities demonstrates that the notion is valid: Huws 2010; Huws 2014.

However, Dussel claims[29] that while alienated labour and alienated capital are symbiotic social forces, labour is ultimately external to such a relation, and it needs to be internalised, which entails its alienation. This represents the core assumption sustaining my claim in this chapter: labour, as embodied subject, enters and exits the labour process, and the labour contract to sell labour-power cannot control such fluidity.[30]

So, the threatening pressure that labour exerts on capital is not just about the potential risk of developing the forces of production to a higher productive potential that is also, at the same time, a higher potential for antagonism; it is also about the constant introduction of this same dynamic into a sphere that is in part outside capital, *non-capital*. This will be reflected in the tension I describe in Chapter 6, with the process of creation of abstract space that irremediably creates new realms for concrete space, that is, non-territorialised space capable of disrupting capitalist spaces of production.

Understanding subsumption from the point of view of the process of producing subjects means understanding not only the ambiguity between coercion and concert but also that between subjection and subversion, alienation and identity constitution. Returning to the interiority/exteriority of labour, subversive subjectivities are not simply the outcome of the inability of capital to completely internalise labour. As Dussel claims,[31] capital requires exteriority because it is the exterior to capital from which – at least in part[32] – labour capacity comes.[33]

---

29 Dussel 2001.
30 For this reason, the most primordial tension, where more determinate supersumptive elements come from, is associated with the notion of fixed capital, that is, capital fixed in the moment of production, and labour as circulating capital, where circulation is not just meant outside the sphere of production but actually outside the whole circulation of capital. Fixed capital and circulating subjective force are united as the two faces of general intellect.
31 Dussel 2001.
32 I say in part, because the surplus is also dialectically internal to the capital/labour relations, as it derives from the attempt of capital to develop the force of prosecution in instrumental ways.
33 An example of this irreducible intractability, that is, incomplete subordination of labour within formal subsumption, is provided by the situation when the worker–employer relation is mediated by legal contracts. Labour capacity is in principle a qualitative characteristic of the worker, associated to his/her specific physical and mental capacities. It is a potential. When we sign a labour contract we can only promise 'we are going to do our best' to deliver an adequate level of labour-power. The legal contract tries to bind this exterior labour capacity and translates into legally compulsory exchange of a commodity, that is, labour-power. Such a translation is, for a change, without guarantees.

Emphasis on subjectivities is not frequently encountered in Marxist scholarship. As Guido Starosta notices,[34] most Marxist scholarship of the last decades tends to privilege social form over social subjects. Similarly, critical social theory passed from seeing the working class as the subject destined to abolish capitalism to the object destined to be abolished by capitalism.[35]

Previously, I showed how the entire social environment shaping and being shaped by subsumptive relations is marked by profound tensions and conditions that make the eternal search for surplus-value production, its continuity and its acceleration unstable and precarious. Particularly relevant for this chapter is the constant process of production of subjectivities adequate to capital, which, predictably, is marked by contradictions. In fact, together with class warfare, a contradiction is synthesised in the phrase 'relations of subjection', by which I mean to capture the tensions of the hegemonic process that at the same time produces subjective identities with their predilections, values, habits and desires. These are capable of moving across the social sphere with a relative degree of freedom on the one hand, while, on the other, they are to an important degree instrumentally produced so as to be adequate to capital; at the same time, both inside and outside the labour process, forces and hegemonic apparati exist that discipline and decompose those subjectivities.

Jason Read[36] argues that at the core of Marx's concerns in his study is the question of how capital subsumes people's species being, the general condition for their subjectivity, which he defines in relation to both active production and its alienated version, labour. Labour is the great articulatory mechanism that constitutes the fundamentals of our subjectivity: its embodied metabolic relation to nature, its primordial social relations, is the basis of general intellect, as well as our practices, habits, institutions and our communica-

---

Thus, the displacement of the labour–capital antagonism at the formal level of formal freedom provided by the contract is subordinated by pre-existing conditions of dispossession and labour markets and the pre-existing indeterminacy of the 'exterior' labour capacity. Similarly, in conditions of real subsumption, the cooperative, socialised character of knowledge and communication recomposes the molecular alienation of legal individualities. In this sense, the distinction Read makes between the narrative of capitalism dying due to 'proletarianisation' and then, in the *Grundrisse*, dying due to socialisation, represents an historic displacement of struggle between capital and labour, which can develop and go in different ways, either by deskilling and alienating the worker or by socialising labour. This position sustains the focus on subjectivities that was central to Negri's and the Operaists' case against subsumption.

34 Starosta 2015.
35 Carrera 2008, p. 9.
36 Read 2013.

tion. The process of abstraction of labour homogenises, in terms of quantity, qualitatively distinct embodied activities, thus rendering irrelevant the particular properties of the person engaged in it. Subjectively, abstract labour implies a reduction in the effort required to bring about surplus-value production. However, this effort is never completely successful. First, even when the worker is not actively opposing it, dynamics such as work intensification are consistently accompanied by what Roland Paulsen defines as 'empty labour'.[37] Secondly, while determinate supersumption does not always necessarily translate into direct politics, in a context that often aggravates exploitation by intensification, precarisation and alienation, labour becomes antagonising.

This composition and decomposition process is already evident if we compare the subsumption of production and subsumption of consumption at the level of relations of subjection. On the one hand, capitalism tries to mobilise 'the animal spirit' of people both as workers and as consumers, while, on the other hand, especially (but not limited to) inside the labour process in many economic sectors, subjective habits and idiosyncrasies are reduced to interchangeable labour inputs abstracted from those subjectivities. The desiring machines[38] capital employs at the level of its subsumption of consumption potentially makes, as Marx suggests,[39] for a rich subjectivity, expressing very nuanced needs; *de facto*, this is very frequently (although not always) negated at the level of subsumption of production in conditions in which the worker feels alienated.

In the current context, in which capitalism that relies on knowledge, information and cognitive skills is often accompanied by underpaid precarious jobs typical of the so-called gig economy, the contradiction becomes stratified and goes both ways: as already mentioned, on the one hand, we see the cultivation of the 'animal spirits' of the consumer, who is set outside the highly constrained production context that is typical of traditional manufacturing jobs; on the other, we see the 'animal spirits' of the cognitive worker who is mentally, and frequently also imaginatively, highly engaged, but who as a consumer is constrained by their reduced purchasing power, and who therefore consumes unimaginatively.

In this context, the hegemonic core that synthesises the coercive and consensual aspects is money, which becomes the supreme object of desires, motivating people to subordinate themselves to exploitative power relations. Money

---

[37] Paulsen 2014, p. 15.
[38] Deleuze and Guattari 1972.
[39] Marx 1973.

also reproduces the same mystified perception of the free perfect marketplace in which we can all participate with equal conditions. Commodities can all be desired, but money internalises the social power that capitalism promises to everybody.

Obviously these are simplifications, polarised examples that are presented here so as to show how capital requires an extremely flexible kind of subjectivity – one capable of navigating the combination of coercion and consent that is typical of hegemonic contexts: 'The advance of capitalist production develops a working class which by education [*Erziehung*], tradition and habit [*Gewohneit*] looks upon the requirements of that mode of production as self-evident natural laws'.[40]

Flexibility and docile bodies are the aim of the real subsumption of subjectivity when subjectivity is required to deal with the sphere of production and consumption, along with their inner contradictions. However, the conditions of production required to deal with such complexity also produce the conditions for determinate supersumption, which problematises relations of subjection as purely one-way power determinations. This is true in several senses: flexibility can make those subjectivities capable of negotiating with power; as Read claims;[41] but at the same time such production seems always to produce a surplus of subjectivity, made up of aspirations, desires, and needs not usable by capital and grounded in the body of the worker.[42]

The very fact that labour is used to mean the category of labour, both as a social function and in terms of the living embodied labourer, is a reflection of the attainment of the subsumption of labour under both exchange-value (as wage-labour) and capital (in its reproductive circulation). However, what determinate supersumption points to in relation to subjects, is that while people as workers may be engaged in power-driven relation of subjection, such subjection is incomplete, unstable, and productive of antagonising subjects. In other words, labour (or the labourer) is a resistant material and not a docile body.[43]

Returning to Read's statement, one could say that the fundamental question of subsumption is the problem of producing adequate-to-capital subjectivities: subjects constituted by their powerfully productive but unpredictable, incon-

---

40   Marx 1990, p. 899.
41   Read 2013.
42   Dussel 2001.
43   While capital has tried discursively to flatten labour complexity into the trope of 'human resources', as Arthur nicely puts it, it still can become a dangerous obstacle for capital reproduction: Arthur 2009.

sistent and uncontainable praxis. From this point of view, subsumption conveys a series of wild and paradoxical capitalist dreams: first of all the hope of exploiting labour capacity with the predictability and immediate responsiveness of dead labour; second, of shaping subjects both in minimalist and maximalist terms, minimal enough to be easily interchangeable, maximal enough to perform the multiple roles expected of such docile working bodies; third: of unleashing their animal spirit as productive labour, creative thinkers and voracious consumers.

Subsumption does indeed aim at synthesising multiple concrete labour categories into one more abstract form, that is, abstract labour, but the abstraction here, as in the whole Marxian materialist perspective, does not necessarily mean the same as being removed from concrete visible tangible physical reality; rather it refers, more simply, to control over the effectiveness of those subjective practices, limiting them (ergo, abstracting).

The basic assumption is that labour is a process necessarily implying both the production of objects and the subjects producing those objects. So, all capitalist investment to develop the means of production also develops the forces of production, in ways never reducible to abstract labour. Knowledge and social relations are incorporated not only into fixed capital as machinery but also as human subjectivity. This new subject is produced during 'free time', outside of waged labour – it is produced 'in and through consumption'.

In summary, we have been looking at the subjective side of determinate supersumption and trying to identify a subject that does not amount to a celebratory fantasy of automatic resistance, but that is instead an expression of a constant interactive relation. It is not a question of whether resistance requires a subject, but rather of whether the subject requires a level of resistance. As Scott has argued, the subjective dimension is even more important than the actual outcome, since resistance might not always have the effects that we intend it to have.[44]

2.3   Consuming Subjectivities

If subsumption is about securing the production of surplus-value, it must entail some varying influence on the realisation of such value, through management of demand and therefore consumption, especially if capital accumulation is assumed to be increasing over time. Marx describes it as follows: 'the discovery, creation and satisfaction of new needs arising from society itself; the cultivation of all the qualities of the social human being, the production of the same

---

44   Scott 1990, p. 290.

in a form as rich as possible in needs, because rich in qualities and relations ... is likewise a condition of production founded on capital'.[45]

Consumption plays two important roles in relation to capital: it realises value and provides the material basis for the reproduction of workers, both socially and biologically. Such a dynamic is certainly not free of tensions. On the one hand, capital's objective of lowering the cost of labour by reducing the bundle of goods necessary for its reproduction, therefore expanding needs, wants and desires, potentially leads to an increase in what the worker perceives to be necessities. (For instance, can most workers do their job and live their lives without a smartphone?) On the other, steady conspicuous consumption must be managed by increasing the workers' needs, wants and desires.

In both aspects, the dispossession at the basis of formal subsumption that deprives people of their means of material survival also makes them into needy consumers: that is, they need to work in order to earn money so that they can then turn to the market to buy commodities. This contradictory situation is also exacerbated by the fact that the capitalist pays the worker with money, which, once in the workers' hands, cannot be easily controlled: the worker is free to spend their wages on card games, drinks or expensive cars, or to save them. In this sense, a significant portion of surplus-value must be invested in marketing and related processes.[46]

From the perspective of subjective subsumptive, this implies the need for the production of an adequate-to-capital subjectivity:

> The capability to consume is a condition of consumption, hence its primary means, and this capability is the development of an individual potential, a force of production. The saving of labour-time is equal to an increase of free time, that is, time for the full development of the individual, which in turn reacts back upon the productive power of labour as itself the greatest productive power. From the standpoint of the direct production process it can be regarded as the production of *fixed capital*, this fixed capital being man himself. It goes without saying, by the way, that direct labour-time itself cannot remain in the abstract antithesis to free time in which it appears from the perspective of bourgeois economy. Labour cannot become play, as [Charles] Fourier would like, although it remains his great contribution to have expressed the suspension not of distribution, but of the mode of production itself, in a higher form,

---

45   Marx 1973, p. 409.
46   Baran and Sweezy 1966.

as the ultimate object. Free time – which is both idle time and time for higher activity – has naturally transformed its possessor into a different subject, and he then enters into the direct production process as this different subject. This process is then both discipline, as regards the human being in the process of becoming; and at the same time, practice [*Ausübung*], experimental science, materially creative and objectifying science, as regards the human being who has become, in whose head exists the accumulated knowledge of society.[47]

Living labour then animates dead labour by infusing it with its labour-power. It also gives the worker a reason to exist, producing the need for production through consumption. In fact:

Production not only supplies a material for the need, but it also supplies a need for the material. As soon as consumption emerges from its initial state of natural crudity and immediacy – and, if it remained at that stage, this would be because production itself had been arrested there – it becomes itself mediated as a drive by the object. The need which consumption feels for the object is created by the perception of it. The object of art – like every other product – creates a public which is sensitive to art and enjoys beauty. Production thus not only creates an object for the subject, but also a subject for the object. ... Consumption likewise produces the producer's *inclination* by beckoning to him as an aim-determining need.[48]

The shaping of functional consuming subjects capable of consuming is a process that has been facilitated by subsumptive dynamics, which have created more easily consumable commodities. For instance, when it comes to food, increased consumability means the increasing presence of pre-cooked or frozen foods. Those commodities are more expensive, but require less work in order to consume. Thus we point to the labour process internal to consumption, which parallels the labour process internal to production: it requires a labouring consumer, tools of consumption, and products whose use-value is related to their consumability. Consumability comprises both specific physical characteristics, but also pre-existing subjects, socialised to know how to consume it. For instance, if I buy an ice pop, and every day I lick it for a few seconds

---

47   Marx 1973, pp. 711–12.
48   Marx 1973, p. 92.

and then put it back in the freezer, that practice is not really conducive to the labour of consumption required by capital; the product would be depleted over a period of weeks, instead of within half an hour, thus depressing the demand for ice-pops.

So does the labour process of consumption homologically imply subsumptive relations? *Ça dépend*. In the case of consumption, the argument in favour of reframing subsumptions as subsumptive relations gains traction, because the distinction between formal and real subsumption becomes fuzzier, and the social environment in which power relations are exerted becomes wider and less controlled.

In fact this environment is so much less controlled that the liberal rhetoric of the worker's freedom to choose – in this case we are talking only about consumer choice – become more substantial, at least in the sense that there is no direct coercion. In the end, the raising of standards of living and the maximisation of consumer choice are the basis for most defences of capitalism.[49] *In principle*, the humblest worker possessing enough money cannot only confront as a peer the capitalist-as-consumer but can even park her yacht close to the capitalist's, and, semiotically, at the level of perception management, can even move the social scale. We can imagine an improbable *Monopoly*-board game situation in which the worker can inherit a fortune from a distant uncle or win the lottery, going on to acquire an even more luxurious yacht than his capitalist boss. So, in principle no subordination ... At the same time, the worker-as-consumer is in principle exempt from the pressure of producing surplus-value, as the act of consumption is in principle unconstrained by socially necessary labour time

However, everything argued up to this point requires an important qualification. Indeed, the very compulsive condition that pushes most of us to *work* is the compulsion to exchange living labour for objectified labour, that is, money, in order to buy commodities. Since most of us are deprived of access to means of independent material subsistence, we are *de facto* obliged to enter the C–M–C circuit, for instance to buy food. As per the allegedly free exchange of labour-power for money, we are indeed free to purchase our bread wherever we want; however, we need eventually to buy food, and moreover to do so in conditions that are sustainable – at an accessible supermarket, using accessible means of transport, and most importantly, at a sustainable cost. This is not a secondary aspect because consumption depends on the moment of realisation and the price of a given commodity. If, for instance, hedge funds controlling the

---

49   See Smith 1990; Friedman 1981; Hayek 1944.

production of medicines for my auto-immune disease decide to raise the price from 25 $ to 250 $ a pill, as a fixed-income worker, I very quickly descend into the realm of crude compulsive needs and even cruder power relations that significantly affect my life.

On the other hand, the capitalist engaged in the M–C–M' circuit must be able to realise value, because if no one buys the products in a reasonable amount of time, the commodities gradually decrease in value, to the point that they may lose their value completely. So, whoever is involved in the business of producing commodities needs to make sure that their value is realised and therefore to manage demand/consumption in certain ways.

In this sense, persuasive communication, and its capability to constitute both needs and the subjects in need, in the advertising industry, is linked to subsumptive relations. Does persuasion replace compulsion? Based on the suggested reinterpretation of subsumptive relations, persuasion represents one of the available key resources for the exertion of hegemonic power.

If subsumption aims at the production of surplus-value, its realisation cannot be implemented without some control over consumption. Thus, I argue that in fact we can talk of subsumption of consumption, which describes how consumer needs can be controlled by capitalist production, but without altering consumer habits. The control can be implemented by several means. For instance, as Paul Baran and Paul Sweezy maintain,[50] this requires heavy investments to induce conspicuous consumption; such marketing targets the consumer by playing on the imperative 'be willing to desire'.[51] Thus, what Costas Panayotakis[52] refers to as real subsumption of consumption corresponds to a desire machine as understood by Deleuze and Guattari,[53] which incessantly works in order to reshape everyday practices, imaginaries and habits of consumption, thus producing adequate subjectivities. In this sense, really subsumed consumption also means a desire for private goods that is not reciprocated by a desire for public services; as Galbraith notices, subsumed consumption is consumption for surplus-value's sake, and is not indicative of the well-being of the consuming population.[54]

While wage-labour is not the only way to access income – think of pensions, subsidies and credit – it represents the fundamental basis for it. The worker is obliged to sell his/her labour-power to acquire his/her bundle of goods to

---

50   Baran and Sweezy 1966, p. 114.
51   Barber 2007.
52   Panayotakis 2021.
53   Deleuze and Guattari 1972.
54   Galbraith 1984.

be consumed for his/her reproduction. In this sense, while not legally framed by a contract, the mostly unpaid labour of consumption presupposes a similar condition of dispossession: people are not only deprived of their means of production, but frequently deprived also of several (but not all) means of consumption; in other words, to consume, we need commodities to be consumed and commodities that facilitate consumption – think of buying a fork in order to eat pasta.

However, supersumption creeps into the continuous struggle to sustain consumption: as we see in the case of workers, consumers must be constantly constructed and reproduced, and this effort is not always successful.

The question of subsumption of consumption, moreover, complicates the narrative that links subsumption to exploitation, alienation and the overall idea of the impoverishment of workers proportional to the production of surplus-value. In fact, consumption nowadays points to the capability of capitalism to raise the material standards of living of a significant portion of the population, despite a rate of exploitation that may well have risen even higher, along with the consequent capability to multiply basic needs. Just to give an idea, if we look at the itemised composition of the basket of goods of a capitalist-led economy such as the UK's, we notice first how the list of items has considerably increased over time but also that, in representing consumer habits and needs, the list has come as of 2022 to incorporate such items as meat-free sausages, canned pulses, sports bras, pet collars and antibacterial surface wipes.[55]

In much of the global North-West, the post-World War II period has meant rising wages and mass consumption, to the point that the class structure of capitalist countries was redefined by the mystifying category of consumption capabilities,[56] the narrative of upward mobility and the belief that high consumption represented the apogee of capitalism.[57] Expanding consumption requires expanding human needs, which in turn and more broadly requires the constitution of subjectivities with new and more complex wants, needs and desires. This is what real subsumption of consumption looks like. As Marx observed in the *Grundrisse*, capital's new anthropology, based on multiplied needs, could produce a richer individuality; and yet, as we shall see, it can also bring about the nightmarish repetition of sameness and alienation denounced by Debord[58]

---

55   See Office for National Statistics 2022.
56   Panayotakis 2021.
57   Rostow 1960.
58   Debord 1995.

and Adorno and Horkheimer.[59] What Adorno and Horkheimer described by the notion of 'cultural industry' is a process of monopolising, standardising and commodifying cultural production. The notion of a culture industry in the end points to the fact that consumption is production; or better worded, that consumption is being subsumed under production:

> Amusement under late capitalism is the prolongation of work. It is sought after as an escape from the mechanised work process, and to recruit strength in order to be able to cope with it again. But at the same time mechanisation has such power over a man's leisure and happiness, and so profoundly determines the manufacture of amusement goods, that his experiences are inevitably after-images of the work process itself. The ostensible content is merely a faded foreground; what sinks in is the automatic succession of standardised operations. What happens at work, in the factory, or in the office can only be escaped from by approximation to it in one's leisure time.[60]

And such subsumption is real insofar as it reshapes subjectivities as well as their relationship with commodities, because the culture industry automatises and standardises the production of stories with interchangeable and predictable plots, so that there is nothing left for the consumer to classify.

Subsumptive relations take place now within the field of consumption by attracting consumers as a 'community of consumption', a sort of audience that responds more to a particular rhetoric on use-values than to genuinely different use-values – which brings us to Braudel's idea[61] that capitalism and the free-market economy are quite different things. In fact, the advertising industry may be understood as a persuasive industry capable of producing distinctions among fairly homogenous use-values in non-free market competition, thus moving towards oligopoly and monopoly. As Panayotakis[62] claims, the domination by a few large corporations of a given market also means the displacement of competition from price wars to rhetorical wars at the level of advertising. Out of the condition of the monopoly of 'sameness' denounced by Adorno and Horkheimer, the advertising industry works on product differentiation and persuades its prospective customers of the alleged superiority of given brands, which, when successful, can charge a higher price. The subsumption of con-

---

59 Horkheimer and Adorno 1972.
60 Horkheimer and Adorno 1972, p. 7.
61 Braudel 1992.
62 Panayotakis 2021.

sumption is then the transformation of people into an audience, preferably, as Adorno and Horkheimer claim, passively receiving meaningful suggestions, rather than interpreting meanings.

To conclude this section, the rhetoric used by advertising leverages existing/emerging values, meanings and practices as means for their persuasive communication. In fact, the redefinition of the use-value is effective when it taps into already operative socially valued practices and habits. When Grant McCraken[63] signals how such a dynamic leads to an instrumentalisation of those socially valued practices as well as socially significant anxieties and fears, therefore instrumentalising culture, he shows implicitly how, again, subsumptive relations are in fact totalising, that is, must incorporate an increasingly broader social terrain in order to guarantee the realisation of surplus-value. This is its way of creating an effective circuit of commodities (c): by tapping into a lifeworld made up of social imagery and practices, which, when consumed or instrumentalised, also change this lifeworld.

Such a totalising process is the result of a class project but is also systemically produced by the goals of individual businesses to valorise their products, through a circuit that leads to the aggregate production of a consumer culture.[64] The commodity becomes the form of representation and material existence of those cultural values. Commodities become the mediator of social action and social imagination: 'Once a sign is appropriated it circulates between advertising discourse and everyday life in a stylised form – this kind of mediation invariably changes the sign's cultural meanings and associations'.[65] Real subsumption of consumption translates into a science and technology of persuasion that enrols social scientists and psychologists, but also public personas such as actors, to sponsor the message.

Finally, I want to conclude this chapter by returning to the subject I touched on lightly when I mentioned Dussel's idea of the exteriority of living labour. Looking at the nexus between subsumption and consumption, we have just confirmed again that subsumptive relations need to be examined in the context of a process of totalisation. In this sense, this is exactly what Dussel problematises: the assumption of the existence of an all-encompassing capitalist totality.

The Bodily Limit to Subsumption: Living Labour: When reviewing the literature on subsumption, the subject seems to vanish, being caught in between

---

63   McCraken 1988.
64   Bordwell 2002.
65   Goldman and Papson 2000, p. 91.

the abstraction-tendencies implied by the labour theory of value and the subsumption of concrete labour under exchange-value, on the one hand, and an historical perspective that tends not to look at subjects but rather at broad phases, such as the dynamic of totalisation, on the other. The body seems to be either presupposed or not posited at all, which betrays a logico-idealist conception of subsumption that I intend to push back against. As Lefebvre explains in his critical spatial inquiry, there seems to be a link between how the subject and its corporeal dimension are conceptualised:

> Western philosophy has betrayed the body; it has actively participated in the great process of metaphorisation that has abandoned the body; and it has denied the body. The living body, being at once 'subject' and 'object', cannot tolerate such conceptual division, and consequently philosophical concepts fall into the category of the 'sign of non-body'.[66]

Such dematerialisation of the body may be linked to the fact that, for capital, workers represent an objective force of production, where the human, subjective and corporeal factors tend to be irrelevant. Paradoxically enough, while the worker is reduced to a mere physical body, his or her bodily needs are disassociated. Joseph Fracchia, discussing Marx's real subsumption and the production of relative surplus-value, claims that 'capital strips workers of bodily and mental skills and dexterities, reducing the qualitative capacity to work to little more than the quantitatively-measured expenditure of energy'.[67] He adds that even when the sustainability of the length of the working day becomes a terrain of confrontation, its resolution does not really consider human corporal needs, but only class antagonisms.

Especially in conditions of real subsumption, when science and technology become fundamental factors for the reorganisation of the labour process towards higher levels of productivity, the body as subjective life disappears under the fetishism of a fictional objectivity. It is dissected into moving parts, turned into a pseudo-machine. Divorced from the active and subjective force of production, bodies become mere means of production:

> Machine labour exhausts the nervous system to the utmost, suppresses the many-sided play of muscles, and confiscates all free bodily and mental activity. Even the alleviation of labour becomes an instrument of torture

---

66 Lefebvre 1991, p. 40.
67 Fracchia 2008, p. 47.

since the machine does not free the worker from work, but empties the work of all content. Every kind of capitalist production, in so far as it is not only a labour-process but also capital's valorisation process has this in common, that it is not the worker who employs the conditions of work, but rather the reverse, the conditions of work employ the worker; but it is only with the [capitalist] employment of machinery that this inversion acquires a technical and palpable reality. Through its metamorphosis into an automaton, the instrument of labour confronts the worker during the labour-process in the shape of capital, dead labour, which dominates and sucks up living labour.[68]

To reintegrate the bodily subject into a discussion of subsumptive relation is not just to push back against what I defined as a logico-idealist and thus incomplete understanding of subsumption; it also has to do with the fact that neglecting it means not understanding how such a dimension constitutes a source of determinate supersumptive conditions.

In the grand narrative of abstraction tied to subsumption of concrete labour under value – and therefore its transformation into abstract labour – we can indeed identify the history of de-corporealisation described by Lefebvre, which in spatial terms he conceptualises as the shift from 'the space of the body to the body-in-space'.[69] What I think is really helpful for my general argument is that, as Kirsten Simonsen observes, the corporeal opens up a perspective with which to understand how people's embodied practices are never completely subsumed by abstract processes:

> For Lefebvre, however, the body serves as a critical figure too. It is not possible totally to reduce the body or the practico-sensory realm to abstract space. The body takes its revenge – or at least calls for revenge – for example, in leisure space. It seeks to make itself known, to gain recognition, as 'generative'. This renders necessary another understanding of the body, not only as the subject of historical abstraction and visualisation, but also as an intrinsic part of social practice.[70]

We are reduced to pure physical tools of production, but our body and subjectivity work both functionally and dis-functionally towards capitalist pro-

---

68   Marx 1990, p. 548.
69   Lefebvre 1991, p. 302.
70   Simonsen 2005, p. 2.

duction needs. As I mentioned before, the dismissal of the embodied subject reveals the dismissal of the subject's agency in relation to wider power relations.

While the perspective of subsumptive relations and determinate supersumption share with the Foucauldian framework the desire to avoid classical dualism, such as power-freedom, structure-agency, heteronomy-autonomy and control-resistance, I think that in order really to see the politics of subsumption/supersumption we must incorporate that kind of social actor that, moving between the levels of the strategic and the tactical,[71] is capable of spontaneous bursts of organisation, can sometimes push back against existing power relations and can consistently renegotiate them.

When it comes to the labour process, the bodily subject is essentially living labour. The assumption of this book is that living labour constitutes an element of indeterminacy *vis-à-vis* capital, a specificity that can potentially approach singularity, in which such potential derives negatively from the fact that living labour can never be completely saturated or exhausted by subsumptive relations. Its indeterminacy derives both from formal/legal and material conditions.

Formally, subsumptive relations, as relations of power aiming at producing surplus-value via control and subordination of labour, remain unfinished because, regardless of the fairness of the legal contract structuring wage-labour, what is really bought and sold is not labour-power but potential labour capacity. Labour capacity, unlike labour-power, is based more on a promise or a statistical estimation than a certainty. The second, certainly connected, reason for their incompletion is that such labour capacity is implemented by a body that does not respond to contracts or correspond to a Cartesian pure will. It is instead a practical, bodily-constituted consciousness made of pain, as Fracchia points out,[72] and defined by material needs and other social and political factors.

Enrique Dussel's conceptualisation of living labour[73] as exteriority or 'interior transcendentality' of capital represents an effective way of explaining a source of constant instability for subsumptive relations – as well as an equally constant existential threat. Dussel introduces the category of the 'distinct' and 'alterity' as foundational for problematising a straightforward power relation between capital and living labour and the absolute domination of the former

---

71 De Certeau 1984.
72 Fracchia 2008.
73 Dussel 2001.

over the latter. For Dussel, living labour is both exterior and anterior to the totality that capitalism tends to create, which in turn tends to create a fundamental and irreducible duality between living labour and objectified labour. 'Exteriority', argues Dussel, 'is the sphere located beyond the foundation of totality. The sphere of exteriority is real only because of the existence of human freedom'.[74]

The bodily dimension of human life represents what for Dussel is defined as the 'analectical' – referring 'to the real human fact by which every person, every group, or people, is always situated "beyond" (anó-) the horizon of totality'.[75] Dussel insists on both reflexive and bodily 'transcendence', conceived as both living and the will to live fused with the material need to exist. For Dussel the exteriority of living labour is not spatial, but since living labour cannot ever be completely subsumed by capital, it is a limit. It is alienated, subsumed, subordinated, but never completely saturated. It is consistent potential for otherness and resistance inside capital. Dussel supports his assertion based on the materialist argument, already mentioned here, that labour capacity depends on the physical existence of the worker, and practical consciousness, the synthesis of body and mind, can never be completely saturated, even under the most overwhelming physical coercion or psychological conditioning.

Sáenz de Sicilia points to the fact that for both Dussel and Marx, living labour, the creative source of all values, the *conditio sine qua non* of capital, cannot undergo self-valorisation.[76] The production of surplus requires capital to subsume living labour from the outside. The Hegelian (and Schellingian) assumption reproduced by Dussel is that the creative source of something precedes and exists outside that being; in other words, capital is not autopoietic. Using the same line of argument, Dussel criticises the Marxist conceptualisation of capital as a self-sufficient totality, because it hides the real condition of living labour as a necessitated exteriority.

Capitalism as a totality can only really integrate living labour in 'the past' as objectified labour, but the future, that is to say living, labour needs to be constantly incorporated. Therefore, subsumption is always at risk of its determinate negation. Dussel explains how:

> ... the price of the labour capacity in the wages, covers an essential fallacy: it is thought that the value of labour is paid when in reality only the value of the labour capacity is paid. The 'labour capacity' has value because

---

74   Dussel 2001, p. 158.
75   Dussel 2001, p. 158.
76   Sáenz de Sicilia 2016.

the corporeality of the labourer has assumed, consumed and incorporated commodities (means of subsistence) which have value. The value of commodities bought in the market with his wages is now the value of his own 'labour capacity'. In a certain way, as the incorporation of wages, the 'labour capacity' is now the fruit of objectified labour also – and thus it shall be. Money becomes capital: from exteriority to totality commensurable, interchangeable, sellable for money: both shall be objectified, past labour. But 'living labour' shall never have value; thus, its non-value could not be determined; it shall not have a price, nor shall it be able to receive wages ... because it is the 'creating source of value'.[77]

Integrating Dussel to my theory of determinate supersumption means emphasising the level of instability of subsumptive power relation, which run the gamut from the conjunctural, accidental and even potentially singular all the way to the generality of surplus-value production. While subsumptive relations are relations of power that are supposed to guarantee a steady level of production and productivity, living labour is constantly subsumed from the outside, and since such subsumption is never complete this always implies a level of contestation. Living labour is 'no-capital' and therefore, if we wish to understand capital as a relation, living labour is also 'no-capital-subsumption'.

Dussel finds the synthesis of such a tension in the frequently neglected distinction between labour capacity, understood as pure creative dexterity that reproduces itself with the value of wages, and labour-power, pertaining to the situation when such a capacity is commodified and produces value, or, in other words, when living labour is subsumed and consumed by capital. For Dussel, Marx's humanism recognises a distinction between the exteriority of living labour and its alienation in the act of production. He maintains that, for Marx, human beings are not reducible to objects because they exist for themselves (as living labour prior to objectification) and are therefore aware of their will to live and develop:

> This living labour, existing as an *abstraction* from these moments of its actual reality (also, not-value); this complete denudation, purely subjective existence of labour, stripped of all objectivity. Labour as *absolute poverty*: poverty not as shortage, but as total exclusion of objective wealth. Or also as the existing *not-value*, and hence purely objective use-value, existing without mediation, this objectivity can only be an objectivity not

---

77 Dussel 2001, p. 47.

separated from the person: only an objectivity coinciding with his immediate bodily existence. Since the objectivity is purely immediate, it is just as much direct not-objectivity.[78]

Sáenz de Sicilia[79] claims that when we understand Dussel's terms living labour in these terms, as excess, then we find in it the foundation of a critique of capital that is essentially similar to Hardt and Negri's[80] claim regarding the excess and incommensurability of biopolitical production with respect to the biopower of capital:

> Living labour is the fundamental human faculty: the ability to engage the world actively and create social life. Living labour can be corralled by capital and pared down to the labour-power that is bought and sold and that produces commodities and capital, but living labour always exceeds that. Our innovative and creative capacities are always greater than our productive labour – productive, that is, for capital. At this point we can recognise that this biopolitical production is on the one hand *immeasurable*, because it cannot be quantified in fixed units of time, and, on the other hand, always *excessive* with respect to the value that capital can extract from it because capital can never capture all of life.[81]

Both perspectives imply the existence of a bodily and vitalist excess that capital harnesses to produce surplus-value but that it cannot completely control. In this sense, capital cannot reduce living labour to a general factor in production; it remains unpredictable. Sáenz de Sicilia argues that this is true of both Dussel's and Hardt and Negri's reading of the *Grundrisse*. Living labour is no-value and simultaneously a source of value which exceeds and escapes capital subsumption. For Dussel, subjectivity is neither a universal subject nor a particular one, but is a collective expression of intersubjectivity, which in turn constitutes an intractable singularity moved by spontaneous activation, as well as tactical, and sometimes strategic and coordinated, kinds of action.

While the legal persona of the worker who signs working contracts lives in theory only during working hours, the body cuts across working and free time, different structural roles (such as those of seller and buyer of commodities),

---

78   Marx 1973, pp. 295–296.
79   Sáenz de Sicilia 2016.
80   Hardt and Negri 2000.
81   Dussel 2001, p. 146.

and labour-power. While the use-value of labour-power relies on the worker's bodily capacity to adapt to the requirements of the labour process, this talent for spontaneous change also presents a threat to capital, therefore constantly modifying subsumptive relations.

CHAPTER 5

Subsuming Communication: The Rising of the Translation Machine and Data-Subjects/Objects

> When labour becomes cognitive – a communicative-relational activity no longer mediated by a rigid system of machines and by a precise separation of labour-time and the time for life – the command (management) over living labour is realised in a determinate emotive tonality, that is, in negative values transformed into professional competences.[1]

∴

Historically, the instability of subsumptive relations can be almost constantly linked to technological dynamism, by which, as already mentioned before, I do not simply refer to innovation in machinery, but also to the technological organisation of social relations. Understood in this way, organisational technology does not only enter the scene with real subsumption but turns out to be crucial across the entire subsumptive domain – and, by extension, all social phenomenology. Thus, while I agree with Matteo Pasquinelli[2] about the tendency of contemporary capitalism to develop through technological abstraction powered by algorithms of the metadata society, the best way to understand the role played by technology in contemporary capitalism is to look at the social relations that operate through it. In other words, we need to be careful not to fetishise technology.

In this chapter, I will engage those social relations through communicative practices, and I will utilise the notion of fixed capital as understood by Marx, Harvey and Read.[3] As I have already mentioned, fixed capital constitutes an

---

1 Marazzi 2016, pp. 40–6.
2 Pasquinelli 2015.
3 See Marx 1973; Marx 1990; Harvey 2003; Read 2013. Both Harvey and Read clearly draw on Marx but they also take two distinct paths, and since I will be taking both paths, it is important here to clarify their differences. On the one hand, I will be using Harvey's elaboration on the idea of a fix as a solution. In other words, Harvey claims that during crises capital focuses

important and recurrent node when it comes to subsumptive relations for a variety of reasons. It is the apogee of the contradiction between two of capital's machinic dreams: on the one hand, to reduce the indeterminacy linked to living labour to the predictability of dead labour, which would reduce the need for constant control and the resources to implement power relation across the whole social field (thus beyond the labour process); and, on the other, to bring about a situation in which production of surplus-value, due to the specific living labour capacity of people, is able to 'animate' dead labour.

Thus, fixed capital will be used as a framework to grasp the interrelation between subsumption, technology and the process of subjection, in this case linked to communicative practices. In fact, fixed capital refers to both motion and stasis of capital but also to the stability and instability of the process of accumulation that requires constant fixes, that is, remedies that frequently push for the subsumption of new spheres of social life. Fixed capital thus embodies the inextricable relations between subsumption and determinate supersumption, a relation that creates *impasses* and new opportunities. In relation to this, in this section I link technological abstraction to the evolution of informational and translational machines and a particular kind of fixed capital that interacts linguistically and cognitively with living labour, at levels unimaginable until a few decades ago.

The discussion in Chapter 4 was meant to introduce the general perspective of the conceptual and practical relationship between subsumptive relations and contradictory processes of subjection. In many ways, adding the aspect of language means providing a concrete example of how those subsumptive dynamics operate at the molecular level. Accordingly, in this chapter, I want to ground this context through a series of specific productive practices that are driven by communication and information communication technology.

When it comes to subsumptive processes, especially in the current context, many aspects of what we could define as digital capitalism can provide interesting examples, where both communicating subjects and their specific mode of communication practices intersect with labour, the labour process, and there-

---

on investment in fixed capital (such as infrastructure or built environment in the process of urbanisation). I will claim that during the Covid-induce crisis, capital in many countries resorted to digital fixes that produced digital abstract space. On the other hand, Read draws on the Autonomist Marxist reading of fixed capital linked to the general intellect, which is not simply materialised in machinery but also in people's social, cultural, and cognitive ('human') capital. In this sense, I will argue that communication/translational practices operate as fixed capital that, by producing translatability, provide means of circulation for capitalist meanings.

fore subsumptive processes, in ways that resonate with the goal of this book: opening up new perspectives on subsumption.

The chapter is structured as follows: I first briefly spell out my materialist approach to language, which is understood in the context of means of production signifying use-values.[4] This is theoretically and practically speaking the node where the tensions between subsumption/supersumption, communication and subjection become manifest most vividly, because the lack of communication is one of the factors that creates alienation, especially from other workers. However, its resurgence is ambiguous, to say the least: it may certainly remediate alienation, but it also creates the condition for a new or more insidious kind of alienation.

I then discuss the pivotal role of language in the implementation of different forms of subsumption, that is, formal, real but also ideal. On the one hand, language substantiates – via a coded and allegedly in its written form *fixed* legal rhetoric – the fiction of labour and capital as equal parties exchanging wages for labour-power. While language materialises this fiction in the realm of real subsumption, language operates as the technological implementation of real subsumption by enhancing cooperation in the division of labour, particularly through particular jargons/language games that each moment/sector of production tends to produce, as well by translating between different jargons and information technologies; finally, language also serves as a bridge to establish capitalist communication practices, thus paving the way for more 'effective' subsumptions.

In the second part of the chapter, I consider the informal and unrecognised form of communicative labour defined as translational labour, that is, the mostly unpaid labour we all do as inhabitants of the social field when we circulate meaning across different social scales and contexts. After a brief discussion of a Gramscian-inspired understanding of translation, I argue that translational labour represents an interesting gateway for subsumptive/supersumptive relations. I then consider various instances where translational praxis sheds light on the dialectic pair subsumption/determinate supersumption: 1) subjectification processes, as 'ideal'[5] and 'hybrid' subsumption of people under neoliberal capitalist forms, which creates both complacent victims and organised antagonism; 2) the notion of the linguistic machine possessed of algorithmic translational capacities.[6] Finally, I examine a Freire-inspired and to

---

4 See Fuchs 2020; Williams 1977; Rossi Landi 1968.
5 Murray 2004.
6 See Marazzi 1999, Pasquinelli 2015.

my mind radical use of language for supersumptive politics, describing the so-called 150-hours project, which, while not as recent as the other cases examined here, still offers opportunities to reflect on language and subsumption in political terms.

Ultimately, I argue that all those cases provide instances in which translational practices of users and workers operate both as powerful means for real and ideal subsumption and their alienating and abstracting tendencies. They furthermore elucidate the fundamental limits of translatability and the potential for linguistic social intercourse to revolutionise subsumptive relations.

1   Communication: Relational Labour and Labour of Relations

The way in which communication is understood in this book requires that I make some brief prefatory comment on its fundamental role in the material production and reproduction of social life. This is especially due to the fact that language is one of the most important mediations of social relations, and thus of subsumptive relations as well. Marx and Engels claim that the capability of making history is first tied to the material sustainment of human life:

> We must begin by stating the first premise of all human existence and therefore, of all history, the premise, namely, that men must be in a position to live in order to be able to 'make history'. But life involves before everything else eating and drinking, a habitation, clothing and many other things. The first historical act is thus the production of the means to satisfy these needs, the production of material life itself. And indeed, this is an historical act, a fundamental condition of all history, which today, as thousands of years ago, must daily and hourly be fulfilled merely in order to sustain human life.[7]

Language represents a fundamental condition of possibility for material activity, both 'mental' and 'manual'. According to Adrienne Harris: 'Language learning is the by-product of entering and altering the ensemble of social relations'.[8] Moreover, if communication is about acting upon social relations, it also implies a non-reductionist kind of materialism, that is, not reducible to simple matter, simple organic life or economics:

---

7   Marx and Engels 1846, p. 156.
8   Harris 1983, p. 99.

> According to the materialist conception of history, the ultimately determining element in history is the production and reproduction of real life. More than this, neither Marx nor I have ever asserted. Hence, if somebody twists this into saying that the economic element is the only determining one, he transforms that proposition into a meaningless, abstract, senseless phrase. The economic situation is the basis, but the various elements of the superstructure: political forms of the class struggle and its results, to wit: constitutions established by the victorious class after a successful battle, etc, juridical forms, and then even the reflexes of all these actual struggles in the brains of the participants, political, juristic, philosophical theories, religious views and their further development into systems of dogmas, also exercise their influence upon the course of historical struggles and in many cases preponderate in determining their form. There is an interaction of all these elements in which, amid all the endless host of accidents (that is, of things and events, whose inner connection is so remote or so impossible of proof that we can regard it as non-existent, as negligible) the economic movement finally asserts itself as necessary. Otherwise, the application of the theory to any period of history one chose would be easier than the solution of a simple equation of the first degree.[9]

Communication provides the basis for the conditions of possibility for a whole way of living,[10] a practical social enterprise to satisfy basic human needs such as eating or providing shelter, but also for the establishing of social, economic and cultural institutions. I assume here that communication's materiality not only goes beyond the debates between the economic and non-economic, the mental and manual, the symbolic and the material, the objective or the subjective, but also that communications do not pertain to a superstructural condition, in which they are immediately determined by a 'structure'.

Based on what we have discussed so far, communication can be considered as a social product, a social tool and a social process.[11] Communication is a social product in the sense that it is not produced by a single individual but by the whole social intercourse; it is a transindividual enterprise.[12] This is true for both linguistic practices as well as means of communication such as the telephone or the internet, which are socially produced beyond individual or

---

9   Marx and Engels 1978, Vol. 49, pp. 760–761.
10 Williams 1977.
11 Artz, Macek and Cloud 2006.
12 Virno 2001.

individual manufacturers. As a social tool, once communication gets produced, it becomes available for the organisation of social action, social relations and social production. Associating a word to an object or an event entails much more than a description; it also involves an assessment of social value and social relations, thus, for instance, identifying roles in productions, hierarchies, labour processes.

Most of all, communication can be described as a social process: it is a 'shared and contested practice that must constantly be negotiated and reconstructed even as it expresses and organises human understandings'.[13] Communication relations are also class relations. Communication mediates class conflicts, class interests, class consciousness, but also class alliances. Christian Fuchs summarises this materialist perspective very eloquently:

> ... humans *communicate productively* and *produce communicatively*. Communication aims at the production of a specific social use-value, namely that humans understand the world and understand each other. Therefore, *communication is productive*. The production of use-values that satisfy human needs cannot be achieved individually, but only in social relations. Communication is the process that organises social relations. Therefore, *humans produce communicatively*.[14]

2   Translatability and Translational Labour

According to the conceptual approach proposed by Kant, and recently reproposed by Sáenz de Sicilia,[15] communication and subsumption processes imply an agency of translation, in the sense that both describe the transposition of meanings and practices from one social context to another: thus, homologies exist between modes of communication as well as between different modes of productions such as the pre-capitalist and capitalist.[16] Furthermore, like

---

13   Artz, Macek and Cloud 2006, p. 18.
14   Fuchs 2020, p. 7.
15   Sáenz de Sicilia 2022.
16   So, for instance in the case of formal subsumption, the taking command by capital of the labour process requires a translational effort in the sense that power, control and subordination, being infused in material social relations, do not act as some kind of ghostly force, but must necessarily operate as a semantic agent. So, for instance: starting from now, Mr John Doe will be addressed as my 'boss', my work as his employee becomes labour, my time becomes his time, answering to his re-significations of it.

subsumption processes, translation mediates between concrete meanings and practices and their abstract extrapolations.

If communication must be understood as fixed capital, what is it that produces, and how can this 'output' become productive of surplus-value via subsumptive dynamics? Drawing on Gramsci's notion of translation/translatability,[17] I argue that communication's main product is translatability, especially in the context of ICT-driven capitalism. Like logistics infrastructures exemplified by highways, airports and the power grid, translatability represents the capital that allows for capital circulation.

Translatability operates both as a principle of exchangeability of concrete translational labour, thus erasing its diversity by abstraction, as well as a power relation that attempts to contain practical signification produced by communication around adequate-to-capital, that is, meaningful productive practices. In a general sense, translational labour helps transition from one capital form of representation to another: so, capital in production, capital as commodities form, and capital as in money and capital as consumption funds.[18]

Thus, the Italian thinker understood translation not simply as a transfer of meanings across natural languages, but as a general act of communication that over time creates homologies between different social spheres. That is to say that it creates a reciprocal translatability between them. Gramsci speaks of translation in various senses that are similar but never completely overlapping: (1) referring to the *correspondence* from historical-political to philosophical in Notebook I; (2) referring to translation as *reduction*, such as the Jacobin phraseology reduced to German idealism; and, finally, (3) referring to translation as a reciprocal translation, as in Notebook III, where discussion is of the relation between spontaneity and conscious leadership, political praxis and theory, etc. This is how he explains it:

> Philosophy, politics and economics are the necessary constituent elements of the same conception of the world, there must necessarily be, in their theoretical principles, a convertibility from one to the others and a reciprocal translation into the specific language proper to each constituent element. Any one is implicit in the others, and the three together form an homogeneous circle.[19]

---

17   Gramsci 1975, especially Notebook 10 and 11.
18   In the various metamorphoses of capital, for example, as production process, as a commodity, as a wage, as money, translational labour is needed to make sense of the various forms of representation.
19   Gramsci 1975, Q 11, § 65.

While capital, language and a given social order are considered by Gramsci to be tightly co-dependent and co-developing, communication is not inherently instrumental, nor is it merely reflective of a given capitalist hegemonic regime. In fact, what makes communication into fixed capital is not its inherent translational element – its nature as a transindividual structure – but rather how such a characteristic is used more or less instrumentally by capital. As a matter of fact, Gramsci was politically interested in translation for the exact opposite reason: because he wished to communicate more effectively the groundbreaking experience of the October revolution in Europe.

Gramsci's take implies the tensions between openness, the possibility of instrumentality, and subjection to the power of communication. This is particularly apparent in his distinction between immanent and normative grammar. Spontaneous or 'immanent grammar'[20] represents an idiolectic way of communicating; while 'normative grammar'[21] represents a hegemonic linguistic mode enforced by social and cultural institutions and by individuals' reciprocal monitoring of themselves, as well as by structures such as the education system or the economy:

> One could sketch a picture of the 'normative grammar' that operates spontaneously in every given society, in that this society tends to become unified both as a territory and as a culture, in other words it has a governing class whose function is recognised and followed. The number of 'immanent or spontaneous grammars' is incalculable and, theoretically, one may say that each person has a grammar of her own. Yet, alongside this actual 'disaggregation', one has to consider the movements of unification, of greater or lesser amplitude both as territorial area and as 'linguistic volume'. Written 'normative grammars' tend to embrace an entire national territory and the entire 'linguistic volume', to create a unitary national linguistic conformism, that, under another respect, places expressive 'individualism' at a higher level, because it creates a more robust and homogeneous skeleton for the national linguistic organism of which every individual is the reflection and the interpreter.[22]

In the same way, on the one hand, we create our own spontaneous translations, by coining metaphors and linking social elements or spheres creatively.[23] On

---

20   Gramsci 1971, p. 453.
21   Gramsci 1971, p. 454.
22   Gramsci 1971, p. 459.
23   Spontaneous grammar represents another way to explain what Dussel had in mind when

the other, we also translate in a normative mode, as the result of both structural forces such as the market as well as conscious hegemonic projects, which are implemented through social and cultural institutions such as education, the family and the media. The normative, by virtue of its hegemonic position, tends to subsume most (but not all) molecular and concrete-immanent grammar into molar, more abstract and normative grammar.

Gramsci understands language as a terrain on which people's ways of living, on the one hand, and the collectively shared 'common sense', on the other, meet and confront each other in many ways:

> It seems that one can say that 'language' is essentially a collective term, which does not presuppose any single thing existing in either time or space. Language also means culture and philosophy (if only at the level of common sense) and therefore, the fact of 'language' is in reality a multiplicity of facts more or less organically coherent and coordinated. At the limit, it may be said that every speaking being has her own personal language [*linguaggio*], that is, her own way of thinking and feeling. ... Since this is the way things happen, the importance of the general question of language comes to light, that is, the question of collectively attaining a single cultural 'climate'.[24]

As a result, the distinctive combination of structural limitations relating to the available transformative potential of communication – in other words, the synthesis of structure and struggle[25] – finds in translation practices its most exemplary case. As already mentioned in the case of grammar, translation mediates the abstract and the concrete of every practice, not just labour. As Maurizio Lichtner observes: 'Abstract discourse is the translation of historical reality, and is, in turn, retranslated into praxis, mainly in historical-political action. Thus, the concept of translation is not simply linked to praxis but leads us to the political nucleus of the philosophy of praxis'.[26] This is what makes translation an instrument that paves the way for subsumption: it creates a necessary prerequisite condition for abstraction and equivalence at the concrete level of practical signification and practical consciousness, that is, at the level of lan-

---

he was arguing that living labour is never completely under the control of capital: Dussel 2001. These spontaneous creations of meanings, even when immediate and not politically strategic, can be incredibly powerful as a disruptive force against capital.

24   Gramsci 1971, pp. 348–9.
25   Aune 2013.
26   Lichtner 2010, p. 195.

guage itself. Therefore, translational practices do not seek identities but homologies. Translational practices both create and rely on social homologies.

Social homologies are possible because of a condition of translatability, and this condition results from pre-existing homological structures. For example, the quantification of concrete labour relies on the existence of abstract labour. Not by accident, the concept of social homology bridges semantic correspondences in linguistic practices and the principle of exchange and equivalence in the economic realm of subsumption. Implying a circular relation between social structure and communicated signification, that is, a condition of translatability, Gramsci claims in Notebook XI that one of the relevant conditions is the existence of a social whole in which all parts are indissolubly interrelated. Accordingly, philosophy, politics and economics:

> ... are the necessary constituent elements of the same conception of the world, there must necessarily be, in their theoretical principles, a convertibility from one to the others and a reciprocal translation into the specific language proper to each constituent element. Any one is implicit in the others, and the three together form an homogeneous circle.[27]

Like other subsumptive dynamics, translatability, whether as a structural condition, as a product of praxis, or as a producer of translatability, can never be perfect. This is because the process constantly produces both a deficit and surplus of meaning: the 'essential root' of phenomena as well as the historic process that generates subsumptive practices is continuously changed by people's living praxis. That is why Lucia Borghese claims that:

> Translation thus becomes a necessary criterion of mediation between two cultures, or conceptions of the world, which can critically mediate between the multiple and ever-changing faces of reality and protect against all kinds of 'metaphysical' rigid thinking: translation allows us to prevent contingent truths from being considered absolute and becoming fossilised as ideologies. In a certain sense, then, the concept of translation gives us a measure of Gramsci's 'absolute historicism' and the value in irony in translation as a detachment from teleological conception of history, as a perennial movement and tension.[28]

---

27 Gramsci 1971, p. 403.
28 Borghese 2010, p. 136.

When Marx describes capitalism as a mode of production characterised by 'blindly operating averages between constant irregularities',[29] he refers to the consistent need to articulate and mediate conflicting aspects of economic forms such as price and money and, more importantly, to the different elements organised by the relations of production. In the same way, translatability allows abstraction and exchangeability within a normative standardised grammar that represses the immanent one.

Thus, as I have already mentioned, we can think of immanent/spontaneous translation as concrete translation, and normative translation as a more abstract form of translation. I refer to a different degree of abstraction because of the 'logistical' need socially to coordinate and cooperate in a context of real subsumption, which is to say to translate across practices, thus guaranteeing the circulation, appropriation and monetisation of linguistic/knowledge of the general intellect: resources continuously and spontaneously created by people such as languages, culture, traditions and knowledge in general.

As previously suggested, communication practices always operate as translational practices because our own 'spontaneous grammar' must be, to a relative and mutable degree, translatable; if it were pure idiolect, it could not sustain social relations. This constant semantic task of circulating meanings becomes vital for a mode of production such as capitalism. Hence, due to its highly developed division of labour – which fragments a common language into separate technical jargons – capitalism requires remarkable levels of social cooperation and coordination, especially under the condition of real subsumption and the accumulation of a particular kind of fixed capital: machines and machinery, or what today we would more broadly define as technology. This is the connection between fixed capital and the vital function of communication as a translation machine.

2.1   *Communicative Fixed Capital*

Historically, capitalism has probably been the most consistent and successful revolutionising agent of all, always on the road, never scared of bad infinities, uninterested in miser-like, irrational hoarding, and always relaunching the game. 'Every limit is just a barrier!', capital proudly proclaims, but, as we have been painfully learning in recent years, every time a crisis hits, all barriers immediately go up again, walls get erected, money goes under the mattress, and the spectacle of capitalism unveils itself, even if for only a few moments.

---

29   Marx 1990, p. 196,.

Still, it is during those critical times that the revolutionising force of capitalism shows its strength, its stubbornness in overcoming difficulties through a particular kind of capitalist endurance, dedicated to increasing production and productivity, that is, fixed capital. For instance, in the 2007–8 crisis, China saved global capitalism[30] through fixed capital accumulation and the consequent Keynesian stimulus of effective demand, by expanding infrastructures such as highways, bridges and high-speed trains. More recently, in the aftermath of the Covid-induced crisis, and in the midst of a supply chain/logistical crisis, analysis of the stimulus packages of the US, EU and China discloses a common remedy: massive investment to consolidate digitalisation, increasing broadband, digital literacy, business digitalisation and e-government.

More than consolidating digitalisation, the Covid-induced crisis accelerated this process, as the employment of information and communication technologies (here and after ICTs) has already possibly become the most distinctive aspect of current capitalism. In this sense, tropes such as 'platform capitalism',[31] 'datafication',[32] 'algorithmic culture',[33] and 'algorithmic life'[34] describe a holistic plane where computational logic meets people's consciousness, practices, knowledge and, last but not least, labour. This is also the same plane where the inextricable relationship of platforms and algorithms creates the condition for our datafied lives – the establishment of subsumptive relations under platforms.

In relation to such an ICTs-driven and data-saturated world, I discuss here the fundamental role played by communication as a form of (communicative) fixed capital, comprising and combining both data-objects (information) and data-subjects (most of us, at this point), with reference to what I define as translational practices.

What do we gain by understanding communication and mediation processes as fixed capital? I posit two analytically discernible, but also linked, lines of arguments. Historically and politically, investments in fixed capital intended to solve capitalism's problems represent an imperfect and unstable solution, one that tends to prepare the conditions for future crises.[35] As we shall see, the tensions that undermine fixed capital derive from its reliance on an active and dynamic combination between people's work and machines, thus leaving

---

30   Harvey 2017.
31   Srnicek 2016.
32   Van Dijck 2014.
33   Striphas 2015.
34   Amoore and Piotukh 2016.
35   Harvey 1982.

room for fluid power relations, resistance and alternatives. In other words, fixed capital provides fixes/solutions that represent a temporal and/or spatial displacement of class antagonism and subsumptive relations.

Theoretically, understanding communication as fixed capital has some important repercussions. First of all, it moves the debate about ICTs beyond technological determinism and beyond the forced polarisation between utopian and dystopian approaches to technology. I will contend that we should conceptualise the machine, or more prosaically technology, not as a product/appliance but as a *fluid organisational social relation*. Linked to that, we will show that the argument that communicative fixed capital creates both data-objects and data-subjects has two further important implications. First, the association of communication and machines provides a needed theoretical bridge between political economy and media and communication studies, which enriches how we understand both technologies as well as communication. In this sense, subsumption becomes an illuminating perspective on surplus-value extractive relations in an ICT environment.

Second, it provides a more robust framework to comprehend how a context saturated by data, algorithmic management and online platforms contributes to the constitution of contemporary subjectivities and their motivation to comply with such systems, that is, how it constitutes subsumption-complying subjects. We need to understand how subjectivities subsumed under the forms of ICTs navigate, negotiate and antagonise power relations.

It can seem counterintuitive to think of machines in terms of capital and communication, which are fluid and always in motion. Indeed, the notion of fixed capital is an oxymoron, designed to describe internal tensions and contradictory circulatory dynamics, such as between stasis and movement; agency and structure; space and time fix; and finally, between living labour (people) and dead labour (machineries).

As Harvey describes it,[36] fixed capital consists of durable instruments of labour produced, exchanged and consumed as commodities inside the labour process. They are ultimately utilised to produce surplus-value. In a well-known passage from the *Grundrisse*, Marx describes fixed capital in a rather interesting way:

> Nature builds no machines, no locomotives, railways, electric telegraphs, self-acting mules, etc. These are products of human industry; natural material transformed into organs of the human will over nature, or of

---

36   Harvey 1982.

human participation in nature. They are *organs of the human brain, created by the human hand*; the power of knowledge, objectified. The development of fixed capital indicates to what degree general social knowledge has become a *direct force of production*, and to what degree, hence, the conditions of the process of social life itself have come under the control of the general intellect and been transformed in accordance with it. To what degree the powers of social production have been produced, not only in the form of knowledge, but also as immediate organs of social practice, of the real life process.[37]

This passage above is usually cited to discuss the massive incorporation of technology into the sphere of production as well as to describe the rise of the general intellect. In fact, this collective and machinic dimension of knowledge is productive in two ways: as embodied in industrial machinery, but also as mass intellectuality[38] that manages the new division of labour of cognitive capitalism[39] and produces 'forms of life' and new services within so-called anthropogenic industries.[40] Thus, fixed capital combines the most mechanised-alienated side of production and the most imaginative/creative side of people's mental capacity.

Such a definition of fixed capital implies first a revision of the 'received' meaning of the machine. For Marx, drawing on Charles Babbage,[41] machines are not simply mechanical tools or autonomous agents, but rather organisational social relations that are only facilitated, and not constituted, by mechanical tools, and which occupy and replace an existent division of labour:

> When, by the division of labour, each particular operation has been simplified to the use of a single instrument, the linking up of all these instruments, set in motion by a single engine, constitutes – a machine.[42]

Following the same logical trajectory, the use-value of translational practices/communication understood as productive fixed capital consists of a machine that articulates people, meanings and actions, linking up previously separated realms and particular practices. As I will now argue in more detail, communic-

---

37   Marx 1973, p. 706.
38   Virno 1996.
39   Vercellone 2007.
40   Marazzi 2005.
41   Pasquinelli 2015.
42   Babbage 1832, quoted in Marx 1990.

ation is essentially a *translation machine* that engages people through translational practices and produces translatability. As a machine, not physically fixed in space, but operating in circulation and by circulating, communication would be considered inside the Marxian framework here proposed as a specific (or independent) form of fixed capital that does not appear as a mere instrument enclosed in the production process, like railways, canals, roads, aqueducts, airports, railway stations, etc., but which instead, like broadbands and servers, belongs to 'the general preconditions of production'.[43]

In the section below, again with help of Gramsci, I will explain in detail how such a machine creates subsumptive dynamics that operate within a hegemonic framework.

3   Digital Platforms as Translation Machines

Communication producing translatability becomes a machine that primes practical meanings in order to create an adequate environment for platform capitalism. According to Paolo Virno,[44] the error of traditional Marxism is to consider the general intellect only as fixed capital crystallised into industrial machinery and not as living labour diffused across the whole linguistic activity of associated productive life.

In order to understand such a scenario, we need to step back briefly and consider many of the intuitions produced by Italian Operaismo, a school of thought that applied Marxist categories in order to examine the employment of machines in the labour process and their interaction with workers. Rendering the factory walls more porous, thus establishing a fundamental bridge between production and social production, Mario Tronti's[45] analysis of the so-called social factory and Romano Alquati's[46] insights about cybernetics and valorising information are very useful in expanding the notion of subsumptive relations. The main insight we can draw from this school of thought is that machines *crystallise* social relations that in turn provide an active nexus between machines and workers.

In his book *Thousands of Machines*, Gerald Raunig[47] observes how, historically, machines have themselves been subject to a process of abstraction that

---

43   Marx 1973, p. 739.
44   Virno 1996.
45   Tronti 1972.
46   Alquati 2021.
47   Raunig 2010.

drastically reduced their realm of action: from being a complex machinic composition comprising an object (that is, the mechanical apparatus), a subject (the worker), a function, a purpose, a location, they were reduced to mechanistic objects with a clear physical delimitation. Accordingly, an open social fabric and a dynamic social process were abstracted into a finite object, what we now visualise in terms of physical appliance.

Subsequently, in the aftermath of the first and second industrial revolution, they were subject to yet another round of abstraction, which turned them into a *dispositif*, operating in production in the context of a given economic activity. Still, for Raunig, despite their instrumentalisation at the will of capitalist production, machines remain fundamentally distinct from simple tools, to the degree that the former constitute a synthesis of mechanical components with the knowledge and skills of workers. Machines actively participate in the process of constituting social relations along with the identity of working subjects, but they also affect the information that is produced by the interaction between these subjects and machines.

In this sense, for Alquati, information operated as *dispositif*, capable of mediating constant and variable capital and establishing a more fluid interaction between workers and machinery. Information was indeed the main social relation that permeated both the production and the valorisation process. It was first produced by workers through observation and assessment, then absorbed by machines, and finally crystallised into products. Subsequently, it informed the decisions taken by workers in the design of the production process itself. Productivity of labour, for Alquati, was proportional to the quality of information produced and transmitted by workers. This was a tendency that was adequate to capital insofar as it left its mark on the design of machines, thus establishing a machinic cybernetic network of production.

Living and dead labour also implied living and dead information that materialises in the machinery. In the machinic link between worker and machines, valorising information is both the means of subsumption of the worker and the end-form under which the worker is subsumed. The machinic nature of this relation also implies that although the worker's labour – that is, his/her signifying practices understood as the valorising 'element' of the information itself – is abstracted and objectified for the sole purpose of producing the use-value of the product, it nevertheless remains the case that his/her production skills also continuously enrich the machines. The machinic is ultimately valorised by this interaction of living information and dead information, in which each reciprocally reshapes the other. At the same time, regardless of how the machinic link evolves, the technological innovations consistently reproduce at the level of their own logic the relations between classes. Thus, in those information machines, the flow of information is asymmetrical, and as a technology of social organisation, it mainly entails social control and social domination.

The reason for this diversion into Alquati's analysis is that the logical basis of what gives value to valorising information is a circuit of translational labour between people and machines. In fact, Alquati states that the most valuable part of labour is information produced by workers that gradually improves the design of the machine, the management of the division of labour, and the final value of products; it is the numeric dimension of digital information that makes it possible to translate knowledge into information, information into numbers, and numbers into value; the cybernetic apparatus of the factory grows and improves thanks to the contribution of workers' socialised intelligence.

Producing valorising information is a task of translational labour. What the machinic nexus between living and dead labour does is refine the level of translatability between these two elements or 'sides'. As it happens, the translatability between computer hardware and software provides evidence of the homological link between material/traditional and linguistic/translational kinds of work.[48] In this sense, digitisation conceptually derives from ideas founded in the computational communication that was developed out of Claude Shannon's information theory,[49] which aimed at universal translatability via the abstraction of information from its material and historical contexts. Idiosyncratic meaning would be converted into consistently translatable information. Thus, when Shannon and Warren Weaver claim that 'the fundamental problem of communication is reproducing at one point either exactly or approximately a message selected at another point',[50] they ultimately refer to a translation process between information partitions, as well as between the hardware and software components of computers.

Examining more recent industrial developments, Christian Marazzi[51] follows a similar line of argument when he claims that the massive incorporation of ICTs constitutes a natural continuum of the Turing machine as a linguistic machine, according to which the most important element is the organisation of a grammar whose symbols move on a magnetic 'assembly line', passing back and forth between one position and another. The linguistic organisation of the production process doesn't characterise only the 'Turing machine' and information technologies. Various management models are also inspired by the prin-

---

48   Rossi-Landi 1968.
49   Shannon 1948.
50   Shannon 1948, p. 3.
51   Shannon 1948, p. 3.

ciples expressed by Alan Turing: their goal is to organise the firm as a 'data bank' able to self-determine its actions by virtue of a smooth, fluid, 'interfaced' linguistic communication process.[52]

The linguistic machine invented by Turing lays the basis for the current context in two ways: first, by providing a universalising computational digital code; second, by ensuring that such code is executable, in other words, making sure that every word in such code is both description and command that operates the machine.[53] The term 'digital code' refers usually to three different things: the binary digits encoding an analogue input into 0 and 1 impulses; the language in which software programs are written (for example, C++, Perl, etc); the script of a software program that translates the logical form of an algorithm.

I am particularly interested in the algorithms that abstract information out of information in order to create a network of reciprocal translatability among different formats of information and different languages. Similarly, the algorithms that extract metadata produce abstraction through subsumption of metadata, which can be logically conceived as the 'measure' of information, the computation of its social dimension, and its transformation into value. As Alquati showed, the cybernetic apparatus needs to be continuously fed and sustained by the flows of valorising information proceeding from workers, but it is specifically the accumulation of valorising information, and therefore the accumulation of information about information (or metadata), that improved the organisation of the production line, the design of machinery and the final value of the product.

Crucially, for Marx, the power of machines does not come from mechanical force, but from socially produced knowledge that has been objectified – in other words, from fixed capital in the form of the general intellect – which would not have emerged without a condition of translatability. Thus, while capitalism has always been intimately linked to translations and a condition of translatability, in this chapter I will be concentrating on a particular trend, namely the platform/digital economy, that exemplifies especially well how those translational tasks could be considered as a kind of labour. I will also examine their function in mediating immanent economic tensions.

By discussing platforms, we can now return to the premises of the chapter, communication as fixed capital that facilitates the establishment of subsumptive relations and that provide fixes to overcome crises. Platforms afford a space where organisations or individuals use online interfaces to access other

---

52   Marazzi 1999, p. 27.
53   Galloway 2004.

organisations or individuals in order to solve specific problems or provide services in exchange for payment. The most common services include creative activities such as software development or graphic design; transportation, for example of people or consumer goods; domestic services such as caregiving, cleaning, or shopping; and finally other micro activities such as tagging images on Web pages.

The last decade of critical inquiry into platform working shows how, beyond the rhetoric on flexibility and autonomy, work is strongly constrained in a structured and systematic way by algorithmic supervision, combined with omnipresent evaluation systems, as well as conditions of wide uncertainty regarding compensation.[54] In many cases, companies do not simply 'match' consumers with the suppliers of services, but aim to control the behaviour of workers through *algorithmic management*.[55] As the Autonomist Marxist tradition would understand it, using the terminology of post-Fordism, the platform economy has expanded the moment of production from the factory to the 'social factory'[56] by moving into areas of social life that were previously external to the economic realm, such as the affective relations of family and friends, voluntary-humanitarian activities and community work, the private and intimate spheres, and finally leisure time.

As a result, platforms and the digital economy have been enhancing the instrumental significance of translatability within capitalism. This is for several reasons. First, the colonising via subsumption of new social spheres essentially means establishing – via the commodity and the value form and other capitalist kinds of social relations – principles of equivalences among previously diverse and even incompatible kinds of meanings and practices. This is fundamental for the possibility of a condition of translatability, because while for a long time the rule of exchange in the marketplace has made any human being reciprocally translatable as one of the two subjects involved in a transaction, now the same principle *tends* to expand towards the whole society. Put differently, we observe the establishment of a condition of reciprocal translations of practices, discourses and language games previously disconnected but now mediated by capital. See, for example, the communication practices enhanced by smartphone etiquette or email.

Secondly, the massive investment in this kind of ITC-oriented fixed capital under a condition of real subsumption has increased the importance of communication as translation because the very technology relies on language;

---

54   Moore 2018.
55   Moore 2018.
56   Tronti 1972.

furthermore, as Alquati noticed in his workers' inquiry,[57] the quality of the interaction between worker and machine became a fundamental aspect of the valorising process. Thirdly, and linked to Alquati's argument about valorising information, while the homology between meaning and value has possibly increased due to the cooperative and social powers of labour that have consistently characterised the capitalist mode of production, with the platform economy it becomes increasingly dependent on social knowledge, cooperation and communicational skills, thus increasing the prominence of fixed capital as a combination of technology and the common mental/cultural resources of a given society, that is, the general intellect. In this scenario, wealth is no longer produced by bodies put to work in the closed spaces of the factory, but rather by knowledge, communication and social interactions,[58] that is, by translational practices and their translatable structures.

Furthermore, such a knowledge/information/communication-based economy establishes vicious cycles that increase the need for translatability. In fact, the existence of knowledge-based commodities that are not depleted by consumption – for example, you can deplete a candy, but you cannot so easily deplete an MP3 – in the context of capital's insinuation into all social spheres, creates both a constant overproduction crisis of knowledge capital as well as fragmentation into specialised languages created by a multiform consumer culture. In turn, both tendencies require constant translation in order to create links between diverse semiotic codes. From this point of view, the very flexibilisation and hyper-connectivity of most platform/digital work can be understood as a response to those needs. In this sense, the kind of algorithms that power cultural entertainment platforms such as Netflix and YouTube must constantly create an area of translatability between diverse interpretive and consumption communities, by creating categories out of very diverse genres.

In this sense, the economic integration of processes of digitisation that took off in the early 1970s provides a striking example of how late capitalism benefits from and attempts to increase translatability. In fact, creating digital versions of analogue/physical objects such as documents or images allows for the possibility of the complete translatability of potentially all knowledge in the form of bits and bytes, which makes the creation, retrieving and consumption of knowledge considerably more effective.

In the second portion of the chapter, I will discuss three examples of communications function as fixed-capital-producing translatability through trans-

---

57 Alquati 2021.
58 Virno 2001.

lational labour. These are app-delivery labour and data-driven journalism and the adult education project of 150 hours. As we shall see with the example of online app-delivery workers, workers' production of information for their companies, digitalisation and information theory are all key aspects of the primordial valorisation process internal to language and knowledge, which can be valorised (for instance) by the translation of 'knowledge into information, information into numbers, and numbers into value'.[59] In the case of data-driven journalism, I will describe the other side of this circuit: how raw information and numbers, that is, big data, are being retranslated into news stories, which then get valorised by being retranslated into numbers, that is, metrics.

4 Who Is Exactly a Translational Worker ...?

While, according to the optic of social subsumption and communications, many of us are translational workers – and also, to a different degree, platform users – I here want to concentrate on a narrower category of worker, in order to clarity how translational work is converted into wage-labour. For instance, academic professors or store clerks are becoming platform workers, but they do not experience it in the same way as workers such as call-centre or delivery workers.

Thus, the first important distinction to introduce is that between 'translational workers' and translational labourers. In the context of translational 'practices', 'work' and 'labour' are clearly linked but are not the same thing. In order to speak about transnational activity in concrete ways, this must involve productive agents. Who are they? In what sense are they 'productive'? To answer these questions, we must first distinguish between working and labouring. While the distinction is never clear-cut, I refer to work as a productive activity that tends to be spontaneous and creative, producing use-values that are qualitatively determined. Think of cooking for pleasure, or building model aeroplanes. By labouring, I refer to a productive activity that creates surplus-value, most frequently for someone else, and is quantitatively determined, like wage-labour. The first activity is concrete in the sense that it is attached to concrete use-values and objects, the second tends to be abstract because it is often considered as a generic unit of labour that adds extra value, regardless of who is producing and what is being produced.

---

59 Pasquinelli 2015, p. 58.

While both analytically and normatively useful, in reality the distinction is much more fluid. Thus, returning to translational practices as communication, as social individuals we are all translational workers and 'social workers'; that is, we operate through social cooperation and with 'the linguistic-relational abilities of humankind, in the complex of communicative and cognitive faculties'.[60]

At the same time, while we are social workers because we all produce, consume and accumulate this 'collective linguistic wealth',[61] corporations take a much bigger share of it for free, as they can both capture and monetise such translational commons through translational labourers. Those of us who are employed by such businesses also become translational labourers, and our translational outcomes tends to be more and more abstract. That is because, especially when mediated by ICTs 'protological' codes,[62] capitalist-mediated translations tend to form a general condition of translatability. Thus it is not just labour that becomes generically quantified by units, but also the kind of translation that labourers produce: a type of communication that tends to be standardised, routinised, instrumental to productivity, ideally indifferent to the identity of the labourer who produces it.

Returning to the fluidity of the work/labour distinction, while clearly most of us do not work as professional translators, nevertheless, as we work and socially interact, we produce the translatability condition necessary for commodities and value to circulate. Furthermore, in the context of 'free labour' we fluidly pass from work to labour and vice versa.[63] This fact has important consequences, however: we enter into class relations with a capitalist insofar as we need to work, thus we continue translating and using commercial online platforms (for example, Facebook, WhatsApp, Google) and connective technologies such as cell phones or emails.

We also enter into exploitative relations because we produce unpaid surplus translational value, such as user-generated content. So, even if we don't sell our translational labour, we create translational value produced by socially necessary translational labour-time: that is, the not-so-easily-pinpointable-but-still-determinable translational time needed to implement a particular translation, such as, for example, when the Facebook platform translates the meaningful practice of 'likes' into clients and friends, or the neoliberal system translates philosophically-based 'freedom' into a culture of consumer 'choice'.

---

60   Virno 2001, p. 84.
61   Rossi-Landi 1968, p. 69.
62   Galloway 2004.
63   Terranova 2000.

Echoing the Gramscian distinction between spontaneous and normative grammar, translational production comprises both free and compulsory aspects. In fact, like Tiziana Terranova's free labour,[64] translational labour is voluntary and freely creative, but also compulsory and often unavoidable, because we need to be able to speak outside the idiomatic circles of our family or social regions – for example, we need to write essays in relatively formal (*ergo* translatable) language when in schools, or when speaking to colleagues who do not perform or who have been trained for the same tasks.

Thus, to summarise, translational labour is essentially a circulatory and logistical activity dealing with practical significations, which is value being productive in the expanded realm of the valorisation process, as is typical of post-Fordism and the digital economy more generally.

As we have already noticed, we translate in spontaneous and subjective ways, and we participate in a larger process with a variable degree of instrumentalisation by social forces like capital. In this sense, we can distinguish between objective and subjective translational labour, which can bring us back to the notion of fixed capital. Understanding communication as fixed capital means acknowledging an assemblage between people and machines and subjective and objective aspects of production.

Thus, on the one hand, translational labour interacting with platforms software creates data objects such as information as well as the overall condition of their reciprocal translatability. In this sense, the best example is metrics information, which is a quantitative assessment used for comparing and tracking performance. When an individual checks his Facebook page, information is created in terms of time spent, number of clicks, content produced, links created and so forth.

This person, the worker, is both numerically assessed and constituted by self-quantification practices, produced by tracking and self-tracking that in turn affects his attitudes, dispositions, relationships, preferences and behaviours.[65] The devices behind the working of the digital machine tend to perform subjectivity by propelling the human capacity in a performance-based direction. Workers feed algorithmic media while they are contemporarily fed by them, in a recursive loop.[66] On the one hand, users become identified as subjects by identifying objects, they are monitored and monitor themselves through tools enabling evaluation, reporting and ranking.[67] Thus they become data-objects.

---

64   Terranova 2000.
65   Moore 2018.
66   Beer 2016.
67   Merry 2016.

In this way, subjectivities can be understood processually, since subjectivity is partly acquired and partly constructed by the process of algorithmic 'individuation'.[68]

On the other hand, I also refer to 'data subjects', in order to capture the ways in which involvement in translation implies processes of subjectification – for instance, via the same metrics mentioned above, produced by a variety of tracking and self-tracking practices. Thus, translational subjects may reflect on themselves and their relationships numerically, within a neoliberal logic that is encoded into the platform. Thus, the subject may be in competition with Donald Trump in terms of impression management or number of friends. The distinction between data objects and subjects is intended analytically to emphasise aspects that are present in both categories. Furthermore, as per our discussion in Chapter 4, in the process of subjectification enhanced by subsumption, we are simultaneously subjects and objects.

The two cases I am about to examine exemplify the link between subsumptive relations and communication via translation, albeit to different degrees. For instance, I will show how both the delivery biker and the journalist are subjectively constantly engaging in translations of data in order to make sense of their work and identity. However, objectively, that is, looking at their primary positionality inside the process of creating translatability – and therefore data-objects – they tend to inhabit different positions. While both subjects are integrated into the overall circulatory network of communication/meanings that makes translatability possible, the delivery gig mainly produces data and metrics via labour that focuses on translatability within a concrete social space, such as the urban environment. Conversely, the data-driven journalist re-translates the abstract universe of translatability of big data into narrativisations, therefore bringing back from the abstract sphere of data a relative, and alienated, sense of the concrete.

5 Data Subjects and Data Objects

In both cases, that is, assuming subjects and objects subsumed by the data-commodity form, I pose the same question: what is the relationship between communication practices, translational practices and subsumptive relations? In this first example, I examine the experience of food delivery workers employed by online apps.[69] While platforms use translational labour to extract

---

68 Prey 2018.
69 This is not the first time I have covered this subject: see Briziarelli 2020a; Briziarelli 2020b.

value at the 'objective' level of the labour process, workers mainly use it to fulfil their tasks as well as to rationalise their subjective condition.

Approaching my first question leads us back to the hegemonic framework of subsumptive relations and how coercive and exploitative economic organisations such as the gig economy can be represented and perceived, that is, translated, into 'a necessity recognised and proposed to themselves [the workers] as freedom, and not simply the result of coercion'.[70] Thus, linguistically but also semiotically, we must look for indicators of how poorly paid, unstable and exploitative work can translate into perceived subjective opportunities.

Translational subsumption takes place when appropriating workers' communicational/relational skills at two levels: first, riders must translate the interpersonal relations they once needed in order to manage orders across the company into a communication with a robot/app, which for instance means accepting orders via phones, becoming familiarised with the app and moving across the urban fabric according to its instructions. From this point of view, as Pasquinelli[71] observes, the connective technology-intensive gig economy relies on the translational labour that riders must mobilise at the machinic level, that is, a people-machine interface.

First, the workers' smartphone operates as the platform through which they sell their labour-power in formal-legal terms. By pushing the button 'accept', they freely accept the task. Moreover, because many riders work for multiple platform companies at the same time, the rhetoric of free choice – 'I accept' – combines with a tactical selection of the best offer.

Identification with the romanticised rhetoric of the venture capitalist serves to constitute both a neoliberal and a data subject: riders must make a bet, as they have limited information and even less time, and therefore must be ready like all good entrepreneurs to grasp the opportunity as it arises. Especially in a kind of job in which the boundaries between employment and self-employment are maliciously opaque, pressing the cell phone button 'accept' means translating a compulsive situation (that is, needing to work multiple jobs) into a partial fiction of self-employed discretional business, as well as initiating the production of metrics/data.

The reason I decided to return to the subject is that it exemplifies a basic problem in a very 'spectacular' way: very physical jobs are mediated by cutting edge IT 'machines' such as digital/connective technology, algorithms, and AI. Furthermore, we see the embodied worker as a node in subsumptive relations, creating fixed machinic capital that in turn mediates machines and workers.

70   Gramsci 1971, p. 178.
71   Pasquinelli 2015.

Accordingly, ideal translational subsumption shows how an ideologically structured imagination shapes our discursive practices even when these are not directly commodified. It is as if those practices were indeed subsumed. For instance, if the dominant labour relation inside capitalism is wage-labour, then calling a gig food delivery rider 'self-employed' reveals the ideal subsumption of a relation not subsumed by wage-labour but operating 'as if it were.'[72]

In most countries where these delivery apps are in business, they operate by taking advantage of hybrid subsumption, according to which surplus-value is extracted with no direct control over the riders' labour, which means the capital-labour relations are not mediated by the traditional labour contract that would indicate formal subsumption. In terms of class relations, the position of subordination and dispossession of riders is very much predetermined. However, it is also true that, formally speaking, when the riders accept an order, they *de facto* re-enter exploitative class relations: surplus-value is extracted by the delivery job but also by the translational job of providing (for instance) logistical data to companies about how effectively workers can cover urban ground and display cognitive promptness.

Thus, a fundamental way in which translational labour creates value is by translating analogue reality into digital data about speed, space, the practice of stopping at lights and the rush-hour times in different areas of the city. At the same time, while the rate of exploitation of translational labour is extremely high (because it goes almost completely unpaid) riders recognise the added flexibility and better pay, at least compared to working as a delivery guy for a restaurant, and taste the thrill of bets on multiple orders and/or earning points/credits within a highly gamified labour process. This is how creating data also creates subjects.

In the case of employees involved in so-called data-driven journalism, the task of translation mainly concerns the other side of the circulatory value attached to translation, that is, retranslating the abstracted communication created by metrics, numbers and quantifications, as well as computational language, into news stories.

The universe of information defined as big data represents one of the most fetishised spheres of translatability – it is not by accident that it is so close to the mystifying world of fictitious-capital cryptocurrencies. And this is not simply because of its abstract and quantitative nature but because it consistently dissembles 'people's agency'. While both scholarly and lay discourse typically asso-

---

72   Murray 2004.

ciate data with scientific objectivity, they are never raw but always processed via specific interests and ideologies.[73]

The reason for the selection of this second example is that the production of news stories represents one of those fields that more closely resembles a mechanised and standardised sphere of production, both in relation to information and communication. Like many fields, journalism has been affected by the rise of digital platforms that try to analyse and quantify work – for instance in terms of performance, audience response and the potential success of a topic. In this sense, analytics platforms deliver almost real-time data about a range of audiences' online behaviours, such as clicks, shares, likes and time per page.

While reporters and editors initially considered the use of data to turn their articles into 'clickbait' content,[74] their acceptance of data as a working tool grew considerably over time, to the point that metrics have been integrated in the news production process. Caitlin Petre, for instance, has looked at how journalists used Chartbeat metrics to get real-time information about page views and visitors, social media metrics, sources of traffic, time engaged, geo-location of readers, pinned tweets and posts, as well as comparisons with historical data. Large amounts of information rapidly scrolling across the screen requires a high level of attention and engagement from users.[75]

When it comes to translational work, two aspects of this data-driven job stand out: how journalists retranslate data into more 'analogue' news stories, and how, in the process, they negotiate their identity.

While the narrativisation of data may depict this particular translational labour as involving the de-fetishising of data, that is, the uncovering of insights and stories hidden behind data, the reality is frequently just the opposite. First, because those stories build on the only apparent condition of raw objective data, so, if anything, they increase the layers of opacity mediating that which is being recounted. Second, translating data into visualisations (for example, the typical graphs comparing, ranking and showing trends) – usually the core part of this storytelling process – does indeed provide an important interpretative frame. However, it hardly provides any information about who produced those data and with what interests. And finally, while those typical stories do indicate important trends, connections, comparisons and ranks, they simply ignore the most important journalistic question: that is, why? This, ironically enough, really seems to exemplify a harmful version of the well-known maxim, 'Show, don't tell!'

---

73   Beer 2016.
74   Anderson 2013.
75   Petre 2021.

As in the case of the delivery gig work, journalists also constitute themselves as data subjects by translating an obvious disciplinary and exploitative aspect of the incorporation of technologies into rationalising arguments about 'choice', 'agency' or 'serving the community'. As a level of subsumption that frequently operates at the level of ideology and practical consciousness, ideal translational subsumption mainly concerns the discourse-based processes of subjectivation, because 'capitalism must constitute itself subjectively ... develop the desires and habits necessary for it to perpetuate itself'.[76] According to Robert Prey,[77] in such an environment subjects become managers of themselves and of all social relationships, extending the logic of costs and benefits to affective relations.

As mentioned before, the translation behind 'as if it were' is both objectively imposed as well as subjectively felt by the individual rider, who monitors his/her own productivity, becoming an entrepreneur of the self. Such subjective translation is the basis for the building of hegemony within the gig economy, because instead of relying on solely coercive and hetero-directed mechanisms (such as the app constantly geo-locating riders), gig workers experience self-direction, self-promotion using subjective resources and self-empowerment.[78] As a result, tensions are resolved in the direction of a model of subjectivity and society based on techniques of self-motivation, flexibility and individual performance.

Furthermore, those subjects partly internalise such flexibility as an apologetic ideology of self-enactment and individual choice. The result is a subjectivity that experiences the digital and platform economy via the ambiguities of exploitation and empowerment, along the realisation/self-exploitation and pleasure/pain axes.[79] Most generally, echoing Gaye Tuchman's insights about the strategic ritual of objectivity[80] that journalists perform, the increasing reliance on big data is justified with reference to objectivity appearance: 'big data provides a systematic, unbiased way of making decisions that would lead to more accurate predictions and greater returns'.[81]

Furthermore, Christin and Petre claim that journalists justify their usage of big data by establishing moral boundaries between 'good' and 'bad' metrics: some of them engage in surveillance practices and intrude on privacy,

---

76   Read 2013, p. 114.
77   Prey 2018.
78   Salcel 2010.
79   McRobbie 2011.
80   Tuchman 1972.
81   Mayer-Schonberger and Cukier 2013.

and some of them 'save lives' and produce important knowledge.[82] They also strategically invoke a 'best-case scenario' rhetoric that negotiates the potential dilemma presented by the need for high traffic numbers and editorial quality. Another strategy they use is to domesticate technologies by creating their own *ad hoc* software. Finally, exploiting the liberal ideology of journalism as the great instrument of a healthy public sphere, they tend to reframe metrics as a way to enhance the democratic process: first, everybody can access metrics, thus everybody can test the sources of a given story; second, by means of such access, journalists join the rhetoric of democratic/citizen journalism; finally, the metrics they receive in real time about their story can be framed as democratic feedback, thus measuring the level of public concerns on a given topic/matter.

Clearly, formal and real translational subsumption often overlap each other. In the case of gig-economy occupations, this happens rather often, as the very 'on-demand' and 'online' nature of jobs such as delivery services causes them constantly to colonise new spheres and more of their workers' time. In this sense, the fluid terrain between formal and real translational subsumption constitutes one of the 'bloodiest' translational battlegrounds between labour and capital in the current political-economic context. That is because translational labour is needed to circulate and exchange information and value across different social spheres.

As I have examined in previous studies,[83] illustrative of this is the online delivery app Deliveroo's communication guideline for managers,[84] which reveals the constant effort to translate subordination of employees into a discourse of self-employment: 'independent supplier' instead of 'employee', 'worker' or 'staff'; 'onboarding' instead of 'hiring'; 'supplier agreement' instead of 'employment contract'; 'working with Deliveroo', instead of 'working for Deliveroo'; 'riders choosing an area of work' instead of 'assigning riders to a zone'; 'Kit', 'equipment' or 'branded clothing' instead of 'uniform'; 'logging in' instead of 'starting a shift', 'starting a session' or 'clocking in'; 'fee per delivery' instead of 'piece rate'; and finally 'rider community' instead of 'fleet'.

Finally, I would like briefly to discuss a kind of hybrid translational subsumption. This kind of subsumption describes how capitalism can take advantage of a particular social activity without necessarily controlling it, thus when no formal or real subsumption has been achieved. Accordingly, hybrid translational subsumption manifests the inherent dialectical agency and outcomes

---

82   Christin and Petre 2020.
83   Briziarelli 2020a.
84   Briziarelli 2020a.

of translation. Therefore, if capitalist translation ideally aims at creating pure abstract communicational space for value exchange purposes, it cannot avoid producing hybrid translational space in the process. As I will be discussing in more detail in the next chapter, these processes can be identified in the domains of urban space and technology.

Thus, while the deployment of information/communication technology is mostly aimed at intensifying and increasing control of the typical post-Fordist labour process,[85] such control is never complete, and the consistent reality of different modes of connectivity (for example, via mobiles and computers) – combined with the implied necessity of constantly translating for communication from one device to another – produces the need for hybridity and reversibility. In fact, delivery workers can exploit such sociality to retranslate flexibility and freedom into a politicised denunciation of unfair working conditions Thus, logistical and instrumental practices are translated into strategies of protest, as the wave of protests of the last three years in Europe so well displays. As I argued elsewhere,[86] gig workers take advantage of such hybridity in order to reappropriate the space of the city as a space for political mobilisation and to antagonise capitalism.

While the main narrative of this chapter conveys a logic of reproduction and capitalist subordination via ICTs, it is important to notice how ultimately, hybrid subsumption reveals the inherently intractable productiveness of translational practices, which cannot produce new abstract-logistical venues for meaning and value without creating conditions that are potentially subversive and antagonistic to capital. Thus, translation, even in its purely subsumptive guise, cannot establish homologies and equivalence without irremediably violating them. In this sense, I would like to conclude this chapter on a more optimistic note, by looking at supersumptive politics in the domain of communication.

6 Active Supersumptive Politics: Freire and the 150-Hours Laboratory on Communication

This chapter has so far explored the relationship between subsumptive relations and communication practices. Based on the theoretical assumption of this book, the question is not simply whether communication can work both

---

85   Moore 2018.
86   Briziarelli 2018.

functionally and 'difunctionally' *vis-à-vis* subsumption, but how it operates concretely. In the following case, I discuss how communication can be utilised to reverse its 'ideal subsumption' /ideological function. The case I am discussing here invites us to consider communication as a tool for adult education, a context in which workers can enrich their knowledge and practical skills, and a crucial political ground, where consciousness, material needs and interests, material limitations and class relations are all in play.

The so-called 150-hours case took place in 1970s Italy, a very particular period for the social history of the country – as a matter of fact, the episode recounted here took place right after so-called 'Hot Autumn' of 1969, which represented one of the few high points of the labour movement in Western Europe. As Italy's decade-long (and so-called) economic miracle started to lose momentum, it gave away to a considerable amount of social unrest, grounded in the organisational capabilities of a very strong labour movement. In fact, the supersumptive politics of 150 hours must be understood in the context of struggles promoted by rank-and-file workers' organisations, rather than with reference to the Communist Party and the main trade unions. Such mobilisation was associated with important debates conveyed by radical publishing venues such as *Quaderni Rossi, Classe Operaia*, and organisations such as Potere Operaio and Lotta Continua.[87] All these initiatives could be grouped under the heading of autonomism, which explicitly promoted antagonism to real subsumption by asserting workers' ability to define their own tasks, interests and ways of class struggle.

The '150 hours' constituted a credit the worker could use for purposes of adult education: it represented the result of hard negotiations between workers in heavy-industry and capital, focused on entitlement to paid leave in order to pursue educational goals such as starting or completing a degree. The scholarly documentation of '150 hours' is surprisingly limited. Maurizio Lichtner, one of the few sources on this subject, defines the experience as follows: 'the 150-hours courses in lower secondary schools have changed their nature, and can be viewed as a "laboratory", awaiting new, more adequate forms of provision'.[88]

The project of adult education was an aspect of workers' material demands, but it also represented an affirmation of the right to access culture and knowledge in the face of the Taylorisation and mechanisation of the labour force, with its implied risk of the alienation of the worker from product, fellow coworker and culture. Self-organised adult education was a way of pushing back

---

87   Wright 2002.
88   Lichtner 1991, p. 5.

against real subsumption's project of constituting an adequate worker. First of all, the access to knowledge that was demanded was not only intended in the Gramscian sense – the acquisition of more and more control over the process of production, as per the case of the 1919–20 factory councils – because it was based on the fact that most workers had not completed the full cycle of mandatory schooling. Frequently, lack of a school degree was preventing many workers from obtaining better contractual conditions.

The assumption was that only by mastering the hegemonic culture could workers critically discern between what was in their interest and what was ideologically mystified. Furthermore, once that critical discernment could be attained, knowledge was supposed to enhance the acquisition of the workers' own collective identity – in autonomist terms, to bring about a process of labour re-composition. Pushing back against the mystification created by their working conditions represented an overt contestation of subsumption as subjectification, but also a way of opposing the tendencies toward deskilling that workers under real subsumption frequently experienced.

The specific proposal consisted of 150 hours that the worker could take off over a period of three years, in order to acquire formal education while still receiving a wage. This reflected the workers' desire to update their skills, but also, more importantly, to change the realm of the factory in social and cultural terms. The idea that part of the salary could be translated into cultural and intellectual capital that was not exploitable within the factory's productive system implied the formulation of a political demand for the humanisation of the worker, but also for an alternative socialisation, outside subsumptive relations. It represented a profound alteration of the relationship between product and producer, commodity and labour, and was also a reappropriation of socially necessary labour relative to surplus labour time, a struggle in the terrain of value.

Once the 150 hours were attained, in 1973 a lively debate about who was to educate whom, why, how, where, when and with what objectives arose among workers. This debate took place in a moment when the revolutionary ideas of Paulo Freire were particularly popular in Europe and in Italy; during that time, Freire was residing in Switzerland and was particularly receptive to factory struggles in Northern Italy. His pedagogic[89] method, the same used to raise consciousness among the peasantry in Latin America, contributed significantly to enriching the 150-hours experience. The philosophy behind the methods was based on attaining knowledge and the use of the language of a given com-

---

89   Freire, 2000.

munity. It was not 'imagined community',[90] but a community of practice, a productive and material one, the expression of the community's concrete perceptions, emotions, vision for life, beliefs, fears, hopes, aspirations and individual and collective identity.

Freire's method worked in developmental ways at the molecular level: from the experience of individuals, it opened out into the experience of collectives. It represented an effort to recompose a sense of class out of the most decomposing aspects of real subsumption and the alienation brought about by the division of labour. The workers themselves needed to become the active agents of a process aiming at an organic construction of knowledge. Freire thought that understanding should not be fragmentary or too focused on the contingent, and had to be considered a social process. His idea was to construct knowledge out of semantic clusters and thematic foci concerning the everyday lives of the workers.

Accordingly, themes for discussion included everyday words like 'car', 'job', 'family' and 'city', which were deconstructed into their component syllables and then reconstructed into new words, presenting daily life from another point of view. For Freiere, such deconstruction and reconstruction of the given represented a method that could be used to enhance critical reflection on social reality. Dialogue was conceived as a fundamental condition of this kind of education. It operated as a counter-translation mechanism, according to which many assumptions about how to associate meanings (and what value to place on them) were reflectively examined, rather than passively received from above. This was the negative moment of a positive re-signification of work and life experience.

Councils were organised so that workers, trade unionists and teachers could work together on the generation of themes. These could emerge from individual stories, first orally narrated, then transcribed into written texts. The narrative stage was based on the idea of self-bibliographies, based on the philosopher and pedagogist Jerome Bruner.[91] Bruner aimed at re-signifying education as a social project that takes proper account of the historical and social context of its participants. The workers' narrations of their own lives were examined as epistemically valuable examples of intuition, as 'the intellectual technique of arriving at plausible but tentative formulations without going through the analytical steps by which such formulations would be found to be valid or invalid conclusions'.[92] From the individual stories, common fea-

---

90   Anderson 1991.
91   Bruner 1971.
92   Bruner 1971, p. 13.

tures gradually emerged: the early abandonment of the school, the formal subsumption experience of the passages from artisanship to industrial work, the urban transition from the rural world, or the migration from Southern Italy.

The workers divided themselves into groups and started to deepen their interest in scientific subjects, which were inspired by individual stories and individual life experiences. Their curiosity, at first spontaneously emerging from lived experience, was supposed to evolve into an epistemological quest, that is, a curiosity framed by a structured epistemological approach. The passage from the spur-of-the-moment mode to disciplined learning constituted the method of study for both the individual and the group. Thus, all topics at first emerged from auto-biographical narration, later to become explicit objects of study: for example, the condition of work inside the factory, health, the rural-urban relationship, the relationship between workers and state, the relationship between workers and culture. Education provided knowledge that could make intelligible the dialectic between immediate lived experiences and the theoretical awareness of broader social processes.

Each topic was then developed through the articulation of sub-topics. For instance, in relation to the working environment, the question might be how the factory works: the role of capital, the labour force and the wage, the internal structure of the factory, hierarchies, qualifications, control of labour and the capitalist organisation of labour. The exploration of specific sub-topics was often supported by the presence of experts in the field, to ensure that each subject could be approached with the highest possible degree of awareness. At the end of each session, both at the individual and the collective level, the participants were required to write a text that was intended as a report on what had been done. This allowed all groups to share in the work of other groups. All texts were then gathered in an annual anthology. This represented the positive and reconstructive moment, where the meanings that had been discovered became a new frame with which to interpret experiences.

According to this new educational method, subjects were not compartmentalised, and there was no differentiation between grammar and history. What was learned about history was then transcribed on the blackboard and the notebook of each person so that they could learn at the same time their own language, a class idiom as a fundamental class composition tool. Similarly, maths did not consist of abstract exercises with numbers anymore. Numbers and formulas were inductively extracted from concrete reality, from indexes of inflation, wages and productivity. Students were taught how to read the graphs that often appear in newspapers or in internal factory reports, and they studied how to calculate the percentages used to assess taxes. The induction of knowledge from material reality was fundamental for the workers and allowed what Lukács defines as the passage from imputed to empirical consciousness.[93]

The experience of the 150 hours was guided by three main principles: the principle of materialist constructivism; the principle of analysis; and the principle of participation. First, the experience was driven by materialist and constructivist principles because education relied on the construction of knowledge based on the concrete and material experience of life and one's own political motivations. This was an epistemology that was very much based on action and the daily experience of both individuals and collectives, rather than (meta) discourse about this experience. The Freirain assumption shaping this experience insisted that knowledge was not transferable; it needed to be constructed and constituted in every single mind.

Another challenge in the construction of knowledge and consciousness was the dilemma between spontaneous curiosity and disciplined examination. The challenge, as Gramsci puts it, was about 'how to move beyond social immediacy without at the same time destroying spontaneous impulses',[94] so that common sense became good sense and spontaneity was transformed into critical consciousness. The tension between creative elaboration and the necessity of structuring knowledge exemplifies a fundamental aspect of the construction of an (alternative) hegemony, which for its attainment and maintenance relies both on structural conditions and human agency, such as the relations of production and the will of the social group, and the idiosyncrasies of individuals.

In other words, experience represented the working out of an analytical principle, because the construction of knowledge implies a method of analysis that explores, in a deep and disciplined way, the objects of its speculations. The objective was to combine spontaneous intellectual interests with a disciplined analytical method. For Gramsci, such a pedagogy aimed to be socially transformative, and, to accomplish that, it needed to become equally focused on the mastering of conventional/traditional knowledge. In this sense, in my view, the analytical facet of the 150 hours' pedagogy represented an attempt to pass from the chaotic and contradictory nature of 'common sense'[95] to the inherently coherent and critical nature of 'good sense'. The transformation of 'common sense' into 'good sense' is thus an 'intellectual unity and an ethic in conformity with a conception of reality that has gone beyond common sense and become, if only within narrow limits, a critical conception'.[96] If subsumption, as we have

---

93 Gramsci 1975.
94 Gramsci 1971, p. 40.
95 Gramsci 1971, p. 422.
96 Gramsci 1971, p. 333.

mentioned several times, is systematically associated with abstractions understood as mystifications, then the project of elevating common sense into good sense represents a powerful instance of supersumptive politics.

Finally, a participatory principle was at work, because the definition of themes and topics and their treatment was based on discussion and dialogue, which was intended as a dialectical tool that could enhance mediation between the individual level and the collective sharing of thought. The collective dialogue generated the schematisation, the problematisation and the approach to consciousness. The thematisation corresponded to the stage of the process in which collectively, through dialogue, the participants could identify particular themes. The problematisation consisted of the process of analysis of themes, which were deconstructed and then re-elaborated. 'Approaching awareness' is a concept used by Freire[97] to refer to the permanent attainment of consciousness: starting from individual experience, which is objectified through theoretical study, one attempts to attain a critical distance that allows for a more mature awareness.

The supersumptive process would start by critically analysing the social reality of the workers: the very words used to describe their environment were the first lexical 'input' to be incorporated into the literacy project. Based on that self-questioning, each group would produce generative topics such as 'work', 'family', 'disposable time', 'dissatisfaction' and 'the boss'.

Freire's alphabetisation method attained the highest level of de-fetishisation and de-alienation of language, in the sense that, contrary to a highly codified language such as computational binary language, the purpose of which is to create data, language for Freire was mostly attached to the practical and productive experience of the speaker. So, for instance, instead of having students memorise phonemes and then combine them together to form words – a mechanical approach to meaning – Freire would start from words deriving from the concrete experience of the workers and proceed through experiential association. In every session, before adding new words, participants would reflect on the meaning of those words in relation to their own lives. Thus, to speak a language meant to understand reality critically, to enter the social community through humanisation and not dehumanisation, with a recognition of the right to exist and to exist freely and happily.

To alphabetise does not mean to treat words as 'bricks' or 'tools' but to allow us to relate to associated life in humanised ways, as a free human being capable of relating to others and to objects. The source of illiteracy was not the

---

97   Freire 2000.

lack of study but the lack of material possibilities of living. So, to alphabetise and learn means actively to perform supersumption against social and mental-conceptual power relations, both inside and outside the labour process.

Speaking/communicating is the inextricable unity of reflection and action, that is, productive praxis, that is, transformative praxis. It is also situated transformative praxis, though the same word may have a different transformative force inside the labour process and out, in one part of the city but not in the rest, at one time but not forever. Freire was particularly fascinated by metaphors as disalienating tools: that is, because the introduction of a new metaphor re-signifies established experience in the same defamiliarising way as poetry; it calls attention to something that is at least peripherally or subliminally relevant to their experience. In metaphors, people re-encounter each other. Freire's careful and strategic attention to the adequate metaphors for collective speech about a given topic represents a beautiful counter-hegemonic aspect of translational labour, which cannot be completely subordinated to capital's command.

CHAPTER 6

Domesticated Living Bodies and the Social Space of Subsumption

The city is subject to contradictory questionings. Wanting to overcome such contradictions is a bad utopia. On the contrary, it needs to be shaped. The city, throughout its history , has been the perennial experiment that shapes contradiction and shapes conflict.[1]

The development of the means of labour into machinery is not an accidental moment of capital, but is rather the historical reshaping of the traditional, inherited means of labour into a form adequate to capital. The accumulation of knowledge and of skill, of the general productive forces of the social brain, is thus absorbed into capital, as opposed to labour, and hence appears as an attribute of capital, and more specifically of *fixed capital*, in so far as it enters into the production process as a means of production proper. *Machinery* appears, then, as the most adequate form of *fixed capital* and fixed capital, in so far as capital's relations with itself are concerned, appears as *the most adequate form of capital* as such. In another respect, however, in so far as fixed capital is condemned to an existence within the confines of a specific use-value, it does not correspond to the concept of capital, which, as value, is indifferent to every specific form of use-value, and can adopt or shed any of them as equivalent incarnations. In this respect, as regards capital's external relations, it is *circulating capital* which appears as the adequate form of capital, and not fixed capital.[2]

∴

---

1 Rizzi, in Gil 2018.
2 Marx 1973, p. 694.

Both the 2007–8 financial crisis and the still ongoing Covid-19-induced crisis have accelerated the emergence and consolidation of the social scenario described by tropes such as 'datafication',[3] 'algorithmic culture'[4] and 'algorithmic life'.[5]

When it comes to labour mediated by ICTs, despite consistent lay and scholarly interest, academic research on this matter has generated little critical theory, by which I mean that particular way of grasping social processes that can inform radical antagonism against capitalism. For instance, in the context of platforms studies, as Simon Joyce[6] has recently pointed out, these mostly uncritical tendencies have produced an oversimplification of our understanding of platform work, which is caught in the binary opposition of techno-optimism and pessimism, as well as being sclerotised by the consistent tendency towards technological determinism. In this sense, while I think the study of capitalism propelled by ICT is fundamental to understanding current subsumptive relations, such perspectives can also help go beyond some of those issues.

More specifically, in this chapter I interrogate how the reconfiguration of space, implemented by organisational technologies of production that have been deployed in response to the Covid-19 confinement lockdown measures (such as 'remote working'), have affected subsumptive relations.

Spatially, the Covid-19-induced crisis has pushed forwards the process of socialisation of production:[7] from the manufacturing plant to the so-called social factory, and now, forcefully and abruptly, from the general social factory that extended beyond the workshop and office, to the private sphere of our homes.

The hybridity of production here derives from the fact that most of the domesticated work is *de facto* formally/contractually independent, but also from the fact that we are still producing surplus-value for our employers, but in an apparently less coercive environment. As we shall see, this creates the opportunity for tactical politics such as *la perruque*. Domestication is then simultaneously a potential reversion to formal subsumption *and* an implementation in terms of real subsumption. Furthermore, referring to Chapter 4's discussion of the contradictory nature of subsumptive relations, this chapter examines through the optic of domestication the co-constitutive tension between labour

---

3 Van Dijck 2014.
4 Striphas 2015.
5 Amoore and Piotukh 2016.
6 Joyce 2020.
7 See Tronti 1972; Bologna and Fumagalli 1997.

control/disciplinisation, *la perruque*-style social practices, and neoliberalism's ideological attempt to shape workers as self-enacted, self-controlled and self-exploited 'machineries'.

1 Space and Subsumption

This manuscript has proceeded as a journey through multiple levels of abstraction of subsumption, that is from the simple abstract to the complex concrete, passing from an essentially conceptual approach to material social relations of subsumption, and finally to practices of subsumption such as communication and translation and now spatial practices. The conceptual link between subsumption and space is of a co-constitutive kind: subsumption produces the conditions for the social production of space under capitalist forms, and the social production of space under capitalist forms provides the conditions to produce subsumption.

Subsumption understood through space is not just an ode to concreteness but, as will be clarified by viewing it through the prism of Henry Lefebvre's work,[8] a synthesis of both the abstract and concrete. In fact, from Lefebvre's point of view, space appears as the paradox of a concrete abstraction, that is, an abstraction that becomes true through social practices.[9] Spatialising subsumption via Lefebvre's perspective means closing the circle of our examination in two ways. First, if the goal of his book was to unpack and open the framework of interpretation of subsumption, via the examination of instances of the intersection between capitalist production of social space and capitalist spaces of production, I articulate the physical, the mental-logical and the historical-political dimensions of subsumption.

Second, subsumption has been frequently treated as a logical and social process understood on a plane well above the social practices of embodied subjects; in this sense, Lefebvre's sensibility for the embodied subject, his idea of an acting intersubjectivity may alter this theoretical prejudice without necessary falling into 'subjectivism' or even some kind of a 'cult of personality' as Althusser reproached Marxist humanism.[10] Thus, synthetically put, subsumption is articulated by social relations, power, immanent contradictions, the social practices of embodied subjects and space. This represents the concrete enrichment I have tried to provide in this book.

---

8   Lefebvre 1991; Lefebvre 2003.
9   Stanek 2011.
10 Althusser 1964.

This effort to maintain a broad but unitary theory of subsumption is also important in relation to, for instance, the just examined link between communication/translation and subsumption: in both cases, subsumption comprises practices that are both material/embodied and mental/symbolic. Furthermore, spatialising subsumption represents another important point of view from which to understand subsumption as the contradictory and unstable (power) relations of a hegemonic system:

> Hegemonic power organises the configuration of space to make it consistent with their social, economic and political objectives. Space thus produced is, however, not just an image of a social relation projected on to screen of the earth. As it is a physical object, space constitutes an active moment, which can be in conflict with hegemonic social power.[11]

In this sense, abstract space, as understood by Lefebvre, is the privileged space of subsumptive relations, and reflects the hegemonic combination of consent and coercion, appeasement and violence:

> Abstract space, the space of the bourgeoisie and of capitalism, bound up as it is with exchange (of goods and commodities, as of written and spoken words, etc) depends on consensus more than any space before it. It hardly seems necessary to add that within this space violence does not always remain latent or hidden. One of its contradictions is that between the appearance of security and the constant threat, and indeed the occasional cruption, of violence.[12]

In capitalism, space indeed forms an indispensable regulatory element within which to contain class struggle and economic crisis. In fact, the social production of space, as understood by Lefebvre, involves real subsumption of spaces by means of spatial bounding and spatial integration.[13] On the one hand, the instrumental reconstitution of space can create boundaries so that its inhabitants are obliged to relate only through capitalist interactions, with all non-capitalist relations sealed off. In space, this may materialise with 'no-trespassing' boundaries, fences, walls or other physical limitations, but also via the need for a fenced community, an administrative building defended by armed force. On the other hand, space is lived by everyday practices tactically

---

11   Mizuoka 1991, p. 8.
12   Lefebvre 1991, p. 223.
13   Mizuoka 1991.

and opportunistically, which means that every limit is just a temporary barrier eventually trespassed or re-territorialised.

Another way in which space is tied to subsumption is through spatial integration. This process of real subsumption of relative space, or spatial integration,[14] is what Marx termed 'annihilation of space' by means of communication and transportation; the phrase currently refers to the processes implemented by highways, high-speed trains, internet and telecommunications. But again, as per fences and borders, lines of communication, even when constructed with a specific capitalist goal in mind, end up confronting the disruptiveness and excess of meaning that social intercourse consistently creates.

In this chapter, I look at this tension between the domination of space and the tendencies that tend to escape such control, with a specific focus on the interregnum between public urban social life and the domestic sphere. Such liminality is contextualised with reference to a moment of abrupt reconfiguration, that is, the pandemic of Covid-19, during which public space became a new battleground in which privative experiences confronted the sense of and for a polity, or public life, and every public space was faced with the threat of becoming a mere place of production and/or consumption.

According to Lefebvre, historically the production of social space entailed the production of a distinguished spatial sphere for social production and biological reproduction, according to the so-called process of 'localisation'.[15] In this sense, capitalism progressively assumes the position of the dominant productive logic; via subsumptive dynamics, it has increased localisation according to the same logic of division of labour that characterises real subsumption. For instance, the domestic sphere in a capitalist society constitutes both the sphere of biological reproduction as well as an important sphere for Marx's small scale circulation, the M–C–M circuit in which labour-power is reproduced via commodity acquisition and consumption; this sphere is distinguished but also inextricably linked to the space where social relations of production are reproduced: Marx's general circulation of capital.

Such complexity is accounted for by Lefebvre via a tendency to approach social-spatial phenomena using a triadic, dialectical framework. When it comes to the general approach and goals of this book, a crucial aspect of Lefebvre's take on space consists in his trying to keep united the theorisation of spatial production, on the one hand, and the ways in which real subjects actually experience space, on the other. Thus, for instance, his triadic model of

---

14 Harvey 1982.
15 Lefebvre 1991, p. 32.

spatial practices, representations of space and representational spaces cannot be understood without acknowledging how embodied subjects live it, which corresponds to space perceived through spatial practices, space conceived through the representation of space and space lived through space of representations.

The approach to the spatialisation of subsumption could start anywhere, as the productive activity takes place in both temporal and spatial dimensions. In this chapter, in order to study the phenomenon of 'domestication' with the help of Lefebvre's insights, we can start with the process of urbanisation. The urban is a social-spatial dimension that I think pertains to the middle-range molecular scale I mentioned in Chapter 4, where both individuals and collective subjectivities concretely move around and interact. As I will elaborate later on, it is where strategic and tactical practices, structure and agency meet. Furthermore, the urban dimension is where the abstractive force of capitalism meets everydayness and localised differences.

The point of view provided by Lefebvre's spatial theory is theoretically extremely important, because it helps me to explore a crucially ambiguous productive potential of subsumption. Subsumption is not just a parasitic dynamic that translates existing social places into capitalist spaces, it also creates its own:

> The reproduction of the relations of production entails the extension as well as the enlargement of the mode of production and its material base. On the one hand, capitalism spread across the entire world to subordinate preexisting productive forces and transform them for its purpose, as Marx understood it. On the other hand, capitalism formed new sectors of production, exploitation and domination. These sectors include leisure, everyday life, knowledge (*connaissance*) and art, and, finally, urbanisation. What are the results of this double process? Capitalism has maintained itself by extending across space in its entirety. Starting from a small number of countries at the time of Marx, it has conquered the globe by constituting the world market and celebrated colossal victories (notably with the creation of leisure, tourism, etc), and this despite a number of serious defeats, revolutions and revolts.[16]

Lefebvre's thesis, going beyond the traditional understanding of the city/countryside, points to a long process in which industrialisation and urbanisation

---

16   Lefebvre 1972, p. 152.

constitute a dialectical unity: while industrialisation provides the conditions and means of urbanisation, urbanisation emerges from the spread of industrial production across the entire globe. Urbanisation dissolves the city as an identifiable social and physical object; it is the social production of social space subsumed by capital production.

What characterises the process of urbanisation is the systematic exploitation and commodification of urban space. Thus, space, as with labour, becomes at the same time a means of production of surplus-value as well as a commodity, produced, valorised and exchanged. Lefebvre does not simply refer to physical lands, like real estate, but social space, the ensemble of social relations inhabiting a given space. Thus, for instance, the value of a gentrified area of a given city, as opposed to a depressed one, does not only depend on the real estate market but also on the capability to attract and sustain particular demographics, classes and social practices.

This intense process of commodification of space tends then to recreate the tension inherent in any commodity: the contradiction between use-value and exchange-value, productive and unproductive space, and abstract and differential space. This tension is reflective of the same tensions characterising subsumptive relations. Again, urban space is not simply capitalist space. The urban represents a meso level of abstraction and analysis between the level of private and ordinary life and the global defined as institutions, the state and the market; it thus mediates the other two levels. Considered as a capitalist social form, urban space is also defined by 'centrality', which refers to the generical possibility of social gathering and communication. This consists of a collection of contradictory and mutually conditioned elements. Centrality does not refer to any physical location but to a form of associated life within a built environment. Its logic represents the synchronicity of objects and people that can be assembled around a given point:

> The urban is defined as the place where people walk around, find themselves standing before and inside piles of objects, experience the intertwining of the threads of their activities until they become unrecognisable, entangle situations in such a way that they engender unexpected situations.[17]

In the end, Lefebvre's conceptualisation of space represents a formidable conceptual framework, one that helps us to see how power relations – such as the

---

17   Lefebvre 2003, p. 39.

one instrumental to the production of surplus-value – operate, at the same time, within a complexity of pre-existing social relations developing in time and space, crucially contributing to their reproduction, reshaping them, and being reshaped by them in turn.

2 The Covid-19 and Determinate Supersumption

The generalised and quick spread of the Covid-19 disease caused an array of restrictions on the mobility of people and goods (that is, curfews, quarantines, stay-at-home and shelter-in-place orders) intended to contain and prevent further infections. As a result, schools, universities, restaurants and other 'non-essential' businesses closed. By April 2020, close to half of the world's population was under lockdown. The effort to flatten the curve of contagions caused what many IMF economists defined as the Great Lockdown 2020, with a projected cumulative GDP loss of nine trillion US dollars.[18]

To explore the concrete ramifications of subsumptive relations considered in spatial terms, I examine the relation between digital labour and production of urban space in the time of the Covid-19 pandemic. I show how determinate supersumption via digital space of production and its domesticated subjects manifest as both the source of and the remedy to the Covid-induced crisis. I claim that one of the most significant aspects of the pandemic crisis has been the production of new social spaces under the pressure of contradictory subsumptive dynamics, more specifically, the tension between the stalling mobility of productive circuits in 'locked-down' conditions and the compensatory increase in productivity through dynamics of real subsumption, which comes to encompass new sites due to the accelerating propagation of digital connectivity and its distinctive realm: space that operates as a digital spatial fix.[19]

Those fixes, as we have already mentioned, represent a materialisation of determinate supersumption: the evidence of the instability of capital's subsuming relations and their resilience.

Such a fix in digital and spatial terms represents a compensatory response to a Covid-19-induced circulatory crisis, which can be described as the manifestation of contradictory subsumptive phenomena in terms of the production and realisation of surplus-value, but also as the opportunity to unleash a new

---

18   imf.org 2020.
19   See Harvey 2001a; Greene and Joseph 2015.

wave of real subsumption based on digital technology. I will exemplify this by examining how the private residences of many workers are being really subsumed as digital abstract space (that is, a logistical space constituted by the synergic encounter between digital platforms and subjects that operate in a machinic fashion), which tend to be shaped by multiple overlapping spheres of action, which makes them *domesticated*.[20]

2.1 Social Spatial Fixes

As we have already mentioned, the built environment produced by the process of urbanisation has become the main stage of the logistical and circulatory dimension of contemporary capitalism.[21] The famous passage already quoted in Marx's *Grundrisse*, describing the annihilation of space through time, gets restated within the context of urban space, which is being reshaped by information and communication technologies as effective tools to overcome space/time barriers in the sphere of circulation.[22]

Such a process of production of urban space via both digital machines and bricks and mortar[23] – the emerging post-pandemic capitalist paradigm, exacerbated by increased digitisation – *allegedly* contributes to the rise of the so-called Fourth Industrial Revolution,[24] based on the integration of AI, big data, robotics into the circuits of capital, and technological automation, all boosted by giant tech companies. The semantic (and social) field inhabited by technological revolutions, artificial intelligence, smart cities and hyperconnectivity points to an ideological dynamic that functions in the domain of ideal subsumption. Many Frankfurt School thinkers such as Adorno, Marcuse and Horkheimer refer to this tendency as a technological rationality that tries to transform all everyday life into a 'world of instrumentalities',[25] in which reason is the rationality of domination, *ergo* of subsumption.

---

20 Bologna 1997.
21 See Andrijasevic and Sacchetto 2017; Bologna 2018.
22 Manzerolle and Kjøsen 2015.
23 Graham 2020.
24 My qualification of the alleged Fourth Revolution reflects the importance of not accepting this notion un-reflexively in its technological deterministic sense of historical change, or its ideological connotations. As Moll recently stated:
>Portraying rapid technological development as a bold, new industrial revolutions a far stronger ideological strategy for those seeking to mobilise political, social and economic forces to secure their position of dominance against these threats than a whimpered appeal that we revive and repair the Third Industrial Revolution in which we actually continue to live. (Moll 2021, p. 30.)

In the last chapter I will take up the discourse on technological revolutions once again.
25 Marcuse 1968, p. 18.

As I will elaborate below, the digitalisation process, propelled by practices such as e-commerce, telecommuting, consumer demands, last-mile delivery, virtual tourism/attendance of events, digitalisation of public services and smart city models, consists of technological changes that reveal a spatial fix of a specific kind: one that simultaneously contains the seeds of crisis while also laying out the conditions for a surge of capital circulation and an increase in its mobility. This is, in my view, another important manifestation of the instability of subsumptive relations, which must consistently renegotiate their control over the social relations of production of surplus-value as well as over the constant production of differential elements, which in turn tend to antagonise or unsettle the homogenising function of subsumption under exchange-value and capitalist forms.

In this sense, digital media constitutes both the material conditions for capital accumulation and circulation as well the necessary disciplinary apparatus to exert control over workers via automation and surveillance, data gathering and interpretation, implementing real subsumption by intensifying worker productivity, for example by integrating algorithms, global-scale production and social reproduction.[26] In other words, digital media works at the same time as a tool of production, circulation and consumption.

Reacting against the circulatory restrictions introduced in the wake of the pandemic, platform capitalism finds in the spaces of the city both its new barriers as well as spatial fixes to cope with such barriers. As we already mentioned in the previous chapter, (spatial) fixes are temporary and contradictory solutions. In fact, *fix* means both investing in fixed capital and fixating capital in place, and those two aspects contradict each other. In fact, the geographical/physical anchoring of capital makes it less prone to be realised because it cannot move:

> The vast quantities of capital fixed in place act as a drag upon the capacity to realise a spatial fix elsewhere ... If capital does move out, then it leaves behind a trail of devastation and devaluation; the de-industrialisations experienced in the heartlands of capitalism ... in the 1970s and 1980s are cases in point. If capital does not or cannot move ... then over-accumulated capital stands to be devalued directly through the onset of a deflationary recession or depression.[27]

---

26 See Baldwin 2020; Casilli 2020.
27 Harvey 2003, p. 116.

Capitalism thus overcomes spatial barriers by fixing infrastructures of production (for example, factories, roads, power supplies), in order to overcome space by reducing transport and communication costs. However, such tension between fixity and mobility is destined to create the need for new spatial fixes, because the physical fixation of capital tends to imprison capital, making it more static and less able to respond to everchanging political and economic scenarios. For this reason, Harvey describes how, historically, spatial fixes tend to create the condition for further future fixes, in order to fix the issues created by the previous round of fixes.

Compared to traditional fixes, platform capitalism has generated digital fixes that operate with considerably fewer geographical and physical fixations. The prompt re-localisation of production during the pandemic points to this dynamism: in a few weeks, a significant part of capital production was able to pass from offices to houses, thus simultaneously moving new elements of production into the private sphere while intensifying those that were already located there.

Especially exemplary are those productive activities that can be performed via digital means, which exacerbate digital labour and the creation of what I will define as digital abstract space. The transition to remote working and the expansion of gig work demonstrated how digital media infrastructures represent fixed capital already in place and capable of responding more effectively to the abrupt changes caused by the pandemic and its consequent circulatory restrictions.

Digitalised work provides the conditions for digital spatial fixes in the sense that the digital realm is currently 'where capital seeks freedom from contemporary limits'.[28] However, while I agree with Marcus Green and David Joseph about digital space being material and not a mere representation, I also think that such space possesses a distinctive way to provide 'fixes', which is exemplified by the pandemic crisis of Covid-19. I argue that digital space relies on a combination of different kinds of capital: on the one hand, internet-based technologies necessitate capital fixated in immovable physical infrastructures such as home computers, servers, power grids, fibre and mined minerals; on the other hand, those fixes are able, comparatively more than other kinds of spatialised fixes, to harness and mobilise flexible capital, that is, people's living labour. More specifically, those fixes do not simply harness labour capacity but also labourers' subjectivity,[29] becoming a new and dynamic form of fixed capital.[30]

---

28   Greene and Joseph 2015.
29   Armano, Murgia and Teli 2017.
30   Read 2013.

Such a tendency to combine fixed and circulating capital was already pointed out by Marx when he said that 'fixed capital' is 'man himself',[31] because while machinery is understood as crystallised human intelligence, human intelligence also absorbs and 'learns' from machines.

The renewed dynamicity of an otherwise less movable capital becoming machinic leads us to frame the Covid-19 pandemic crisis from a particular perspective, which demonstrates contradictions at two levels: one, crisis as inner contradictions within the capitalist system; and two, the dialectics of crisis which can be understood as both contractive and expansive capital circulation and accumulation. The regressive/contractive side of crisis would suggest a connection between economic downturns and the unmaking of the conditions of subsumption; as such, subsumptive capitalist forms seem to lose their grip on society. Clover[32] advances a persuasive insight about the intimate link between crisis and expansion of subsumption, which takes place in two main ways. Firstly, crisis can lead to recognition of the idea of a spatial fix: such processes trigger subsumptive dynamics in order to provide fixes to the economic downturn. Secondly, and similar to the case of machinic fixed capital, crisis can actually trigger a massive expansion of the 'subsumed' sector of the economy, as exemplified by the spectacular growth of the gig economy during the last months.

As a whole, this dynamicity of digital fixes provides surplus-value through subsumption at two levels: real subsumption of labourers' subjectivity, which becomes domesticated, and the formal subsumption of environments such as the private sphere of homes, which hitherto have been relatively untouched by the productive instrumentalisation (at least in modern capitalist history). As a result, the dynamism of machinic capital goes beyond the fix, becoming an expansive capitalist force (as opposed to a limited and temporary solution) insofar as it implies subsumption of new space as well of worker subjectivity.

3   Digital Abstract Space

Digital abstract space represents the intended outcome of the digital spatial fix; its goal is to displace subsumptive relations. By digital abstract space, I refer to a capitalist space mediated but also constituted by digital technology,

---

31   Marx 1973, p. 712.
32   Clover 2010.

which draws from Lefebvre's notion of abstract space as a space almost entirely instrumental to capitalism. For Lefebvre, abstractions refer to the description of a space that is artificially purified (thus preventing the flow of capital circuits) and that privileges quantifiable and commensurable elements rather than qualitatively distinctive ones.

Digital abstract space constitutes a conjunctural social field: a preponderant logistical venue for digital capitalism, inhabited by self-directed and self-exploited neoliberal subjectivities that partly buy into the disingenuous narrative of 'flexibility';[33] a highly intrusive ideology of digital connectivity; and finally a protocological approach[34] to management that emphasises computational logic. Abstract space is an ensemble of social relations infused by power and disciplinary apparati. In this sense, the technological side of such space doubles down on practices of control, since technology does what it can do when employed by capitalist relations. It implements productivity and control.

Ideally, digital abstract space aims at being minimalist – it is reduced only to its functionality. In this sense, it seems compatible with the sense of emergency, and the politics of 'essentialism' (that is, everything is shut down except essential services) has indeed made this realm a primary abstracting force. In fact, the lively debate about the health/economics dilemma conveyed by current public discourse demonstrates that in a capitalist society everything that is not about value production-realisation can be stripped out, because it is non-essential.

In the context of the digital spatial fix prompted by the circulatory/pandemic crisis, digital abstract space is generated by digital machines of different kinds (that is, machines such as IoT, big data, virtual reality, AI, cloud and robotics), which by convergence generate the capitalist social form that seems to impose itself on every other social form: production, consumption, sociality and social reproduction. All those different digital tools share the common tendency of shaping environments in which algorithmic instructions travel across connection points that enable the dialogue between the physical world, people and machines. It is indeed the systematic production of those digital environments and their systematic conduciveness to capital flows (regardless of concrete subjects and physical context) that makes those machines productive of abstract space in the Lefebvrian and Marxian sense.

Accordingly, qualitatively different kinds of spaces, through means of connectivity, can from the mere point of view of value production be subsumed

---

33   Huws 2010.
34   Galloway 2004.

as digital abstract space: space that is able to redefine organisational and productive logics, and to reconfigure them into more commensurable sites and relations of production. Commensurability is indeed another main facet of 'abstraction'; this is something we already touched upon in the previous chapter about translatability. While I discussed abstraction as a reduction of concrete complexity into artificial essentiality, here I also point to abstraction as providing the condition of replicability and the possibility of technological automation. We are, after all, dealing with another important example of the translation machined discussed in Chapter 5.

Finally, the same digital spatial fix that transformed traditional modes of work into remote structures while increasing digital abstract space shapes its agents by subsuming them as domesticated subjectivities within this kind of 'homey and cozy capitalism'. However, as I'll point out in the last section of the chapter, domestication is what dynamises traditional fixed capital into machinic capital, but is not free of contradictions.

Returning to abstractions, abstract space is the product, the process of production, and the agent of production of the space of capitalism *par excellence*. It is a privileged space adequate to capitalism in its abstract quality as well as in its abstracting function.

Capitalism and neocapitalism have produced abstract space, which includes the 'world of commodities', its 'logic' and its worldwide strategies, as well as the power of money and that of the political state. The space is founded on the vast network of banks, business centres and major productive entities, as well as on motorways, airports and ICT apparati. Within this space, the town – once the forcing house of accumulation, fountainhead of wealth and centre of historical space – has disintegrated.[35]

Qualitative differences represented by particular bodies, imperfections in physical space, and instability of social relations (linked for instance to transportation and communication issues) are all indeterminate and unpredictable variables that may interrupt, slow down or derail the essence of capital, that is value in motion. In this sense, abstract space constitutes the social, physical and practical environment in which the ideality – the theoretical 'flawlessness' – of capital's dynamism is implemented:

> It has nothing of a 'subject' about it, yet it acts like a subject in that it transports and maintains specific social relations, dissolves others and stands

---

35   Lefebvre 1991, p. 53.

opposed to yet others. It functions positively *vis-à-vis* its own implications: technology, applied sciences and knowledge bound to power. Abstract space may even be described as at once, and inseparably, the locus, medium and tool of this 'positivity'.[36]

In this sense, digital abstract space represents almost the apogee of abstraction: a binary world made of 1 and 0. That is possibly the closest thing to absolute abstraction, that is, while the concrete is made of many determinations, absolute abstraction would be only one number, only one determination, which then would replace difference with identity or accomplish the reduction of social reality to one value, for example, all 1s or all 0s. However, according to the dialectical take suggested by Lefebvre, the more intense the tendency to abstraction, the stronger the process of creating difference (that is the differentiation between the place abstracted *vis-à-vis* the concrete space that surrounds it), therefore the constant possibility for its negation.

Thus, digital abstract place radicalises its own dialectical nature: on the one hand, both the digital labour process and the ICT that supports it radicalise the production of abstract space identified by Lefebvre, by means of further commodification and subsumption of social life, as well as the employment of scientific and computational management; on the other hand, the fluidification and delocalisation of digital labour processes are such that the subsumption of labour under exchange-value, that is, its commodification, tends to create connective two-way venues that link digital workers' subjectivities with personal motivations while exploiting them, contradictorily qualifying and disqualifying their work, and finally decomposing and recomposing labour.

Lefebvre notices how abstract space is not so easily detectable:

> Abstract space is not defined only by the disappearance of trees, or by the receding of nature; nor merely by the great empty spaces of the state and the military – plazas that resemble parade grounds; nor even by commercial centres packed tight with commodities, money and cars. It is not in fact defined on the basis of what is perceived. Its abstraction has nothing simple about it: it is not transparent and cannot be reduced either to a logic or to a strategy.[37]

---

36 Lefebvre 1991, p. 52.
37 Lefebvre 1991, p. 50.

However, while abstract space frequently manifests itself visibly as the logistical space of capitalism – clearly exemplified by the physical space of commercial malls, suburbia, airports and highways – digital abstract space is less detectable.

Such space appears at the same time as more 'laminar' and purely semiotic, because it can operate as an invisible layer, like a Google map laid across urban space. I am not simply referring to the semi-ethereal nature of digital substance, but also to the fact that digital abstract space, while supported by tangible hardware (such as computers, power grids, cables and offices), locates its power in its capability to produce and reproduce capitalist social relations – thus subsumptive relations as well – and to facilitate all the necessary processes required for capital accumulation, such as those relating to value, commodities and workers.

Digital abstract space is also more territorialising,[38] because it not only reorganises the social relations of a particular space but does so inter-textually, that is, by connecting and geo-locating people and things on digital maps. Thus, digital abstract space generates abstractions by standardisation as well as high degrees of individualisation, able to locate, 'quantify' and therefore control individual workers. In this sense, digital abstract space is potentially more value extractive than Lefebvre's abstract space because it reflects the increased subsumptive power of a post-Fordist capitalism enhanced by digital media connectivity and blurring private/public life, work/home, work/leisure time, formal/informal relations, instrumental/non-instrumental relations. Thus, while in the Fordist abstract space capitalism is accumulated by investments in constant and variable capital,[39] in the context of digital abstract space, value is captured outside traditionally productive processes, including from affective cognitive and communication practices.

Furthermore, digital abstract space increasingly replaces the analogic interconnectedness of the social with digital connectivity. Digital connectivity implies the passage from formal to real subsumption of space as productive in capitalist terms: from layers of superimposed abstract Fordist space to a deeper reconstitution of (abstract) space through digitalisation, but also through the operationalisation that follows a protocological rationale,[40] digital abstract space uses metadata to measure the value of social relations, thus mapping them as a set of valorised social relations; digital codes transcend the status of

---

38 Deleuze and Guattari 1972.
39 Marazzi 2005.
40 Galloway 2004.

language to become a machine that executes meaning and information into action. As a result, digital abstract space creates a realm of power relations where digital management methods can operate as the means of algorithmic control and measure over most phases of the labour process as well as over workers.[41] The general potential intrusiveness of digital abstract space resides mostly in its symbiotic and machinic nature. Such symbiosis has consistently characterised the practical relationship between people and technology, as Marx points out in the *Grundrisse*'s section 'Fragment on Machines'.[42] In this sense, while Lefebvre recognises the reciprocal relationship between the production of abstract space and the integration of machines in the capitalist process of production, we claim that such a symbiotic relationship has become even more integrated with the emergence of digital technology and its varied configuration of connectivity.

While in the dialectical framework of space provided by Lefebvre, abstract space tends (not so dialectically) to violently 'grind down and crush',[43] the production of digital abstract space emphasises a contradictory process in which lived practices along with the human bodies originating them are not crushed but instead subsumed via complex connective dynamics. Thus, in the current digital realm of connectivity, while the production of digital abstract space points to a process that possibly has even accelerated the progress of capitalist social relations, it has done so through digital technology that circumstances may, under specific circumstances, allow to counteract such progress, as we will illustrate with our example below.

A prominent example of digital machines' co-production is provided by algorithms that operate as a vital interface between machine and human labour,[44] as software coordinating the sequence that machines must carry out at different degrees of complexity, from linear to retroactive-AI tasks. Generally understood as 'any set of instructions, with specific steps, that lead to certain results'[45] for manipulating data or reasoning through a problem, algorithms constitute a significant step towards the implementation of the earlier mentioned vision of computational 'universalism'.

The proficiency of algorithms in producing digital abstract space derives from their capability to resolve complex problems and rearticulate complex

---

41   Wood 2021.
42   Marx 1973, pp. 690–712.
43   Lefebvre 1991, p. 285.
44   Finn 2017.
45   Ingraham 2014 p. 6.

spaces through a limited number of elementary, homogenous and fixed steps, which are integrated through the active combination of human capabilities.[46]

Thus, recalling and applying Deleuze and Guattari's thought,[47] we could define such an active arrangement that allows the digital machines to generate abstract space as *agencement*, which coordinates living human capabilities with the procedures codified by the algorithm. Such a combination becomes increasingly prominent in digital labour. Especially when it comes to digital capitalism, algorithms should then be considered as machinic forms of hybridisation between bodies and the informational network of digital space, vital for both production and reproduction.

Indeed, digital abstract space tries to subsume the body of workers. For Lefebvre, abstract space denies sensuality and sexuality unless understood as a mere reproduction of labour capacity and social and biological reproduction; 'lived experience is crushed, vanquished by what is "conceived of"'.[48] However, all the power and violence that can be associated with abstract space cannot reduce its immanent contradictory development:

> The reproduction of the social relations of production within this space inevitably obeys two tendencies: the dissolution of old relations on the one hand and the generation of new relations on the other. Thus, despite – or rather because of – its negativity, abstracts space carries within itself the seeds of a new kind of space. I shall call that new space 'differential space', because, inasmuch as abstract space tends towards homogeneity, towards the elimination of existing differences or peculiarities, a new space cannot be born (produced) unless it accentuates differences.[49]

4   The Contradictory Facets of Domestication, or Subsumption as Always

In Chapters 4 and 5, I mentioned how subsumption depends on the legal framework and the state's intervention in a given society. For instance, a crucial aspect of the process of neo-liberalisation, beginning in the 1980s, was the erosion of the welfare state and the significant cuts in public spending, which transferred the burden of several services back onto families. As a res-

---

46   Sacchetto et al. 2013.
47   Deleuze and Guattari 1972.
48   Lefebvre 1991 p. 51.
49   Lefebvre 1991 p. 52.

ult, homeworkers such as housewives had been overexploited in the private territory of nuclear families and their own homes.[50] This is the historical base of current 'domestification', which does not only concern unpaid or underpaid labour but all sorts of 'knowledge work' relegated to home by Covid-19. The household becomes the terrain of confrontation between digital abstract space and differential space (with a variable degree of digital mediation). This *domus* intersects various tasks attributable to home working, homeschooling and disposable/leisure time.

In terms of space, the process of digital abstraction describes a space that is fetishised and impoverished – as well as the conditions for more effective exploitation – and posits the condition for potentially replacing workers with machines. At the same time, part of the differential space this kind of abstract space produces can be understood in terms of subjectivities. This is because domesticated subjectivities and domestication constitute a subsumptive relation.

First, specific digital space produced by the Covid-19 fix must be found in the reconfiguration of space. Restrictive measures dealing with the crisis have regimented and brought about significant changes: examples include the appropriation of public space for private use (as in the case of restaurant patios and street closure for open-air dining),[51] or how abandoned/dormant public space is reconfigured for mutual aid like unused parking lots or how space previously used for cars now is being reconverted to bike-paths.[52]

However, in my view, the most preponderant tendency in space production exacerbates the general neoliberal tendency to privatise public space, accomplished by measures of partition and sanitation. Public spaces are considered 'impure' and 'dangerous' spheres, repressed by measures such as social distancing, mask mandates and sanitation stations. The previous relative openness of public space acquires new internal boundaries that facilitate its control via processes of segmentation and partition in quantifiable parcels (for example, the six-foot rule in the US or the two-metre rule in Europe), which operate when people agglomerate, for example when they are waiting in line outside a business or a governmental building.

Conversely, private space becomes a refuge from contagion/human contact and freedom from state-imposed restrictions. At the same time, due to digital platforms and technology, it becomes a super-locale[53] in which the intimate

---

50 Mies 1986.
51 Trudeau and Wareham 2020.
52 Sarkin 2020.
53 Fuchs 2020.

sphere is mobilised to become a productive sphere and a new sphere of socialisation via digital connectivity. This is especially true for the so-called knowledge workers,[54] with their experience of domestication as hybrid subsumption of the private sphere, which becomes what Fuchs has recently defined as a supra-locale.[55] Drawing on Anthony Giddens,[56] Fuchs claims that localisation, occuring through particular space and time and the particular social interactions in the space of the household where a remote worker lives and works, can be problematised as follows:

> In the coronavirus crisis, the social spaces and locales of work, leisure, education, the public sphere, the private sphere, friendships, family converge in the locale of the home. The home is at the same time workplace, family and private space, school, nursery, leisure space, natural space, a public space from where we connect to friends and professional contacts, etc. Social spaces converge in the home. In this convergent social space, it can easily become difficult to organise everyday life by breaking up time into small portions of which each is dedicated to specific activities in a routinised manner. In the coronavirus crisis, the home has become the supra-locale of everyday life.[57]

The space of the house is inhabited by multiple social spaces and multiple social interactions, which hybridise previously differentiated, localised, spaces.

In this new productive sphere (that is, integrating public and private) inside homes, the spatial fix manifests through a re-compression of space and time (previously decompressed by the lockdowns, Covid-19 restrictions, etc.) by pushing production towards more (social) space and more time: overlapping and superimposing working time/space over leisure time/space; by compensating the disconnection from the traditional office, now 'contagious', with a permanent connection to a safer one. Such a digital and logistical safe zone has materialised by means of smartphones, digital platforms, endless intrusion of

---

[54] Richard Barbrook was possibly one of the first to use the notion of knowledge working to describe how in the information economy a specialised kind of worker provides services, information, ideas (Barbrook 2006). In the context of increased digitalisation, knowledge workers play an essential role as producers and users of the general intellect by employing creativity, knowledge and communication skills: Fuchs 2014. It is an expansive category of intellectual labour whose collective workforce comprises professionals such as scholars, software designers, journalists, call-centre and micro-logistics workers.

[55] Fuchs 2020.

[56] Giddens 1984.

[57] Fuchs 2020, p. 379.

ads on our computer screens, a never-ending buzzing of delivery trucks carrying food and consumer goods and waste management workers getting rid of Amazon boxes and packaging material.

The subject at home thus pays for their privileged freedom from contagion through exposure to new intrusive forms of value production and extraction. She experiences an intensification of the pressure on individuals to combine operativity and productivity, that is, the capability to manage and reproduce activities outside of formal working hours, to demonstrate flexibility, and also the capability to react to the new and exceptionally transient demands thrown up by the pandemic crisis.[58]

If space is a social relation, and its production is active social intercourse, then people working from home are shaped by home working, and the home is affected as well, becoming first of all a digitalised household, the overdetermined outcome of home-office, home-schooling and the use of the home as a setting for a social-media-constructed identity. The family once again becomes the framework for both healthcare and schooling.

In this context, the worker is *domesticated* in a twofold sense: secured from contagion, as well as subjected/controlled for smoother exploitation, while living a fundamental contradiction between an abrupt separation from the contagion risks of public social life and a simultaneous reconnection by digital means. The home itself, meanwhile, becomes one of the few venues considered to be safe from the perspective of hygiene/anti-contamination measures. Domestication then implies a paradoxical reciprocal appropriation: capitalism spills over into the worker's intimate space, while the worker confronts capital in a contest literally played in the space of the worker's own home – thus potentially possessing more tools with which push capital back. Thinking relationally and not simply physically about domestification, we come to treat productive space in the 'negative':

> This phenomenon leads to the definition of non-places of labour, as opposed to classic forms of domestication. In this case, indeed, we should not talk about a convergence of labour-place and life-space but, rather, about the expropriation of the workplace and of all possible consequences that this process might have on work identity. We are witnessing the overcoming of the separation between production and reproduction. This is the first consequence of life becoming work. When we talk about life, we do not only mean it as directly finalised to productive activity, but

---

58 See Burchi 2020.

also to the social reproduction of life itself, a clear example of which is the almost exclusively female caretaking work.[59]

Sergio Bologna and Andrea Fumagalli[60] observe that while salaried workers used to spend their active productive time in a place that was not theirs, organised by someone else, now the workers' own private sphere is subsumed under capitalist forms, while they at the same time subsume their work within their own private forms of life. The domesticated worker apparently defines her own physical space of work, but the relations of force infused into digital abstract space constantly and significantly constrain this autonomy. Such a relation of power is indirectly visible in the domesticated space and very directly visible in the socially necessary time of work: the domesticated worker geometrically alienates herself by feeling less alienated in the time and space of her own house or bedroom. Perceived socially necessary time expands because it is appropriated by and intermingled with disposable time.

For instance, the digital spatial fix and the consequent creation of digital abstract space led to a material reconfiguration of many homes in terms of consumption and social reproduction, which adds up to a reconfiguration of production. For example, households mimic on a smaller scale the logistical space of the city with its landscape made of fixed capital and circulating capital: leisure and/or spare rooms become home offices. Many users increased their bandwidth allowances for remote working and schooling; entrance halls become hubs where micro-logistics workers deliver and pick up packages; and the multifunctional operativity of homes is enhanced by the creation of corners for *uber-sport,* which reinscribes the neoliberal preoccupation with consumption and nurtures the individualised consumer subject (one can think in this connection of the treadmill, or exercise bike).[61]

The paradox of digital abstract space is that while it establishes an order apparently instrumental to the circulation of capital, it also overloads the physical environment of workers' homes by creating potential new frictions. For instance, overloaded subjects such as working mothers experience an exacerbation of the unfair sexual division of labour inside their home; this in turn may well affect their productivity and general well-being.[62]

Reflecting on what I just described, the Marxian labour theory of value suggests that the magnitude of value is determined by socially necessary labour-

---

59 Fumagalli and Morini 2013, p. 114.
60 Bologna and Fumagalli 1997.
61 Clevenger, Oliver and Bustad 2020.
62 Burchi 2020.

time. When capitalism is understood as a circulatory process, one could argue that digital abstract space represents a kind of socially necessary labour space; if capitalism's tendencies imply the disappearance of different concrete forms of labour, such that 'labour-power [is] expended without regard to the form of its expenditure',[63] then an important form of its expenditure is its spatial localisation. Digital abstract space represents capitalism's attempt radically to de-territorialise and re-territorialise in purely instrumental terms the concrete physical environment. Regardless of whether one finds oneself in the office or home kitchen, in a business suite, or in the restroom at Heathrow Airport, thanks to digital connectivity one can provide hours of productive work.

4.1   La Perruque, *Gamification and a Rhetoric of Choice*

There is indeed a constitutive link between overwork and underwork and unemployment and how the worker understands herself and acts accordingly. This is not certainly new:

> The over-work of the employed part of the working class swells the ranks of its reserve, while conversely the greater pressure that the reserve by its competition exerts on the employed workers forces them to submit to over-work and subjects them to the dictates of capital. The condemnation of one part of the working class to enforced idleness by the over-work of the other part, and *vice versa*, becomes a means of enriching the individual capitalists, and accelerates at the same time the production of the industrial reserve army on a scale corresponding with the progress of social accumulation.[64]

Especially in the current context of gig work,[65] the above-mentioned notion of free labour can be in good part explained by the motivation to increase the chance of employability – we do things to reduce the chance of being laid off. In other words, the perspective of moving from being employed to being unemployed and vice versa powerfully shapes our habits and practices. In fact, possibly the most 'fascinating' aspect of ideal subsumption is that when people are looking for a job, living the life of the unemployed – as I did for a consid-

---

63   Marx 1990, p. 128.
64   Marx 1990, pp. 789–90.
65   The notions of gig work and gig economy are meant to distinguish traditional stable employment from gig jobs that are defined through the rhetoric of flexibility, variety, self-actualisation, temporality, precarity, overexploitation and alienation. Not accidentally, these 'gigs' are defined by digital technology: Zwick 2018.

erable amount of time – they feel the need to operate *as if* they were working under socially necessary labour-time. This is true both for people in the process of finding a new occupation and for people just retired.

In this sense, domestication implies navigating the semiotics of unemployment, of staying home and working at the same time (in fact, working more intensely): permanent connection. However, domestication does not mean absolute subordination of the space of the household to work and capitalist forms. There are ways in which the worker consistently negotiates the space of work, which is always a space of contention. Paul Edwards et al. claim that while organised resistance has always been more visible, workers have always made use of other forms of resistance as well:

> The majority of research studies have tended to focus on the visible, explicit and collective oppositional practices such as output restriction ... and sabotage ... Most of these studies have also tended to focus primarily upon (male) manual workers in the traditional unionised manufacturing sectors ... Yet there are also many other oppositional practices that are often more subtle, covert and secretive and frequently less collective and organised ... The disruptive effects of such oppositional practices should not be underestimated for in certain cases the 'mental strike' or indifference of one individual or the public disclosure of 'sensitive' information by a disaffected or ethically motivated employee could be more damaging to management than a strike by an entire workforce.[66]

While the clearly organised rejection of subsumption through strikes and collective bargaining represents important aspects of determinate supersumption, it also points to a level of class struggle that is historically conjunctural, depending on a combination of circumstances that are possible but by no means invariant.

As Gramsci observes, the elevation of class struggle to the level of organised movement passes through activities of a molecular kind. As already mentioned, the outcomes of determinate supersumption are not just resistance; they also entail tensions, or even new reproductive dynamics of power, which can affect the dominant relations of power in various different ways. At the same time, it is fair to say that understanding those relations of power within a hegemonic framework also means assuming that, while mutating and inherently unstable, those relations tend to favour capital over labour, albeit to different degrees.

---

66 Edwards, Collinson and della Rocca 1995, p. 291.

In this section, we are focuses on practices that can be read as renegotiating subsumptive relations via the reclamation of working time. The negotiation is predominantly moral: in terms of value, it does not really secure a higher share of the value produced, but instead aims at creating alternative values that the worker can freely appropriate.

Those practices go by several names. The phenomenon is alluded to in the United States with phrases like 'homers',[67] and doing 'government jobs';[68] and in Great Britain with terms such as 'idling', 'skiving' or 'pilfering'.[69] 'Homer' consists of 'the use of materials and tools by a worker in the workspace, during work hours, to manufacture or transform artifacts outside of the organisation's [official] production'.[70] 'Homers' can refer to work done in order to produce gifts for family and friends or on the occasion of retirement ceremonies; it can also refer to creative activity performed during working hours. Colleagues who manufacture them attest openly to the homer quality of the gift. In all those different circumstances, what really remains constant is not *production* for oneself but rather *work* for oneself, in other words, resistance to subsumptive relations in terms of subsumption under wage-labour, via the reappropriation of working time, tools, or raw materials belonging to the employer.

One of the most iconic examples was discussed by De Certeau using the notion of *la Perruque*:

> *La Perruque*, the French word for wig, also refers to the colloquial expression used to describe when the worker's own work disguised as work for his [sic] employer. It differs from pilfering in that nothing of material value is stolen. It differs from absenteeism in that the worker is officially on the job. … The worker who indulges in *la perruque* actually diverts time (not goods, since he uses only scraps) from the factory for work that is free, creative and precisely not directed toward profit. In the very place where the machine that he must serve reigns supreme, he cunningly takes pleasure in finding a way to create gratuitous products whose sole purpose is to signify his own capabilities through his work and to confirm his solidarity with other workers or his family.[71]

---

67   Haraszti 1978.
68   Dalton 1985.
69   Ackroyd and Thompson 1999.
70   Kosmann 1999, p. 1.
71   De Certeau 1984, pp. 24–26.

La perruque-related practices do not address the reality of the unpaid labour extracted from the worker by issuing a claim for more money or less working time. Rather, as De Certeau argues, they represent a diversion and a challenge against alienation, a reclaiming of mental imaginative labour against monotony and the necessity of Taylorised production. They are a sort of micro-prefigurative politics, implying a successful evasion of control and subordination.

As the French author observes, *la perruque* is also indicative of a potential alternative to the capitalist law of value, which could potentially be replaced by a gift economy *à la* Mauss. De Certeau offers a hint of this when he claims that:

> *La perruque* is no doubt related to the potlatch described by Mauss, an interplay of voluntary allowances that counts on reciprocity and organises a social network articulated by the 'obligation to give'. ... It survives in our economy, though on its margins or in its interstices. It is even developing, although held to be illegitimate, within a modern market economy ... the loss that was voluntary in a gift economy is transformed into a transgression in a profit economy: it appears as an excess (a waste), a challenge (a rejection of profit), or a crime (an attack on property).[72]

La perruque is non-capitalist reciprocity and a collectivising of playfulness; it represents a way to trick the system of labour-control by blurring the line between worker and leisure. It thus constitutes a form of irreverence directed against the subsuming power of legality and the work ethic shaped by it. Such tactics point to circumstances in which workers are not subjects fixed in space, wearing determinate masks/social roles, but are instead nomadic. That is, workers can carve out creative spaces with the materials to hand, without taking over their working environments entirely.[73] For De Certeau, *la perruque* represents individual agency exercised within the imposed space of work; a differential spatial practice re-territorialising abstract space.

While de Certeau considers these to be acts of micro-resistance, micro-diversion of power, they cannot be considered as some kind of class struggle, unified action, 'Voice', a 'Culture' of its own – or of the great 'Others'.[74] *La perruque* is not the same as 'sabotage', which 'primarily means working slowly

---

72 De Certeau 1984, p. 27.
73 Dawkins 2010.
74 De Certeau 1984, p. 132.

and lowering the quality of what is produced'.[75] It is a covert, everyday type of revolutionary rehearsal in which workers assert their subjectivity: 'As long as people feel cheated, bored, harassed, endangered or betrayed at work, sabotage will be used as a direct method of achieving job satisfaction – the kind that never has to get the bosses' approval'.[76] There is also the notion that sabotage is a reaction against managerial strategies.

Peter Fleming and Graham Sewell[77] concentrate on a kind of supersumption that does not tend to produce 'reactionary' measures by capital, because, just as for James Scott's hidden transcripts, it remains essentially invisible to labour control. *La perruque* indicates a kind of struggle against subsumption as production of docile subjectivities. It does not want to become public and overt, because that would undermine the very process of inner dis-alienation. Those who try to capture resistance beyond (or beneath) formalised, organised acts are dependent upon a kind of transcendental principle, 'which remains hidden under the strict disciplinary surveillance apparatus'. For them, 'subjectivity is the very terrain that is being contested'.[78]

La perruque represents the worker acknowledging the struggle over labour-time and acting upon its necessary value, understood as socially necessary labour-time. It is thus a reappropriation of time, especially of creative personal time. Based on De Certeau's distinction, strategies are able to produce, tabulate and impose these spaces, whereas tactics can only 'use, manipulate and divert these spaces'; one should thus say that '*perruquing*' is a tactical action. For De Certeau, determinate supersumption at the subjective level seems to be taking place at the tactical level:

> The space of a tactic is the space of the other. Thus, it must play on and with a terrain imposed on it and organised by the law of a foreign power. It does not have the means to *keep to itself*, at a distance, in a position of withdrawal, foresight and self-collection: it is a manoeuvre 'within the enemy's field of vision', ... and within enemy territory. It does not, therefore, have the options of planning general strategy and viewing the adversary as a whole within a distinct, visible and objectifiable space. It operates in isolated actions, blow by blow.[79]

---

75   Dubois 1979, p. 103.
76   Sprouse 1992, p. 7.
77   Fleming and Sewell 2002, p. 862.
78   Fleming and Sewell 2002, p. 863.
79   De Certeau 1984, p. 37.

But when interpolating tactics and strategy with Gramsci's spontaneity/organisation, it is important to add that the worker's standpoint is never completely reactive or purely spontaneous. There is a level of systematic subversion. In my view, the tactical practice is important to show the internal dialectics of the power relation, but also its alterity and the foreignness of the subordinating power. It also seems to confirm that the most resistant material to subsumption is the worker himself. Tactical practices are opportunistic and follow essentially the logic of *kayros*. Debatable is whether tactical practices can turn into strategic ones. De Certeau claims that tactics can evade, subvert and defy structures, but not destroy them. In this sense, *la perruque* as determinate supersumption produces the conditions of devaluation, or more precisely, reclaims value in terms of labour-time, but also does the opposite, creating the condition for the production of more surplus-value.

Reclaiming time requires a social space, or more precisely worded, reclaiming socially necessary labour-time requires a socially necessary labour space, or at least one perceived to be such. In fact, in our case of domestication, on the one hand, domesticated labour simply exacerbates the same indistinction that affects socially necessary labour-time and surplus labour in the manufacturing plant. On the other hand, while we cannot precisely determine when we stop working to reproduce our life needs and when we start producing for the capitalist, at least we can distinguish between the physical space of the factory and our own space. In this sense, we at least know that outside of the 'production space', there is a good chance that we are not working.

As far as *perruquing* is concerned, in the domesticated space, I see two main kinds of practices: the first involves literally trying to carve out time for hobbies and what has been offensively defined as cyberslacking.[80] In the first case, I refer to activities typical of leisure time, done when supposedly working: from reading to baking. The second reproduces *la perruque* ethics more closely, even though it is less production-oriented. Here I refer to the particular ways in which people decide to work at home.

In this sense, the considerable number of humorous memes of workers, posted especially during the first months of pandemic-domestication – memes depicting workers who have been caught in inappropriate attire or adopting inappropriate postures while remote working – is indicative of the paradox: on the one hand, the worrying experience of work that has reached our bedroom and caught us in pyjamas; on the other, a work that is *partly* domesticated by our own environment, needs and desires.

---

80   Garrett and Danziger 2008.

The comic relief represented by memes depicting people working in pyjamas, inside the bathroom or drinking alcohol 'on the clock' is also indicative of a double-edged re-territorialisation: those practices represent the intrusion of work inside the intimate sphere and the intrusion of the intimate sphere into work, reflecting how the dialectic of crisis that expands abstract space also expands the abstraction of abstract space, that is, its potential re-concretisation.

In the blog of the critical collective *Crimethinc*,[81] the collective, commenting on the practice of stealing from work, discuss *la perruque* as a consolidating tactic, allowing workers to reclaim their time during working hours even when they have little chance of bringing about significant change. The blog discusses how several corporations have pushed their workers to dedicate some of their working time to doing their own personal creative activities. For instance, 3M corporation, in the aftermath of the Second World War, encouraged its employees to allocate up to 15 percent of their work time to the development of any project or ideas they wanted; this was the context in which the well-known post-it note was invented. In more recent times, Google encourages its employees to spend 20 percent of their time on the development of personal projects.

In my view, in the domesticated context, there is a continuum between *la perruque* and the techniques used by corporations to find new ways to use workers' time; in the current context of digital capitalism, this sheds light on determinate supersumption as a double-edged sword. The interesting development of *la perruque*'s logic as critically interpreted by Crimethink is the strategy behind the intersection of play and labour. Play-labour in fact reveals the ambivalence of subsumptive relations in which capitalist command seems to be traded for more workers' agency.[82] The nightmare capitalism of the future will consist only of 'One Hundred Percent Time', constant freedom in conditions of total capture. Workers who engage in tactics of *la perruque*, *but* use the reclaimed hours to participate in digital capitalism that commodifies user attention, merely sneak from one job to another.

While the very nature of subsumption of labour requires control and a disciplinary apparatus that keeps leisure and labour-time separated[83] – with the former considered to be unproductive – digital and platform capitalism pushes for a playful kind of labour that emotionally engages workers.[84] For Thi Nguyen,

---

81   *Crimethink* 2013.
82   Nguyen 2020.
83   Caillois 2001.
84   Kücklich 2005.

gamification of work involves both worker agency and capitalist strategy to capture value. As Alessandro Delfanti shows,[85] Amazon warehouses gamified work to intensify exploitation and control over work and at the same time to provide motivation and a sense of agency. Games increased competition among workers while working; the winner obtained Amazon-branded gear and electronic gadgets.[86] Amazon's gamification program is called FC Games and comprises six arcade nostalgia games involving the completion of tasks inside the warehouse.

One of them is called Mission Racer, which consists of moving the car around a track while picking and placing products into their storage slots and boxes. In most cases, winners get Amazon currency, which can be exchanged for Amazon merchandise, snacks and (in the busiest times, when productivity must be boosted) more valuable electronic gadgets such as consumer electronics. The application of game logic to labour, by pushing competition, point-scoring and tracking accomplishment, has been enabled by the increasing presence of jobs with a high level of connectivity, such as internet based, data-intensive sensors and smartphones.[87]

Determinate supersumption is not salvation, revolution or simply capitalist reproduction; more frequently it is instability, it is a reminder that capitalist reproduction is always under threat. Practices such as *la perruque* point to an understanding of determinate supersumption involving the same ambiguity that Jamie Woodcock and Johnson[88] find in the phenomenon of gamification. They cite Roger Caillois's[89] distinction between '*paidia*' (playing), a liberational, spontaneous and anarchic playing, and '*ludus*' (gaming), structured by rules and motived by competition.

Gamification contains both aspects: a playful sense of agency and freedom with a decisive push towards effective control from above over the labour process. In effect, gamification is a prototype of subsumptive relations, especially present in post-Fordist kinds of work. Determinate supersumption relates dialectically to subsumption: it creates both constraints and opportunities to expand, reproduce or re-articulate subsumption. In fact, gamification, while an important example of determinate supersumption, to the degree it alters or destabilises a given structure of power relations inside production (e.g. by

---

85   Delfanti 2021.
86   Statt 2021.
87   See Deterding 2019; Warmelink, Koivistob, Mayer, Vesa and Hamari 2020.
88   Woodcock and Johnson 2017.
89   Caillois 2001.

providing increased agency), also becomes a new alternate mode to spy on and exploit workers, enabling exploitation and control.[90]

Gamification inside the labour process re-ignites the debate about coercion and consent. While the instability of subsumptive relations is not limited to this problem, one important factor is the indeterminacy of labour-power, which, as a commodity, is purchased as a potentially productive capacity. In this sense, subsumption and tools like management and technology try to overcome indeterminacy by exercising control over work and the modalities of exploitation. However, while Harry Braverman sees in management and Taylorism purely coercive power, Michael Burawoy's effort to shed light on the consensual aspect of those power relations links to gamification. Consent responds to the issue that control, coercion and surveillance are not reliably conducive to workers' motivation to work, and to do so at a pace that can be productive of surplus-value.

Paradoxically enough, gamification introduces an element of agency that instead of increasing indeterminacy, reduces it in the interests of capital. Gamification is a 'new mode of governmentality' in the context of subsumptive relations. This is how Schrape puts it:

> Why, therefore, do people want gamification? The answer is that people seek to optimise their lives, find easier ways to achieve their own goals, deal with meeting the drives of capital, and so on. As Read points out, neoliberalism entails an 'effective strategy of subjectification', in which individuals are increasingly encouraged to view themselves as 'companies of one', seeking more efficient ways to mobilise and improve their own human capital.[91]

Gamification implies real subsumption,[92] the transformation of something which is not a game into a game, fundamentally altering the nature of the activity in question, not merely the manner in which the activity is performed. Woodcock and Jonson cite Woodcock's[93] study on call centres, pointing out how workers would hack gamification, turning so-called 'buzz sessions' into their own games:

> Workers would turn the extension of the 'buzz sessions' – or indeed any other opportunity for breaks – into their own type of game. This involved

---

90 Dragona 2014.
91 Schrape 2014, p. 21.
92 Woodcock and Johnson 2017.
93 Woodcock and Johnson 2017.

subverting the 'buzz session' by asking questions of the supervisors, an act that could only be maintained by ensuring that no one worker asked too many questions, and required a playful dimension the questions skirted the line of feigning interest and sarcasm.[94]

Woodcock and Johnson claim that their case studies offer examples of an important difference between what they call gamification-from-above and gamification-from-below; they show how these can, and often do, exist alongside each other:

> The existence of gamification-from-below does not reduce the exploitative intentions of gamification-from-above, as the two involve very different dynamics. What is important to reiterate here is that elements of games cannot, and indeed should not, be separated from the context of social relations and power in society.[95]

While both gamification from below and from above may represent the ways in which determinate supersumption manifests itself, gamification from below is more explicitly aimed at subversion of work, because it adds a 'playfulness' to gaming, reclaiming time and work intensity, and in the end echoing what in the Italian autonomist and workerist tradition was thought of as the active and subjective refusal to work.

Finally, the condition of working from home, in other words, the lack of direct physical interaction with colleagues, may affect class composition as work becomes, as we mentioned, privatised and privative in relation to social experience. Furthermore, while this book represents the result of reflections inspired by my own experience both as a scholar and worker in-between Europe and United States, this particular experience does not reflect others in other parts of the world. For instance, Chattopadhyay and Pandit[96] observe how, working in developing countries such as India, many of those working from home did not have the space and the technological means to carry on their professional tasks:

> One of the major problems of working from home, especially in a developing country like India, is the unequal access or distribution of equipment and services necessary for conducting work from home. It is import-

---

94 Woodcock and Johnson 2017, p. 8.
95 Woodcock and Johnson 2017, p. 9.
96 Chattopadhyay and Pandit 2021.

ant to mention that unequal access to or distribution of equipment and services does not only entail personal computers, webcams and smartphones but also such basic infrastructures such as uninterrupted electricity, access to clean water, separate room, or space for a work-set up, availability of broadband connection.[97]

All in all, the pandemic crisis has abruptly reconfigured social space and social praxis, by reformulating a utopia consistently accompanying modern media: action at a distance, that is, the exertion of influence upon an object that does not require physical interaction. While such capabilities have been traditionally associated with a power of magic or mystical magnetism, the Covid-19 pandemic mostly invokes a vernacular of the 'new normal'. The infrastructures required so as to develop contactless social practices are already in place, thanks to the increasing preponderance of digital machines in both the production and circulation of capital. In fact, the spatial fix to the crisis was so rapid that the narrative of digital technologies as the best and safest way to keep working during the pandemic restrictions, quickly established itself as the only one that was viable.

Consequently, the pandemic has transformed most of our cities into living social laboratories: we observe an experimental attempt to carry out the permanent integration of digital technology into every aspect of life. The city becomes the sounding board for an *all-shut-in economy*,[98] which keeps exploiting the rhetoric of 'smart cities' coupled with 'smart working' in the domestic space. As a result, social spaces are reinvented, re-territorialised, secured, distanced, eroded, and re-mediated by digital connectivity.

In such a scenario, domestication represents then the first dialectical limit of digital abstract space. To this limit should be joined a second: while enjoying an organic composition of capital that exploits the dynamism of living labour *vis-à-vis* constant capital, this form of capital also tends towards automatisation, thus replacing living labour with machines. If we grant the Marxian assumption that value production only derives from living labour, then the digital spatial fix would entail a *Catch 22* situation.

These domestication phenomena lead us to keep asking questions about subsumption under digital capitalist forms, especially regarding the broader and possibly quintessential capitalist tendency of abstraction. These only become more relevant as universal computational languages and black-boxed

---

97 Chattopadhyay and Pandit 2021, p. 143.
98 Sadowski 2020.

algorithmic management become more prevalent. Are those changes inevitable? Can they be reversed? After all, part of the argument here advanced is that crisis is eminently but also unpredictably productive; crises always oscillate between destructive creation and creative destruction.

While capitalist crises represent in themselves the most fundamental argument against it, so-called 'technological solutionism'[99] constitutes a powerful rhetoric that keeps threatening our capability to voice our concerns and to envision alternative uses of technology, rooted in communitarian social relations founded in solidarity.[100] In fact, the terms of the so-called return to post-Covid-19 normality also depend on our ability to remain vigilant of the changes now taking place, that is, to carry on interpreting and critiquing them.

---

99 González, Rendueles Menéndez de Llano 2020.
100 See Scholtz 2016.

CHAPTER 7

Conclusions: Two 'Futures' of Work

The transformation of the means of labour into machinery, and of living labour into a mere living accessory of this machinery, as the means of its action, also posits the absorption of the labour process in its material character as a mere moment of the realisation process of capital. The increase of the productive force of labour and the greatest possible negation of necessary labour is the necessary tendency of capital, as we have seen. The transformation of the means of labour into machinery is the realisation of this tendency. In machinery, objectified labour materially confronts living labour as a ruling power and as an active subsumption of the latter under itself, not only by appropriating it, but in the real production process itself; the relation of capital as value which appropriates value-creating activity is, in fixed capital existing as machinery, posited at the same time as the relation of the use-value of capital to the use-value of labour capacity; further, the value objectified in machinery appears as a presupposition against which the value-creating power of the individual labour capacity is an infinitesimal, vanishing magnitude; the production in enormous mass quantities which is posited with machinery destroys every connection of the product with the direct need of the producer, and hence with direct use-value; it is already posited in the form of the product's production and in the relations in which it is produced that it is produced only as a conveyor of value, and its use-value only as condition to that end. In machinery, objectified labour itself appears not only in the form of product or of the product employed as means of labour, but in the form of the force of production itself.[1]

∴

---

[1] Marx 1973, pp. 693–4.

CONCLUSIONS: TWO 'FUTURES' OF WORK

As I write this concluding chapter, the future of work in the quasi-post-pandemic scenario is subject to lively discussion, especially in the light of the recession forecast for the autumn of 2022 in Europe, ongoing automation and outsourcing. Elon Musk, the CEO of Tesla, a symbol of a new generation of venture capitalists all about cutting-edge technology – grouped under the fancy category of 'big tech' – recently said that all employees working remotely must return to their offices for at least 40 hours per week or otherwise will be considered to have resigned. While the official rhetoric justifying this move is about the need to show engagement with the company environment, other colleagues and with the company's product, the real motivation boils down to a single point of contention: concern over loss in productivity.

The question of productivity is interesting because, while the study of remote working is not yet conclusive, most research seems to suggest that most workers tend to be more productive while working from home as opposed to working from the office.[2] This debate about remote working and productivity seems to be very much in tune with the discussion this book has offered regarding subsumption, and poses an important question: Can we distinguish between a sort of, for lack of better words, tactical and strategic subsumption? Where one concerns surplus-value extraction and the other the reproduction of adequate class relations? Or can the two objectives be decoupled?

Following the discussion in the last two chapters, I also would like to conclude by reflecting on pressing questions concerning the specific relation of technology in our societies to work and the economy at large. Can technology really replace human labour and its associated law of value? This is a line of inquiry that directly touches on a central argument of this book, albeit now slightly rephrased: can technology break from socially necessary labour-time (that is, value) and the whole hegemonic apparatus, that is, totalising subsumptive relations, needed to extract surplus labour and surplus-value? The short and imperfect answer is no, it cannot.

I would like to elaborate on my short answer by discussing what I consider as two cautionary cases linking work, money and digital technology. Technology has always been fundamental in capitalist ventures, as an effective tool to subordinate and control workers while pressuring them to increase their productivity. Consistent with the main approach of this book, the problem is not technology, but technology subsumed under capitalist relations, which is employed to enhance profitability, to reduce costs – including hiring costs – thus replacing workers.

---

2 *Forbes* 2022.

In a very important note in the chapter on 'Machinery and Large-Scale Industry',[3] Marx urges the necessity of carrying out a critical study on the history of technology:

> A critical history of technology would show how little any of the inventions of the eighteenth century are the work of a single individual. Hitherto there is no such book. Darwin has interested us in the history of Nature's Technology, that is, in the formation of the organs of plants and animals, which organs serve as instruments of production, or sustaining life. Does not the history of the productive organs of man, of organs that are the material basis of all social organisation, deserve equal attention? And would not such a history be easier to compile since, as Vico says, human history differs from natural history in this, that we have made the former, but not the latter? Technology discloses man's mode of dealing with Nature, the process of production by which he sustains his life, and thereby also lays bare the mode of formation of his social relations, and of the mental conceptions that flow from them.[4]

Marx decisively pushes back against technological fetishism. Technology is a social process that instrumentally organises social relations, it thus still responds to the needs of a specific mode of production. It is a social organisation effort, sometimes mediated by physical tools and appliances; it allows the capitalist to exercise the power needed to increase production, productivity and profitability.

Though I have already mentioned it, it is important to keep stressing the perspective of technology as social organisation, a repertoire of ideas, practices, social spaces, knowledge and machines taking the form of a social machine that we tend to see crystallised into a physical 'black box'. Such a perspective thus rejects the various forms of fetishism. The first concerns the individual: 'the individual man of genius, who has now arisen and who understands the truth. That he has now arisen, that the truth has now been clearly understood, is not an inevitable event, following of necessity in the chains of historical development, but a mere happy accident'.[5]

The second form of fetishism concerns agency. Technology is not (yet, maybe) a living Frankenstein's monster, with its own volition, capable of making or shaping history according to its own plan. Still, even prior to *Franken-*

---

3 Marx 1990.
4 Marx 1990, pp. 493–494.
5 Engels 1908, p. 11.

stein, technology has always involved an Oedipal, patricidal relationship to its Demiurge. As Nathan Rosenberg[6] notes, the form and logic of machinic motion mimic the mechanics and the operational styles of the human body – hence the recurrence of the image of the cyborg. The decisive step in productive development involved the machine's transcendence of its original archetype, as it tried to become independent from human skills; thus the shift towards automation. And while Marx never wrote about this tendency, he nevertheless gave us enough material to begin to crack open the black box, by linking technology to class warfare, disciplinary apparati and the tools of relative surplus-value, as well as to science as instrumentalised general intellect.[7]

Machines are tools used by a given social group to fight the worker: strategically, machines contribute to the production of relative surplus-value by reducing the necessary labour-time needed to produce the worker's wage, thus leaving more time for surplus labour. Tactically, machines are placed in an antagonistic relation to skilled work; once workers have been replaced, the labour process comes to be controlled by machines, and the pace of work is intensified:

> But machinery not only acts as a competitor who gets the better of the workman and is constantly on the point of making him superfluous. It is also a power inimical to him, and as such capital proclaims it from the roof tops and as such makes use of it. It is the most powerful weapon for repressing strikes, those periodical revolts of the working class against the autocracy of capital. According to Gaskell, the steam-engine was from the very first an antagonist of human power, an antagonist that enabled the capitalist to tread underfoot the growing claims of the workmen, who threatened the newly born factory system with a crisis. It would be possible to write quite a history of the inventions, made since 1830, for the sole purpose of supplying capital with weapons against the revolts of the working-class. At the head of these in importance, stands the self-acting mule, because it opened up a new epoch in the automatic system.[8]

Class warfare needs to be waged rhetorically as well, especially when it hides behind the fetish of technological subsumptive relations. In this sense, both of

---

6　Rosenberg 1983, p. 42.
7　MacKenzie, like Rosenberg, insists on a key point, problematising the assumption that Marx was a technological determinist by deconstructing the assumption that forces of production are all about technology: MacKenzie 1998.
8　Marx 1990, p. 496.

the cautionary tales that I mentioned earlier deal with this alleged capability of capital to go beyond the material relations that have created it.

1   The 'First Future of Work': Remote Working and Class Relations

Let us go back to the trope I have already mentioned, about the alleged Fourth Industrial Revolution. The trope of Fourth Industrial Revolution mystified the threat posed to work by automation with the promise of more work.

The employment of technology to fight and replace human labour finds two great limits: the first, which we have already mentioned, is the tendency for profitability to fall when capital 'over-invests' in technology to replace living labour; the second is that any labour-replacement technology – whether mechanisation in the past or automation via AI today – needs a huge amount human labour in order to be trained. This involves feeding of the machines with information and the opaque category of work referred to as 'ghost work', an incredibly intensive form of piece-work focused on tasks such as data cleaning, coding and categorising information.[9]

The question is not simply about whether labour is created or destroyed by this 'revolution': the International Labour Organisation has provided data showing a consistent loss of jobs in the manufacturing sector,[10] but also a decline quality of work. Its study shows a sharp increase in precarious jobs that are not regulated by formal contracts. A 2019 report from the ILO[11] documents how, by the end of 2019, 3.3 billion workers were employed in unstable and underpaid jobs.

This brings me to the post-Covid-19 phenomenon called the Great Resignation, and to the related problem of remote working. In April 2022, the economist Michael Roberts[12] published a blogpost discussing lockdowns and the phenomenon of working from home. He observed the futility of the violent opposition of many industrial and venture capitalists (such as Elon Musk) to remote working, which by now characterises almost 20 percent of jobs in many Western countries. Given the fact that the official reason for this hostility – decreasing productivity due to remote working – is not tenable, Roberts wished to know why this form of work has been so frequently opposed by bosses all

---

9   Gray 2019.
10   International Labour Organisation 2019.
11   International Labour Organisation 2019.
12   Roberts 2022.

over the world. The real reason, he argues, is that it 'is not just lower productivity but that management starts to lose control over its employees, both in terms of time and in dictating activity'.[13]

The so-called Great Resignation is not about the refusal of work but simply about workers demanding a healthier work–life balance; in fact, most people who have left their jobs did so merely to take up better employment. Part of the problem of phenomena such as domestication that were discussed earlier is that they affect the quality of work. In fact, in the hybrid and informal realm of the household, both absolute and real subsumption is increasing. As a result, most of us have been working longer and harder hours. While formal and real subsumption frequently tend to exist in a dialectical relation to one another, in this case, they turn into co-developing indices of the *informal* subsumption of precarious gig jobs. Not accidentally when it comes to labour-intensification, technology is key: instantaneous communication, which requires an instantaneous response; ubiquitous monitoring; the process of quantification and self-quantification. This amounts to a sort of bio-political neo-Taylorism, in which we are made to keep up with machines whose sensors and surveillance mechanisms embrace all spheres of life.

An ILO report demonstrates that, until 2018, the number of working hours per week was constantly decreasing,[14] but that this trend stopped at almost exactly the moment of the Covid-19 outbreak, with its massive restructuring of the work process. Furthermore, the intensity of work is constantly increasing, along with shift-work and the imposition of hyper-flexible schedules. Again, this is typically taking place in the overlap between work-leisure space, work-leisure relations, and work-leisure time.

So, if we work harder and longer at home, with similar levels of productivity, why do capitalists oppose remote working? In my view, and according to the broader perspective of the present book, I hypothesise that many bosses realise that what really counts is not the ephemeral gain of relative surplus-value but the preservation of the hegemonic relation of control and leadership; in other words, an advantageous position in relation to class warfare may be more productive than a short-term temporary gain. Thus, this brief discussion may confirm one of the central arguments of the present work: that in trying to understand subsumptive relations, surplus-value and power relations must be considered as united but also distinct aspects.

---

13   Roberts 2022.
14   International Labour Organisation 2019.

2 Another Future of Work, or Cryptocurrency as a Technological Fetish

Talking about the future in terms of the sociological imagination and prefigurative politics, we can see that, in many ways, financial capital stakes a claim on the future. It precludes the horizon of possibility, trying to subsume it, as Marx beautifully describes:

> Now, the concept of capital as a fetish reaches its height in interest-bearing capital, being a conception which attributes to the accumulated product of labour, and at that in the fixed form of money, the inherent secret power, as an automaton, of creating surplus-value in geometrical progression, so that the accumulated product of labour, as the *Economist* thinks, has long discounted all the wealth of the world for all time as belonging to it and rightfully coming to it. The product of past labour, the past labour itself, is here pregnant in itself with a portion of present or future living surplus-labour. We know, however, that in reality the preservation, and to that extent also the reproduction of the value of products of past labour is *only* the result of their contact with living labour; and secondly, that the domination of the products of past labour over living surplus-labour lasts only as long as the relations of capital, which rest on those particular social relations in which past labour independently and overwhelmingly dominates over living labour.[15]

In relation to this, in the last two decades finance capital transactions have been increasingly digitalised. In the case of purely electronic money, digitalisation has been utilised not just to increase the speed of circulation but also to try to eliminate the necessity of intermediaries, offering instead peer-to-peer online payment and online production of receipts, supported by blockchain technology.

Several aspects of the discourse connecting digital technologies and the economy are worth discussing. One that is particularly worth mentioning is the tension between the idealist metaphysics of the immaterial (for example, binary codes rather than metallic coins ...) versus the matter and the body. According to Blanchette,[16] the digital – as immaterial – allegedly provides considerable advantages: it is immune to practical/logistical problems that beset non-digital economies, it is incorruptible, accessible, reproducible and consumable almost at zero cost, etc.

---

15   Marx 1991, p. 91.
16   Blanchette 2011.

Seen from this fetishistic perspective, digitality represents the triumph of purity over the messiness of matter. The digital as ethereal information is what abstract space, if it could dream, would be dreaming about: a pure will to (capitalist) power, liberated from the burden of workers' bodies. This is not a philosophical digression, or poetic license that I am granting myself as I come to the conclusion of my book; it is rather about finding a basis in cultural and social imagery for the utopia of (digital) abstraction[17] as it relates to subsumption under IC technologies. This is especially so when we focus on one central node of subsumptive dynamics in particular: the will to abstract from complex social substance so as to control and exploit it.

As I have tried to argue on several occasions in this book, the prism of subsumption allows us to see that digital capitalism rests on the ideology of computational universalism. In my view, this resembles a transcendental religion that expiates sins by exceeding the body and the metabolic theory of value that is linked to it. So, we go back to the question I posed earlier: can technology go beyond the labour theory of value? Can it supersede a theory of value that is logically and ontologically based on the mental and physical faculties of concrete workers? Let us consider the case of cryptocurrencies.

One emerging topic in the sphere of digitalised financial capital is cryptocurrency, which, according to its cheerleaders,[18] could one day provide the universal currency of a more democratic decentralised future. These are the words attributed to the pseudonymous Bitcoin programmer Nakamoto:

> It's completely decentralised, with no central server or trusted parties, because everything is based on crypto proof instead of trust. The root problem with conventional currency is all the trust that's required to make it work. The central bank must be trusted not to debase the currency, but the history of fiat currencies is full of breaches of that trust. Banks must be trusted to hold our money and transfer it electronically, but they lend it out in waves of credit bubbles with barely a fraction in reserve. We have to trust them with our privacy, trust them not to let

---

17 It is more than a utopia; it is a mystification. Kirschenbaum observes how:
    All forms of modern digital technology incorporate hyper-redundant error-checking routines that serve to sustain an illusion of immateriality by detecting error and correcting it, reviving the quality of the signal, like old-fashioned telegraph relays, such that any degradation suffered during a subsequent interval of transmission will not fall beyond whatever tolerances of symbolic integrity exist past which the original value of the signal (or identity of the symbol) cannot be reconstituted. – Kirschenbaum 2008, p. 12.
18 Nakamoto 2008; Nakamoto 2009; Kelly 2015.

identity thieves drain our accounts. ... With e-currency based on cryptographic proof, without the need to trust a third-party middleman, money can be secure and transactions effortless.[19]

Cryptocurrencies, which appeal to a vast public, speak to various concerns, including centralisation, the role of economic intermediaries, monopolies and surveillance. In the end, however, these consistently reflect a libertarian and neoliberal understanding of the world. According to such a perspective, the main villain is the state – conceived as an exemplification of centralised power *par excellence* – supported by major actors like corporate banks, with their constant interference in the economic activity of free individuals. However, if the state is the artificial name we give the agencies enforcing hegemonic relations, to pretend that it does not exist, or that its existence is merely counterproductive, simply pushes us deeper into the mystification.

Not surprisingly, the utopia of cryptocurrencies proposes the reabsorption of the functions of the state within the arena of free economic activities, that is, civil society. To the question of where the 'fiat' of the fiat currency principle will come from after state intervention as such has been superseded, cryptocurrencies such as Bitcoin answer that they are backed by the trust of individuals in civil society and by their goodwill – the 'goodwill' of the hidden hand, in other words. These arguments refer, first of all, to the aggregate computational power of people,[20] in which every single individual has to document and check transactions in exchange for a fee. In doing this, the individual also pursues the common good. In this universe, goodwill and honesty are about simply doing your computational work, that is, a cryptographic proof replaces the central arbiter; and this proof is rewarded by a transaction fee, the incentive for people to engage in such triple entry accounting.

Secondly, the advocates of cryptocurrencies argue that the aggregate of trust-providing agents assumes the social shape of a network. In relation to the powerful rhetoric of the immaterial I mentioned before, as David Berry acutely observes,[21] the fetish of the network represents an almost natural continuation, because it aims to replace a central body with its deconstructed parts linked into a network.

In theory, this may work, but even when trust is universal, it does not follow that the currency will be universally accepted or stable enough to become a reliable measure and store of value. As the arguments of this book perhaps suggest,

---

19 Nakamoto 2008.
20 Noizat 2012.
21 Berry 2008.

the transformations in our social arrangements that would need to take place in order to sustain such a currency are quite vast. The failure of cryptocurrency as a universally accepted medium of exchange, its instability as a measure, and its unreliability as a store of value, is thus perfectly predictable. In fact, I would argue that a currency that is designed to move value around must rely on the total social arrangement that I have defined as social subsumption. This is the fairly stable – even though in the long run by no means guaranteed – power relation that allows surplus-value to consistently be created and to circulate with fairly stable forms of representation.

The recent dramatic falls in cryptocurrency prices supply a demonstration of this thesis. Equally exemplary is the case of El Salvador. Since September 2021, El Salvador has purchased 106 million US dollars of Bitcoin, with the stated goal of raising funds via national cryptocurrencies and issuing its own Bitcoin denominated bonds. As I finish writing this chapter, in June 2022, El Salvador has already lost almost 50 percent of its initial investment.

As a whole, subsumptive relations depend on material relations of force, such as the ones mobilised in labour relations. This can currently be experienced in almost any aspect of our lives. These relations are indeed significantly mediated by technology, but what the two cases briefly discussed here teach us is that technology acquires meaning only inside those material relation, and not the other way around.

Bibliography

Ackroyd, Stephen and Paul Thompson 1999, *Organisational Misbehaviour*, London: Sage.
Adorno, Theodor W. 1987. 'Late Capitalism or Industrial Society?' In V. Meja, D. Misgeld and N. Stehar, eds. *Modern German Sociology*, pp. 232–247. New York: Columbia University Press.
Adorno, Theodor 2005, *Minima Moralia*, London: Verso.
Alquati, Romano 1962, 'Composizione organica del capitale e forza-lavoro alla Olivetti, Part 1', *Quaderni Rossi*, 2.
Alquati, Romano 1963, 'Composizione organica del capitale e forza-lavoro alla Olivetti, Part 2', *Quaderni Rossi*, 3.
Alquati, Romano 2000, *Nella società industriale d'oggi*, Torino: Working Paper, unpublished.
Alquati, Romano 2021, *Sulla riproduzione della capacità umana vivente oggi. L'industrializzazione della soggettività*, Roma: Derive Approdi.
Althusser, Louis 1964, *Marxism and Humanism*, Paris: Cahiers del ISEA.
Althusser, Louis, Étienne Balibar, Roger Establet, Pierre Macherey and Jacques Rancière 2015, *Reading Capital*, London: Verso.
Amoore, Louise and Volha Piotukh 2016, *Algorithmic Life: Calculative Devices in the Age of Big Data*, London: Routledge.
Anderson, Benedict 1991, *Imagined communities: reflections on the origin and spread of nationulism*, London: Verso
Anderson, Perry 1976, *The Antinomies of Antonio Gramsci*, London: Verso.
Anderson, C.W. 2013. What aggregators do: Towards a networked concept of journalistic expertise in the digital age. *Journalism*, 14 (8), 1008–1023.
Andrejevic, Mark 2011, 'Social Network Exploitation', in *A Networked Self: Identity, Community and Culture on Social Network Sites*, edited Zizi Papacharissi, New York: Routledge.
Andrijasevic, Rudvika and Devi Sacchetto 2017, 'Il just-in-time della vita. Reti di produzione globale e compressione spazio-temporale alla Foxconn', *Stato e Mercato*, 3, 383–420.
Armano, Emiliana, Annalisa Murgia and Maurizio Teli 2017, *Platform capitalism e confini del lavoro negli spazi digitali*, Milano: Mimesis.
Arthur, Chris 2002, *The New Dialectic and Marx's 'Capital'*, Leiden: Brill.
Arthur, Chris 2009, 'The Possessive Spirit of Capital: Subsumption/Inversion/Contradiction', in *Re-Reading Marx: New Perspectives After the Critical Edition*, edited by Riccardo Bellofiore and Roberto Fineschi, New York: Palgrave MacMillan.
Artz, Lee, Stephen Macek and Dana Cloud 2006, *Marxism and Communication Studies: The Point Is To Change It*, Chicago: Peter Lang.

Aune, James 2013, 'An Historical Materialist Theory on Rhetoric', *American Communication Journal*, 6:4, 1–15.
Babbage, Charles 1832, *On the Economy of Machinery and Manufactures*, London: Charles Knight.
Balbus, Isaac 1977, 'Commodity Form and Legal Form: An Essay on the "Relative Autonomy" of the Law', *Law and Society Review*, 11:3, 571–588.
Baldwin, Richard 2020, *Rivoluzione globotica, globalizzazione robotica e future del lavoro*, Bologna: Il Mulino.
Ball, Terence 1991, 'History: Critique and Irony', in *The Cambridge Companion to Marx*, edited by Terrell Carver, Cambridge: Cambridge University Press.
Banaji, Jairus 2003, 'The Fictions of Free Labour: Contract, Coercion, and So-Called Unfree Labour. Historical Materialism-research in Critical Marxist Theory', 11: 69–95.
Baran and Paul M. Sweezy 1966, *Monopoly Capital*. New York and. London: Monthly Review Press.
Barber, Benjamin 2007, *Consumed: How Markets Corrupt Children, Infantilize Adults, and Swallow Citizens Whole*, New York: Norton.
Barbrook, Richard 2006, *The Class of the New*, London: OpenMute.
Beer, David 2016, *Metric Power*, London: Palgrave Macmillan.
Beirne, Pierce and Robert Sharlet (eds) 1980, *Pashukanis: Selected Writings on Marxism and Law*, London: Academic Press.
Benhabib, Seyla 2012, 'Obligation, Contract, and Exchange: The Opening Arguments of Hegel's Philosophy of Right', *in North American Critical Theory After Postmodernism*, edited by P.M. Nickel, Palgrave Macmillan, London.
Berman, Marshal 1982, *All That Is Solid Melts Into the Air*, New York: Penguin.
Berry, David 2008, 'The Problem of Networks', *Theory Culture and Society*, 25:7–8, 364–372.
Bidet, Jaques 2005, *The Dialectician Interpretation of Capital*, Leiden: Brill.
Blackledge, Paul 2012, *Marxism and Ethics: Freedom, Desire and Revolution*, New York: SUNY Press.
Blanchette, Jean-François 2011, 'A Material History of Bits', *Journal of the American Society for Information Science and Technology*, 62:6, 1042–1057.
Bobbio, Norberto 1979, *Gramsci and the Conception of Civil society*, London: Routledge.
Bologna, Sergio and Andrea Fumagalli 1997, *Il lavoro autonomo di seconda generazione. Scenari del postfordismo in Italia*, Milano: Feltrinelli.
Bologna, Sergio 2018, *Per un breve panorama della logistica dal 1070 a oggi*, Intervista, http://www.intotheblackbox.com/author/sergio-bologna, observed 24 June 2021.
Bonefeld, Werner 2014, *Critical Theory and the Critique of Political Economy: On Subversion and Negative Reason*, London: Bloomsbury.
Bordwell, Marilyn 2002, 'Jamming Culture: Adbusters' Hip Media Campaign Against

Consumerism', in *Confronting Consumption*, edited by Thomas Princen, Michael Maniates, and Ken Conca, Cambridge: MIT Press.

Borghese, Lucia 201, 'Aunt Helene on her bycicle: Antonio Gramsci as translator from German and as Translation Theorist', in *Gramsci Language and Translation*, edited by Peter Ives and Rocco Lacorte, New York: Lexinton Books.

Bosteels, Bruno 2014, 'Toward a Theory of the Integral State', *Historical Materialism*, 22:2, 44–62.

Bourdieu, Pierre 1977, *Outline of a Theory of Practice*, Cambridge: Cambridge University Press.

Brassier, Ray 2020, 'Concrete-in-Thought, Concrete-in-Act: Marx, Materialism, and the Exchange Abstraction', *Idealism, Relativism, and Realism: New Essays on Objectivity Beyond the Analytic-Continental Divide*, edited by Dominik Finkelde and Paul M. Livingston, Berlin, Boston: De Gruyter, pp. 175–192.

Brass, Tom 2011, 'Unfree Labour as Primitive Accumulation?', *Capital and Class*, 35:1, 23–38.

Braudel, Fernand 1992, *Civilisation and Capitalism, 15th–18th Century: The Structures of Everyday Life: The Limits of the Possible*, California: University of California Press.

Braverman, Henry 1974, *Labor and Monopoly Capital*, New York: Monthly Review Press.

Breman, Jan 2007, *The Poverty Regime in Village India*, New Delhi: Oxford University Press.

Brito, Jerry 2011, 'Online Cash Bitcoin Could Challenge Governments', *Techland, Time Magazine*, 4 April, http://techland.time.com/2011/04/16/online-cash-bitcoin-could-challenge-governments.

Briziarelli, Marco 2018, 'Spatial politics in the digital realm: the logistics/precarity dialectics and Deliveroo's tertiary space struggles', *Cultural Studies*, 33:1–18.

Briziarelli, Marco 2020a, 'The Social Production Of Radical Space: Machinic Labour Struggles Against Digital Spatial Abstractions', *Capital and Class*, 44:2, 173–189.

Briziarelli, Marco 2020b, 'Translational Labor as Subsumption: A Gig Economy Illustration', *Democratic Communiqué*, 20, 1–18.

Bruner, Jerome 1971, *The Relevance of Education*, New York: Norton.

Buci-Glucksmann, Christine 1980, *Gramcsi and the State*, London: Lawrence and Wishart.

Burchi, Sandra 2020, *Ripartire da casa. Lavori e reti dallo spazio domestic*, Milano: Franco Angeli.

Burawoy, Michael 1979, *Manufacturing Consent*, Chicago: University of Chicago Press.

Caillois, Roger 2001, *Man, Play and Games*, Chicago: University of Illinois Press.

Camatte, Jacques 1988, *Capital and Community: The Results of the Immediate Process of Production and the Economic Work of Marx*, London: Pattern Books.

Carrera, Iñigo 2008, *El capital: razón histórica, sujeto revolucionario y conciencia*, Buenos Aires: Imago Mundi.

Casilli, Antonio 2020, *Schiavi del clic. Perché lavoriamo tutti per il nuovo capitalism*: Milano: Feltrinelli.

Chattopadhyay, Saayan and Sushmita Pandit 2021, 'Freedom, Distribution and Work from Home: Rereading Engels in the Time of the COVID-19-Pandemic', *Triple C*, 19:1, 140–153.

Christin, Angele and Caitlin Petre 2020, 'Making Peace with Metrics: Relational Work in Online News Production', *Sociologica*, 14:2, 133–156.

Cleaver, Henry 1979, *Reading Capital Politically*, Austin: University of Texas.

Clevenger, Samuel, Rick Oliver and Jacob Bustad 2020, 'Critiquing Anthropocentric Media Coverage of the COVID-19 Sport "Hiatus"', *International Journal of Sport Communication*, 13, 559–65.

Clover, Joshua 2010, 'Subsumption and Crisis', in *The Sage Handbook of Frankfurt School Critical Theory*, edited by Benjamin Best, Werner Bonefield and Chris O'Kane, London: Sage.

Colletti, Lucio, 1973 *Il marxismo e Hegel*, Roma-Bari: Laterza.

Collins, Hugh 1982, *Marxism and the Law*, Oxford: Oxford University Press.

Crimethink Workers Collective, 2013, *Expect Resistance: A Crimethink field Manual*. London: Crimethink Workers Collective.

Čyras, Vytautas & Lachmayer, Friedrich 2014, 'Compliance and software transparency for legal machines', *Frontiers in Artificial Intelligence and Applications*, 10.

Dalton, Clare 1985, 'An Essay in the Deconstruction of Contract Doctrine', *The Yale Law Journal*, 94, 5: 997–1114.

Das, Raju 2012, 'Reconceptualising Capitalism: Forms of Subsumption of Labor, Class Struggle, and Uneven Development', *Review of Radical Political Economic*, 44, 2: 178–200.

Dawkins, Cedric 2016, 'A Test of Labor Union Social Responsibility: Effects on Union Member Attachment', *Business & Society*, 55, 2: 214–45.

Deakin, Simon and Frank Wilkinson 2005, *The Law of the Labour Market: Industrialisation, Employment, and Legal Evolution*, Oxford: Oxford University Press.

Debord, Guy 1995, *Society of the Spectacle*, Cambridge: MIT Press.

De Certeau, Michel 1984, *The Practice of Everyday Life*, Berkley: University of California Press.

Deleuze, Gilles and Felix Guattari 1972, *Anti-Œdipus*, New York: Continuum.

Deleuze, Gilles and Felix Guattari 1980, *Mille Plateaux*, Paris: Editions de Minuit.

Delfanti, Alessandro 2021, 'Machinic Dispossession and Augmented Despotism: Digital Work in an Amazon Warehouse', *New Media and Society*, 23: 1: 39–55.

Deterding, Sebastine 2019, 'Gamification in Management: Between Choice Architecture and Humanistic Design', *Journal of Management Inquiry*, 28: 131–36.

Ditton, Jason 1977, 'Perks, Pilferage, and the Fiddle: The Historical Structure of Invisible Wages', *Theory and Society* 4, 1: 39–71.

Dragona, Daphne 2014, 'Counter-Gamification: Emerging Tactics and Practices Against the Rule of Numbers', in *Rethinking Gamification*, edited by Sonia Fizek, Mathias Fuchs, Paolo Ruffino and Niklas Schrape Leuphana, Lüneburg: Meson Press.

Dubois, Morgan 2022, 'La perruque de lutte universitaire: dépasser les contradictions entre activités militante et académique à la frontière', *e-Migrinter* [En ligne], 23.

Dumenil, Gerard and Levy Dominique 2012, *Crisis of Neoliberalism*. Cambridge, MA: Harvard University Press.

Dunayevskaya, Raya 1988, *Marxism and Freedom: From 1776 Until Today*, New York: Columbia University Press.

Durkheim, Emile 1997, *The Division of Labour in Society*, New York: Free Press.

Dussel, Enrique 2001, *Towards an Unknown Marx: A Commentary on the Manuscripts of 1861–63*, London: Routledge.

Dyer-Witheford, Nick 2000 *Cyber-Marx: Cycles and Circuits of Struggle in High-Technology Capitalism*, Urbana: University of Illinois Press.

Edwards, Paul, David Collinson and Giuseppe della Rocca 1995, 'Workplace Resistance in Western Europe: A Preliminary Overview and a Research Agenda', *European Journal of Industrial Relations*, 1:3, 283–316.

Ekbia, Hamid and Bonnie Nardi 2017, *Heteromation and Other Stories of Computing and Capitalism*, Cambridge: MIT Press.

Endnotes, 2010 'A History of Subsumption', *Endnotes*, 2, http://endnotes.org.uk/articles/6.

Engels, Frederick 1908, 'Introduction', *Socialism: Utopian and Scientific*, Chicago: Kerr.

Engels, Frederick 1959, *Anti-Dühring*, Moscow: Foreign Language Press.

Esping-Andersen, Gøsta 1990, *The Three Worlds of Welfare Capitalism*, Princeton, New Jersey: Princeton University Press

Federici, Silvia 2019, 'Social Reproduction Theory History, Issues, and Present Challenges', *Radical Philosophy*, 2:4, https://www.radicalphilosophy.com/article/social-reproduction-theory-2.

Feenberg, Andrew 1999, *Questioning Technology*, London: Routledge.

Finn, Ed 2017, *What Algorithms Want. Imagination in the Age of Computing*, Cambridge MA: MIT Press.

Fine, Robert 1984, *Democracy and the Rule of Law: Liberal Ideals and Marxist Critiques*, London: Pluto.

Fine, Robert 2009, 'An Unfinished Project: Marx's Critique of Hegel's Philosophy of Right', in *Karl Marx and Contemporary Philosophy*, edited by Andrew Chitty and Martin McIvor, New York: Palgrave MacMillan.

Fisher, Eran 2012, 'How Less Alienation Creates More Exploitation? Audience Labour on Social Network Sites', *Triple C*, 10: 2: 171–83.

Fleming, Peter and Graham Sewell 2002, 'Looking for the Good Soldier Švejk: Alternative Modalities of Resistance in the Contemporary Workplace', *Sociology*, 36, 4: 857–73.

Flora Peter and Alber Jens 1981, *Development of Welfare States in Europe and in America*, London: Routledge.
Forbes 2022, 'The Impact of Remote Working on Productivity and Creativity', https://www.forbes.com/sites/forbestechcouncil/2022/01/14/the-impact-of-remote-work-on-productivity-and-creativity/.
Fortunati, Leopoldina 1995, *The Arcane of Reproduction: Housework, Prostitution, Labor and Capital*, Brooklyn, NY: Autonomedia.
Fracchia, Joseph 2008, 'The Capitalist Labour-Process, and the Body in Pain: The Corporeal Depths of Marx's Concept of Immiseration', *Historical Materialism*, 16: 4: 35–66.
Freire, Paulo 2000, *Pedagogy of the Oppressed*, New York: Bloomsbury.
Lawrence J. Friedman 1981, 'Historical Topics Sometimes Run Dry': The State of Abolitionist Studies, *The Historian*, 43: 2, 177–94.
Lichtner, Maurizio 1991, *Traduzioni e metafore in Gramsci*, *Critica marxista*, 29 1, pp. 109–31.
Fuchs, Christian 2014, *Digital Labour and Karl Marx*, New York: Routledge.
Fuchs, Christian 2020, 'Everyday Life and Everyday Communication in Coronavirus Capitalism', *Triple C*, 18, 1: 375–98.
Fuchs, Christian and Lara Monticelli 2018, 'Marx @ 200: Debating Capitalism and Perspectives for the Future of Radical Theory', *Triple C*: 16:2, 406–741.
Fumagalli, Andrea and Cristina Morini 2011, 'Life Put To Work: Towards a Theory of Life-Value', *Ephemera*, 10, 234–252.
Fumagalli, Andrea and Cristina Morini 2013, 'Cognitive Bio-Capitalism, Social Reproduction and the Precarity Trap: Why Not Basic Income?', *Knowledge Cultures*, 1, 4: 106–26.
Gabel Peter and Jay Feinman 1998, 'Contract Law as Ideology', in *The Politics of Law*, edited by David Kairys, New York, NY: Basic Books.
Galbraith, John Kenneth 1984, *The Affluent Society*, Boston: Houghton Mifflin.
Galloway, Alexander 2004, *Protocols: How Control Exists After De-Centralisation*, Cambridge: MIT Press.
Garnham, Nicholas and Christian Fuchs 2014, 'Revisiting the Political Economy of Communication', *Triple C*, 12, 102–141.
Giddens, Anthony 1984, *The Constitution of Society: Outline of the Theory of Structuration*, Cambridge: Polity.
Gil, Pamela 2018, 'Exploring Lefebvre's Dialectic of Space in the Right of the City', unpublished paper.
Godelier, Maurice 1986, *The Mental and the Material*, London: Verso.
Goker, Davut 2018, 'Leadership Workplace Deviance Behaviours'. intechopen.com. Retrived from https://www.intechopen.com/chapters/60399.
Goldman, Robert and Stephen Papson 2000, 'Advertising in the Age of Accelerated

Meaning', in *The Consumer Society Reader*, edited by Juliet Schorand and Douglas Holt, New York: New Press.

González, Aitor and Cesar Rendueles Menéndez de Llano 2020, 'Capitalismo digital: fragilidad social, explotación y solucionismo tecnológico', *Teknokultura. Revista de Cultura Digital y Movimientos Sociales*, 17:2, 95–101.

Gordon, Todd 2019, 'Capitalism, Neoliberalism and Unfree Labour', *Critical Sociology*, 45:6, 921–939.

Graham, Mark 2020, 'Regulate, Replicate and Resist: The Conjunctural Geographies of Platform Urbanism', *Urban Geography*, 41, 3: 453–57.

Gramsci, Antonio 1971, *Selections from the Prison Noteebooks of Antonio Gramsci*, edited by Quintin Hoare and Geoffrey Nowell-Smith, London: Lawrence and Wishart.

Gramsci, Antonio 1975, *Quaderni del Carcere*, four volumes, Turin: Einaudi.

Gray, Mary 2019, *Ghost work: how to stop Silicon Valley from building a new global underclass*, Boston: Siddharth Suri.

Greene, Marcus and David Joseph 2015, 'The Digital Spatial Fix', *Triple C*, 13:2, 223–47.

Halliburton, David 1997, *The Fateful Discourse of Worldly Things*, Stanford: Stanford University Press.

Haraszti, Miklos 1978, *A Worker in a Worker's State: Piece-Rates in Hungary*, New York: Universe Books.

Hardt, Michael and Antonio Negri 1994, *Labor of Dionysus: A Critique of the State-Form*, Minneapolis: University of Minnesota Press.

Hardt, Michael and Antonio Negri 2000, *Empire*, Cambridge: Harvard University Press.

Harris, Adrienne 1983, *Language and Alienation*, in *The Sociogenesis of Language and Human Conduct*, in B. Bain, Boston, MA: Springer.

Harvey, David 1982, *The Limits to Capital*, Chicago: University of Chicago Press.

Harvey, David 2001a, 'Globalisation and the Spatial Fix', *Geographische Revue*, 2, 3: 23–31.

Harvey, David 2001b, *Spaces of Capital: Towards a Critical Geography*, London: Taylor and Francis.

Harvey, David 2005, *The New Imperialism*, Oxford: Oxford University Press.

Harvey, David 2013, *Companion to Marx's 'Capital'*, Volume 2, London: Verso Books.

Harvey, David 2017, *Marx, Capital and the Madness of Economic Reason*, Oxford: Oxford University Press.

Harvey, David 2020, *The Anticapitalistic Chronicles*, London: Pluto.

Hayek, Fredrich 1944, *The Road to Serfdom: The Collected Works of F.A. Hayek*, Chicago: University of Chicago Press.

Hazard, John 1951, *Soviet Legal Philosophy*, Cambridge: Harvard University Press.

Heinrich, Michael 2012, *An Introduction to the Three Volumes of Karl Marx's 'Capital'*, New York: Monthly Review Press.

Horkheimer, Max and Theodor Adorno 1972, *Dialectic of Enlightenment*, Stanford: Stanford University Press.

Hunt, Alan 1985, 'The Ideology of Law: Advances and Problems in Recent Applications of the Concept of Ideology to the Analysis of Law', *Law and Society Review*, 19:1, 11–37.

Huws, Ursula 2010, 'Expression and Expropriation: The Dialectics of Autonomy and Control in Creative Labour', *Ephemera: Theory and Politics in Organisation*, 10, ¾: 504–21.

Huws, Ursula 2014, *Labor in the Global Digital Economy: The Cybertariat Comes of Age*, New York: Monthly Review Press.

International Labour Organisation 2019, *The Future of Work in Textiles, Clothing, Leather and Footwear*, Working Paper, no. 326, Geneva: International Labour Organisation Sectoral Policies Department.

International Monetary Fund Report 2020, *imf.org 2020*. Retrieved from https://www.imf.org/external/pubs/ft/ar/2020/eng/

Jay, Martin 1973, *Marxism and Totality*, Berkley, CA: University of California Press.

Jhally, Sut and Bill Livant 1986, 'Watching as Working: The Valorisation of Audience Consciousness', *Journal of Communication*, 36, 3: 124–43.

Joyce, Simon 2020, 'Rediscovering the cash nexus, again: Subsumption and the labour–capital relation in platform work', *Capital & Class*, 44, 4: 541–52.

Kant, Immanuel 1998, *Critique of Pure Reason*, Cambridge: Cambridge University Press.

Garrett, R. Kelly, & James Danziger 2008, 'On cyberslacking: Workplace status and personal internet use at work', *Journal of Cybertherapy and Rehabilitation*, 11, 3: 287–92.

Kosmann, Robert 1999, *La perruque ou le travail masqué*, Renault, Boulogne: Billancourt.

Kücklich, Julian 2005, 'Precarious Playbour: Modders and the Digital Games Industry', *The Fibreculture Journal*, 5.

Ingraham, Chris 2014, 'Toward an algorithmic rhetoric', in *Digital rhetoric and global literacies: Communication modes and digital practices in the networked world*, edited by G. Verhulsdonck, & M. Limbu, Hershey, PA: Information Science Reference.

Lebowitz, Michael 2003, *Beyond 'Capital': Marx's Political Economy of the Working Class*, Second Edition, Basingstoke: Palgrave.

Lemaitre Ripoll, Julieta 2007, 'Legal Fetishism at Home and Abroad', *Unbound*, 3: 6.

Lefebvre, Henry 1972, *La Pensée Marxiste et la Ville*, Paris: Casterman.

Lefebvre, Henry 1991, *The Social Production of Space*, Oxford: Basil Blackwell.

Lefebvre, Henry 2003, *The Urban Revolution*, Minneapolis: University of Minnesota Press.

Lefebvre, Henry 2009, *Dialectical Materialism*, Minneapolis: University of Minnesota Press.

Levine, Norman 2012, *Marx's Discourse with Hegel*, New York: Palgrave Macmillan.

Levine, Norman 2021, *Marx's Resurrection of Aristotle*, London: Palgrave Macmillan.

Lichtner, Maurizio 1991 *Insegnanti 150 ore, Esperienze e Prospettive di Formazione*. Roma: CEDE.
Liguori Guido, 2015, *Gramsci's Pathways*, Leiden: Brill.
Liskov, Barbara and Jeannette Wing 1994, 'A Behavioral Notion of Subtyping', ACM *Transactions on Programming Languages and Systems*, 16, 6: 1811–41.
Lucas, Rob and Nick Gray 2009, 'Capital, Subsumption and the History of the Class Relation', *Marx, Theory and Philosophy*, edited by Tom Bunyard, London: Goldsmith University Press.
Lukács, György 1971, *History and Class Consciousness*, Cambridge: MIT Press.
Luxemburg, Rosa 1951, *The Accumulation of Capital*, London: Routledge.
MacKenzie, Donald 1998, *Knowing Machines: Essays on Technical Change*, Cambridge: MIT Press.
Mandel, Ernest 1976, 'Introduction', in Karl Marx, *Capital*, Volume 1, New York: Vintage Books.
Mandel, Ernest 1984, *Delightful Murder: A Social History of the Crime Story*, London: Pluto.
Manovich, Lev 2001, *Language of New Media*, Cambridge: MIT Press.
Manzerolle, Vincent and Mikkola Kjøsen 2015, 'Digital Media and Capital's Logic of Acceleration', in *Marx in the Age of Digital Capitalism*, edited by Vincent Mosco and Christian Fuchs, Brill: Leiden.
Marazzi, Cristian 1999, *Il posto dei calzini. La svolta linguistica dell'economia e i suoi effetti sulla politica*, Torino: Bollati Boringhieri.
Marazzi, Cristian 2005, 'Capitalismo digitale e modello antropogenetico del lavoro. L'ammortamento del corpo macchina', in *Reinventare il lavoro*, edited by Federico Chicchi, Jean Lois Laville, Rosa La Mand and Cristiano Marazzi, Rome: Sapere.
Marazzi, Cristian 2016, *Che cos'è il plusvalore*, Bellinzona: Casagrande.
Marchi, Alessandra 2021, 'Molecular Transformations: Reading the Arab Uprisings With and Beyond Gramsci', *Middle East Critique*, 30:1, 67–85.
Marcuse, Herbert 1968, *One-Dimensional Man*, London: Sphere.
Marx, Karl 1970, *Critique of Hegel's Philosophy of Right*. Oxford, Oxford University Press.
Marx, Karl 1973, *Grundrisse: Foundations of the Critique of Political Economy*, New York: Random House.
Marx, Karl 1990, *Capital: A Critique of Political Economy*, Volume I, New York: Penguin.
Marx, Karl 1992, *Capital: A Critique of Political Economy*, Volume II, New York: Penguin.
Marx, Karl, 1996, *Capital: A Critique of Political Economy*, Volume III, New York: Penguin.
Marx, Karl 1992a, *Early Writings*, London: Penguin.
Marx, Karl 1992b, 'Economic and Philosophical Manuscripts', in *Early Writings*, London: Penguin.
Marx, Karl and Friedrich Engels 1848/2004, *The Communist Manifesto*, Peterborough: Broadview.

Marx, Karl and Engels Frederick 1867/ 2010, *Marx and Engels Collected Works. Volume 34. Marx 1861–64*, London: Lawrence & Wishart.
Marx, Karl and Engels Frederick 1867/2010, *Marx and Engels Collected Works, Volume 40. Letters 1856–59*, London: Lawrence & Wishart.
Marx, Karl and Engels Frederick 1867/ 2010, *Marx and Engels Collected Works. Volume 47. Letters 1883–86*, London: Lawrence & Wishart.
Marx, Karl and Engels Frederick 1867/2010, *Marx and Engels Collected Works. Volume 49. Letters 1890–92*, London: Lawrence & Wishart
Marx, Karl and Engels Frederick 1846/1998, *The German Ideology*. London: Prometheus Books.
Mayer-Schönberger, Viktor and Kenneth Cukier 2013, *Big Data: A Revolution That Will Transform How We Live, Work and Think*, London: John Murray.
McCraken Grant 1988, *Culture and Consumption*, Bloomington: Indiana University Press.
McRobbie Angela 2011, 'The Los Angelesation of London: three short waves of young people's microeconomies of culture and creativity in the UK', in *Critique of Creativity: Precarity, Subjectivity and Resistance in the 'Creative Industries'*, G. Raunig, G. Ray and U. Wuggenig, London: MayFly, pp. 119–132.
Merry, Sally Engle 2016, *The Seductions of Quantification: Measuring Human Rights, Gender Violence, and Sex Trafficking*, Chicago: University of Chicago Press.
Mészáros, István 1995, *Beyond Capital*, New York: Monthly Review Press.
Mezzadri, Alessandra 2016, 'Class, Gender and the Sweatshop', *Third World Quarterly*, 37:1, 1877–1900.
Mies, Maria 1986, *Patriarchy and Accumulation on a World Scale: Women in the International Division of Labour*, London: Zed.
Mizuoka, Fujio 1991, 'Subsumption of Space into Society', *Hitotsubashi Journal of Economics*, 32:2, 71–89.
Moll, Ian 2021, 'The Myth of the Fourth Industrial Revolution', *Theoria: A Journal of Social and Political Theory*, 68:167, 1–38.
Moore, Phoebe 2018, *The Quantified Self in Precarity: Work, Technology and What Counts*, London: Routledge.
Morton, Adam 2007, *Unravelling Gramsci: Hegemony and Passive Revolution in the Global Political Economy*, London: Pluto.
Moseley, Fred 2015a, *Money and Totality*, Leiden: Brill.
Moseley, Fred 2015b, *Marx's Economic Manuscript of 1864–1865*, Leiden: Brill.
Muelenbach, Andrea 2012, *Moral Neoliberal: Welfare and Citizenship in Italy*, Chicago: Chicago University Press.
Mundle, Sudipta 1979, *Backwardness and Bondage: Agrarian Relations in a South Bihar District*, Delhi: Indian Institute of Public Administration.
Murray, Patrick 2004, 'The Social and Material Transformation of Production: Formal

and Real Subsumption in *Capital*, Volume 1', in *The Constitution of Capital: Essays on Volume I of Marx's Capital*, edited by Riccardo Bellofiore and Nicola Taylor, London: Palgrave.

Murray, Patrick 2009, 'The Place of "The Results of the Immediate Production Process" in *Capital*', in *Re-Reading Marx: New Perspectives After the Critical Edition*, edited by Riccardo Bellofiore and Roberto Fineschi, New York: Palgrave Macmillan.

Nguyen, Thi 2021, *How Twitter Gamifies Communication*, in *Applied Epistemology*, edited by Jennifer Lackey, Oxford: Oxford University Press.

Nakamoto, Satoshi 2008, 'Bitcoin: A Peer-To-Peer Electronic Cash System', https://bitcoin.org/bitcoin.pdf, observed 17 April 2022.

Nakamoto, Satoshi 2009, 'Bitcoin Open-Source Implementation of P2P currency', http://p2pfoundation.ning.com/forum/topics/bitcoin-open-source, observed 11 May 2017.

Negri, Antonio 1989, *The Politics of Subversion: A Manifesto for the Twenty-First Century*, Cambridge: Polity.

Negri, Antonio 1996, 'Twenty Theses on Marx, Interpretation of the Class Situation Today', in *Marxism Beyond Marxism*, edited by Saree Makdisi, Cesare Casarino and Rebecca Karl, London: Routledge.

Nguyen, Thi 2020, *Games: Agency As Art*, Oxford: Oxford University Press.

Neilson, David 2007, 'Formal and real subordination and the contemporary proletariat: Re-coupling Marxist class theory and labour-process analysis', *Capital & Class*, 31: 89–123.

Noble, David 1983, *Forces of Production: A Social History of Industrial Automation*, London: Routledge.

Noizat, Patrick 2012, 'Bitcoin: A Universal Complementary Currency?', *ParisTech Review*, 20 January, http://www.paristechreview.com/2012/01/20/bitcoin-universal-complementary-currency/.

Norman, Richard and Sean Sayers 1980, *Hegel, Marx and Dialectic: A Debate*, Sussex: Harvester.

Notes From Below 2018, 'The Workers' Inquiry and Social Composition: No Politics Without Inquiry', https://notesfrombelow.org/issue/no-politics-without-inquiry.

Offe, Claus 2020, *The Contradiction of the Welfare State*, London: Routledge.

Office for National Statistics 2022, 'Consumer Price Inflation Basket of Goods and Services 2022', https://www.ons.gov.uk/economy/inflationandpriceindices/articles/ukconsumerpriceinflationbasketofgoodsandservices/2022.

O'Kane, Chris 2017, 'Fetishistic Concrete Abstraction, Social Constitution and Social Domination in Henri Lefebvre's Writings on Everyday Life, Cities and Space', *Capital and Class*, 42: 2, 253–71.

Panayotakis, Costas 2021, *Capitalista Mode of Destruction: Austerity, Ecological Crisis and the Hollowing out of Democracy*, Manchester: Manchester University Press.

Pashukanis, Yevgeny 1987, *The General Theory of Law and Marxism*, London: Pluto.
Pasquinelli, Matteo 2015, 'Italian Operaismo and the Information Machine', *Theory, Culture and Society*, 32:3, 49–68.
Paulsen, Roland 2017, *Empty Labour*, Cambridge: Cambridge University Press.
Petre, Caitlin 2021, *All the News That's Fit to Click: How Metrics Are Transforming the Work of Journalists*, Princeton: Princeton University Press.
Postone, Moishe 1993, *Time, Labour and Social Domination: A Reinterpretation of Marx's Critical Theory*, Cambridge: Cambridge University Press.
Prey, Robert 2018, 'Nothing Personal: Algorithmic Individuation on Music Streaming Platforms', *Media, Culture and Society*, 40:7, 1086–1100.
Propp, Vladimir 1968, *Morphology of the Folk Tale*, Austin: University of Texas Press.
Ramachandran, V.K. 1990, *Wage Labour and Unfreedom in Indian Agriculture*, Oxford: Clarendon Press.
Raunig, Gerald 2010, A *Thousand Machines: A Concise Philosophy of the Machine as Social Movement*, New York: Semiotexte.
Read, Jason 2013, *Micro-Politics of Capital: Marx and the Pre-History of the Present*, New York: SUNY Press.
Reiman, Jeffrey 1987, 'Exploitation, Force and the Moral Assessment of Capitalism: Thoughts on Roemer and Cohen', *Philosophy and Public Affairs*, 16:1, 3–41.
Ricoeur, Paul 1981, *Hermeneutics and the Human Sciences*, Cambridge: Cambridge University Press.
Risi, Elisabetta and Riccardo Pronzato 2021, 'Smartworking Is Not So Smart: Always-On Lives and the Dark Side of Platformisation', *Work Organisation Labour Globalisation*, 15:1, 107–125.
Roberts, Micheal 2022, 'The Future of Work-Remote Working', https://thenextrecession.wordpress.com/2022/06/07/the-future-of-work-1--remote-working/.
Roberts, William 2009, 'Abstraction and Productivity: Reflections on Formal Causality', in *Marx and Contemporary Philosophy*, edited by Andrew Chitty and Micheal McIvor, New York: Palgrave Macmillan.
Rosenberg, Nathan 1983, *Inside the Black Box: Technology and Economics*, Cambridge: Cambridge University Press.
Rossi-Landi, Ferruccio 1968, *Il linguaggio come lavoro e come mercato*, Milan: Bompiani.
Russell, Eric-John 2015, 'The Logic of Subsumption: An Elective Affinity Between Hegel and Marx', *Revista Opinião Filosófica*, 6:2, 201.
Rostow, Walt W. 1960 *The Stages of Economic Growth: A Non-Communist Manifesto*. Cambridge University Press
Sadowski, Jathan 2020, *Too Smart: How Digital Capitalism Is Extracting Data, Controlling Our Lives, and Taking Over the World*, Cambridge: MIT Press.
Sáenz de Sicilia, Andres 2007, 'Living Labor in Marx', *Radical Philosophy Review*, 10, 1: 1–31.

Saenz de Sicilia, Andres 2016, *The Problem of Subsumption in Kant, Hegel and Marx*, Kingston: Kingston University Press.

Saenz de Sicilia, Andres 2022, 'Being, Becoming, Subsumption: The Kantian Roots of a Marxist Problematic', *Radical Philosophy*, 12.

Salcel, Renata 2010, *Choice*, London: Profile.

Sarkin, Georgia 2020, 'Cities at the Front Line: Public Space in the Time of the COVID-19 Pandemic', https://www.smithgroup.com/perspectives/2020/cities-at-the-front-line-public-space-in-the-time-of-the-covid-19--pandemic, observed 24 June 2021.

Sartre, Jean-Paul 1991, *Critique of Dialectical Reason: Theory of Practical Ensembles*, London: Verso.

Schiller, Daniel 1993, *Theorising Communication: A History*, Oxford: Oxford University Press.

Scholtz, Trebor 2016, 'Platform Cooperativism Challenging the Corporate Sharing Economy', http://platformcoop.net/about, observed 24 June 2021.

Schrape, Niklas 2014, 'Gamification and Governmentality', in *Rethinking Gamification*, Sonia Fizek, Mattias Fuchs, Paolo Ruffino and Niklas Schrape, Lüneburg: Meson Press.

Scott, James 1990, *Domination and the Art of Resistance: Hidden Transcripts*, New Haven: Yale University Press.

Screpanti, Ernesto 2019, *Labour and Value. Rethinking Marx's theory of Exploitation*. Cambridge: Open Book Publishers.

Shannon, Claude 1948, 'A Mathematical Theory of Communication: Bell System', *Technical Journal*, 27, 3.

Simmel, Georg 1971, 'The Metropolis and Mental Life', in *Simmel: On Individuality and Social Forms*, edited by Daniel Levine, Chicago: Chicago University Press.

Simonsen, Kirsten 2005, 'Bodies, Sensations, Space and Time: The Contribution from Henri Lefebvre', *Human Geography*, 87: 1, 1–14.

Skepton, Simon 2010, *Alienation after Derrida*, London: Bloomsbury.

Skillman, Gilbert 2013, 'The Puzzle of Marx's Missing "Results": A Tale of Two Theories', *History of Political Economy*, 45: 3, 475–504.

Skillman, Gilbert 2015, 'Production Relations in Agrarian Capitalist Development: A Comment on Das, "Review of Radical Political Economics"', *Review of Radical Political Economics*, 49: 1.

Smith, Tony 1990, *The Logic of Marx's Capital: Replies to Hegelian Criticisms*, Albany: State University of New York Press.

Smythe, Dallas 1981, *Dependency Road: Communication, Capitalism, Consciousness and Canada*, Norwood: Ablex.

Soderberg, Johan 2013, 'Determining Social Change: The Role of Technological Determinism in the Collective Framing of Hackers', *New Media and Society*, 15: 8: 1277–1293.

Sohn-Rethel, Alfred 1978, *Intellectual and Manual Labour: A Critique of Epistemology*, London: Macmillan.

Sprouse Martin, 1992, *Sabotage in the American Workplace: Anecdotes of Dissatisfaction, Mischief, and Revenge*, 1st ed. San Francisco, CA: Pressure Drop Press.

Srnicek, Nick 2016, *Platform Capitalism*, Cambridge: Polity Press.

Stanek, Leonid 2011, *Henri Lefebvre on Space: Architecture, Urban Research, and the Production of Theory*, Minneapolis: University of Minnesota Press.

Starosta, Guido 2015. *Marx's Capital, Method and Revolutionary Subjectivity*, Leiden: Brill.

Statt, Nick, 2020, Amazon expands Gamification programm that encourages wharehouse employees to work harder. *verge.com*. Retrieved from https://www.theverge.com/2021/3/15/22331502/amazon-warehouse-gamification-program-expand-fc-games

Steinfeld Robert and Engerman, Stanley 1997 Labor – Free or Coerced? An Historical Reassessment of Differences and Similarities in Free and Unfree Labour: The Debate Continues 107 (Tom Brass & Marcel van der Linden, eds.) London: Peter Lang.

Steinfeld Robert 2001, *Coercion, Contract, and Free Labor in the Nineteenth Century*, Cambridge: Cambridge University Press.

Striphas, Theodor 2015, 'Algorithmic Culture', *European Journal of Cultural Studies*, 18:4–5, 395–412.

Szadkowski, Kristina 2016, 'Towards an Orthodox Marxian Reading of Subsumption(s) of Academic Labour under Capital', *Workplace*, 28, 9–29.

Terranova, Tiziana 2000, 'Free Labour: Producing Culture for the Digital Economy', *Social Text*, 18, 33–58.

Théorie Communiste 1997, 'Théorie Communiste', *Théorie Communiste*, 14.

Théorie Communiste 2004, 'Réponse à Aufheben', *Théorie Communiste*, 19.

Thoburn Nicholas 2001, 'Autonomous production: on Negri's "new synthesis"', *Theory, Culture & Society*, 18, 5: 75–96.

Thomas, Peter 2007, *The Gramscian Moment*, Leiden: Brill.

Thompson, Edward Palmer 1963, *The Making of the English Working Class*, London Harmondsworth: Penguin.

Titmuss, Richard 1958, *Essays on the Welfare State*, London: Allen and Unwin.

Tomba, Massimiliano 2012, 'Historical Temporalities of Capital: An Historicist Perspective', *Historical Materialism*, 17:4, 200.

Tomlins, Christopher, 2012 Freddom Unbond: Law, Labor and Civic Identity in Colonizing English Amnerica 1580–1865. New York: Cambridge University Press.

Tönnies, Ferdinand 2001, *Community and Civil Society*, Cambridge: Cambridge University Press.

Tronti, Mario 1966, *Operai e Capitale*, Turin: Turion Einaudi.

Tronti, Mario 1972, 'Struggle Against Labor', *Radical America*, 6:3, 22–25.

Trudeau, Dan and Elliot Wareham 2020, 'COVID-19 is Spurring a Reinvention of Public Space', https://www.minnpost.com/community-voices/2020/08/covid-19--is-spurring-a-reinvention-of-public-space, observed 24 June 2021.

Tuchman, Gaye 1972, 'Objectivity as Strategic Ritual: An Examination of Newsmen's Notions of Objectivity', *American Journal of Sociology*, 77, 4.

Uno, Kozo 1980, *Principles of Political Economy: Theory of a Purely Capitalist Society*, Sussex: Harvester.

Van Dijck, José 2014, 'Datafication, Dataism and Dataveillance: Big Data Between Scientific Paradigm and Ideology', *Surveillance and Society*, 12, 197–208.

Van Dijck, José 2018, *The Platform Society: Public Values in a Connective World*, Oxford: Oxford University Press.

Vercellone, Carlo 2007, 'From Formal Subsumption to General Intellect: Elements for a Marxist Reading of the Thesis of Cognitive Capitalism', *Historical Materialism*, 15, 13–36.

Virno, Paolo 1996, 'Notes on the General Intellect', in *Marxism Beyond Marxism*, edited by Saree Makdisi, Cesare Casarino and Rebecca Karl, London: Routledge.

Virno, Paolo 2001, 'General Intellect', in *Lessico Postfordista*, edited by Zadini Adelino and Ubaldo Fadini, Milano: Feltrinelli.

Voloshinov, Valentin 1973, *Marxism and the Philosophy of Language*, Cambridge: Harvard University Press.

Warmelink, Harald, Johana Koivistob, Igor Mayer, Mikko Vesa and Junho Hamari 2020, 'Gamification of Production and Logistics Operations: Status Quo and Future Directions', *Journal of Business Research*, 106, 331–340.

Weber, Max 1978, *Economy and Society*, Berkeley: University of California Press.

White, James 1994, 'Marx: From "The Critique of Political Economy" to Capital', *Studies in Marxism*, 1: 89–105.

Wightman, John 1996, *Contract: A Critical Commentary*, London: Pluto Press.

Williams, Raymond 1977, *Marxism and Literature*, London: Verso.

Wood, Ellen 2002, *The Origin of Capitalism: A Longer View*, London: Verso.

Wood, Alex 2021, 'Algorithmic Management. Consequence of work organization and working conditions', JRC Technical report, retrived from https://joint-research-centre.ec.europa.eu/system/files/2021-05/jrc124874.pdf.

Woodcock, Jamie 2016, *Working the Phones: Control and Resistance in Call Centres*, London: Pluto.

Woodcock, Jamie and Mark Johnson 2017, 'Gamification: What It Is and How To Fight It', *Sociological Review*, 66:3, 442–458.

Wright, Steve 2002, *Storming Heaven: Class Composition and Struggle in Italian Autonomist Marxism*, London: Pluto.

Zwick, Austin 2018 'Welcome to the Gig Economy: Neoliberal Industrial Relations and the Case of Uber', *GeoJournal*, 83:4, 679–691.

Zuboff, Susana 2019, *The Age of Surveillance Capitalism: The Fight for a Human Future at the New Frontier of Power*, London: Profile.

Index

Abstraction   5–7, 11–21, 40, 49–52, 60, 72–73, 96–97, 167, 183, 187–190
Arthur   45–46, 59

Braverman   37, 39, 63, 108

Camatte   27, 35, 92–93, 97
Covid-19   211–14, 217
Cryptocurrency   250–253

Data subjects   196–200
   Objects   195–197
Digital abstract space   174, 218–226, 231–232
Determinate Supersumption   10, 14, 29–31, 140–172, 217, 233
   Molecular   145–149
   Molar   151
Domestication   31–33, 211, 214–215, 227–230
Dussel   154, 165, 168–171, 180–181

Fixed Capital   11, 24–25, 80–81, 95, 154, 159, 173–174, 183–187, 190–191, 195, 210, 219–221, 223
   Communicative fixed capital   183–187
Fuchs   56–57, 178

Gamification   232, 239–241

Harvey   12, 16, 55–56, 143, 185, 218–220
Hegel   12, 34, 39–52, 121–122, 143
Hegemony   23–24, 95–96, 110–120, 122–124, 127

Kant   35, 40–45

Labour   15, 18
   Abstract   21–22, 50–53
La Perruque   211–212, 232–239
Lefebvre   151, 166–167, 213–217, 222–227

Marx   44–90, 101–120, 135–139, 185–188, 214–215, 246
Murray   35, 57–59, 86–91, 102

Negri   11, 80, 92–95

Saenz-DeSicilia   8, 35, 41–42, 47, 52, 60, 169–171
Subsumption   60–91, 140–172
   Formal   64–69
   Real   69–74
   Ideal   74–86
   Hybrid   86–90
Surplus Value   64–69

Technological fetish   248–254
Tomba   55, 87, 123
Totalisation   18, 27, 165–166
Translation   32, 39, 127, 173–209

Welfare state   29, 103, 121–127

www.ingramcontent.com/pod-product-compliance
Lightning Source LLC
Chambersburg PA
CBHW070615030426
42337CB00020B/3807